Legalizing Prostitution

Legalizing Prostitution

From Illicit Vice to Lawful Business

Ronald Weitzer

NEW YORK UNIVERSITY PRESS

New York and London

NEW YORK UNIVERSITY PRESS
New York and London
www.nyupress.org

Library of Congress Cataloging-in-Publication Data

Weitzer, Ronald
Legalizing prostitution : from illicit vice to lawful business /
Ronald Weitzer.
p. cm.
ISBN 978–0–8147–9464–7 (paperback : acid-free paper)
ISBN 978–0–8147–9463–0 (hardback : acid-free paper)
ISBN 978–0–8147–8463–1 (ebook)
ISBN 978–0–8147–7054–2 (ebook)
1. Prostitution—United States. 2. Prostitution—Law and legislation.
3. Prostitution—Netherlands—Case studies. 4. Prostitution—Belgium—
Case studies. 5. Prostitution—Germany—Case studies. I. Title.
HQ144.W447   2011
306.74′209051—dc23   2011028190

Contents

Tables and Figures

Preface

In recent years, America has witnessed major trends in the normalization of some types of vice or previously stigmatized behavior. Marijuana has been decriminalized in some places; gay rights are increasingly protected by the law; casino gambling and state-sponsored lotteries have become quite popular; and pornography, strip clubs, and other sexual entertainment have proliferated. Prostitution is a glaring exception to these trends, not only in the United States but in many other countries as well. The very notion of legal prostitution is alarming to many people; they simply cannot fathom it.

Yet in some nations, prostitution has been decriminalized and is regulated by the government. People who live outside these countries know very little about legal prostitution—what is permitted, how it is regulated, and what the effects of legalization are on those involved. Likewise, many Americans are unaware that prostitution is legal and regulated by local authorities in a number of counties in Nevada and that this legal order has existed for four decades, beginning in 1971. Americans might also be surprised to learn that, until recently, Rhode Island had no prostitution law on the books. The state controlled street prostitution with a loitering law, but indoor prostitution was not an offense and was freely carried out in the state's many massage parlors and by escorts who worked either independently or for an agency. This situation ended in 2009 when the legislature voted to criminalize those who buy and sell sex as well as landlords who allow prostitution on their premises.

The Rhode Island and Nevada cases show that decriminalized prostitution is not a totally foreign idea in modern America. But there are several other countries where prostitution has been legalized as well, and I think that we can learn much from their experiences. *Legalizing Prostitution* sheds light on these systems, with a special focus on three cases—Belgium, Germany, and the Netherlands. The book is intended to help readers think outside the box, to consider alternatives that may be superior to the criminalization approach that reigns almost everywhere in the United

States and in many other nations as well. After describing key dimensions of prostitution, contrasting alternative theoretical perspectives, and considering a variety of policy issues in chapters 1–4, the book presents my research on the red-light landscapes in three cities: Antwerp, Frankfurt, and Amsterdam.

Amsterdam hosts one of the most famous red-light districts in the world, so it is an obvious choice for investigating legal prostitution. But several other cities—including Bangkok, Brussels, Hamburg, The Hague, Singapore, Tokyo—also have well-established and officially tolerated red-light districts featuring a variety of sex businesses and attracting large numbers of customers. The three cities that I studied were selected because they share some basic features as well as differing in some intriguing respects. Antwerp, Frankfurt, and Amsterdam are major northern European cities hosting at least one geographically distinct red-light district that has existed for decades. The national contexts differ somewhat in their legal regimes—certain types of prostitution are de facto legal in parts of Belgium, whereas they are de jure legal in Germany and the Netherlands. They are regulated by the government in all three places, but the regulations differ across the settings. In addition, each city's sexual geography differs in at least some respects from that of other cities. Each red-light district can be distinguished by its social organization—including the constellation of businesses (sex related and other) in the area, the district's appearance and ambience, the location and visibility of sex workers, and the kinds of people who visit or work in the area. Each city also differs in the kinds of sex businesses that are located *outside* the parameters of the red-light district, in other parts of the city. In this book, a red-light district is defined as an area where sexually oriented businesses are clustered and does not include areas where prostitution is confined to street-level transactions.

Scholars are just beginning to draw connections between the social ecology of different red-light areas and the experiences and perceptions of workers, clients, residents, and visitors. These structural-experiential links are explored in the book with the help of ethnographic material on the three red-light landscapes. In addition, the social structure of a commercial sex district can have important public-policy implications. Different kinds of arrangements present unique challenges for authorities responsible for maintaining order and public safety; they affect workers and clients in different ways; they are more or less likely to generate complaints from local residents and merchants; and they influence whether the commercial sex sector will become politicized and perhaps subjected to greater restrictions. Comparative analysis of different cases can help in assessing the strengths and weaknesses of various models and contribute to the larger enterprise of identifying best practices in the legal regulation of prostitution, a theme explored in the book's conclusion.

I conducted countless hours of street observations in the three cities: photographing and mapping the configuration of businesses in each red-light area; recording observations of people on the street and their interactions with each other and with local sex workers; and talking with some workers in each setting. I conducted in-depth interviews with key players, including government officials, brothel and window owners, and sex worker advocates. The data are more extensive for Amsterdam and Frankfurt than for Antwerp, largely because Antwerp's red-light district is small, fairly isolated, and single purpose, whereas the other two are major commercial sex emporiums and thus more complex and challenging study sites. I have studied Amsterdam (and other Dutch cities) for more than a decade, whereas my fieldwork in Antwerp and Frankfurt was more limited and more recent. My ethnographic data are presented in conjunction with information from other sources, including government documents, newspaper reports, scholarly articles, public opinion polls, and online discussion boards where clients converse about their experiences in and observations of the various red-light districts.

The field research would not have been possible without the assistance and insights of local experts and friends who have helped me tremendously over the years. I owe a huge debt of gratitude to Sietske Altink, Frank Bovenkerk, Sander Flight, Juanita Henning, Lorraine Nencel, Joyce Outshoorn, Maurice Punch, Marieke van Doorninck, Jan Visser, Henk Wagenaar, Gerhard Walentowitz, and Hans Willems. These experts informed me about policy changes, shared their own research findings, and advised me on practical matters, such as whom to interview and how to gain access to them. I am extremely indebted to my interviewees in Amsterdam, Antwerp, and Frankfurt as well as the individuals in the sex industry who provided information but were not formally interviewed. Juanita Henning deserves special thanks, for helping me arrange and conduct interviews in Frankfurt. The Frankfurt data would have been very thin had it not been for her extraordinary help and insights. Additional help with the German situation was provided by Gerhard Walentowitz, who clarified many issues for me.

Shannon Dolan served as my research assistant during the final years of the project and deserves special thanks. Michael Goodyear, Christine Milrod, John Dombrink, Henk Wagenaar, Gerhard Walentowitz, Sander Flight,

Hans Willems, Sietske Altink, and Kathy Guidroz read various chapters and provided extremely valuable feedback, as did the anonymous reviewers of the manuscript. Finally, my wonderful editor at NYU Press, Ilene Kalish, supported this project enthusiastically from the very beginning, and I am delighted that we had a chance to work together on the book.

PART I

Sex Work

Understanding Prostitution

It is taken for granted by most people that buying and selling sex is degrading, dishonorable, or despicable, and there is a deep-rooted belief that prostitution has always been and will forever remain taboo. Mention prostitution to someone and you will usually see them react with disgust, while any mention of legalizing prostitution is often met with laughter, incredulity, or shock. There is a widespread sense that prostitution simply cannot be taken seriously or ever achieve the status of other service occupations. Yet this folk wisdom is just that—a narrow, surface understanding that does not come close to recognizing the myriad dimensions of sex for sale, how it is experienced by workers and clients, and the value of considering policy alternatives "outside the box" of criminalization and marginalization.

There are many myths about prostitution—myths that shape both the popular imagination and public policies throughout the world. This chapter examines these myths, as well as the facts. I show that many popular assumptions about prostitutes, their clients, and their managers are either entirely fictional or valid for only a segment of the trade.[1] I begin by sketching the basic dimensions of the sex industry.

Contours of the Sex Industry

The sex industry refers to the workers, managers, owners, marketers, agencies, clubs, and trade associations involved in sexual commerce, both legal and illegal varieties. Sex work involves the exchange of sexual services for material compensation as well as the selling of erotic performances or products. It includes acts of direct physical contact between buyers and sellers (prostitution, lap dancing) as well as indirect sexual stimulation (pornography, stripping, telephone sex, live sex shows, erotic webcam performances).

Sex for sale is a lucrative growth industry. In 2006 alone, Americans spent $13.3 billion on X-rated magazines, videos and DVDs, live sex shows, strip clubs, adult cable television films, computer pornography, and commercial telephone sex,[2] and the estimated earnings for these sex sectors in the 16 nations where data were available in 2006 was $97 billion.[3] In just one decade, the number of X-rated films released annually in the United States more than doubled, from 5,700 in 1995 to 13,588 in 2005, but these figures are now eclipsed by the ubiquity of porn on the Internet.[4] The number of strip clubs in the United States has also risen over the past two decades, to around 3,500 today.[5] Prostitution is another booming sector, though its size and earnings are unknown due to its illegality.

There are many consumers. In 2008, one-quarter of Americans (34 percent of men, 16 percent of women) reported that they had seen an X-rated video in just the past year.[6] Many Americans also visit strip clubs or call a phone-sex number. And more people buy sex from prostitutes than is commonly recognized. The General Social Survey reports figures on the number of men who say that they had ever paid for sex—between 15–18 percent in ten polls from 1991 to 2008 (with about 3–4 percent saying that they had done so in the past year).[7] Remarkably similar figures are reported for Australia (16 percent) and the average within Europe (15 percent).[8] Given the stigma of prostitution, the real figures may be significantly higher.[9] An unusual question was included in a recent British survey: respondents were asked whether they would "consider having sex for money if the amount offered was enough": 18 percent of women and 36 percent of men said yes.[10] This does not imply that they would consider a career in prostitution, but it is clear that a sizeable number of people would be amenable to engaging in an act of prostitution.

Over the past three decades, there has been a steady trend toward the *privatization* of sexual services and products. Instead of having to buy a copy of an adult magazine in a store, today one can view thousands of nude photos online. Adult theaters are a thing of the past, supplanted by the abundant videos on cable television and the Internet, and the peep show has given way to the live webcam broadcast. The advent of telephone-sex agencies and escort services also has contributed to the privatization of commercial sex. And the Internet has changed the landscape tremendously—providing a wealth of erotic services, information, and connections for interested parties. Internet-facilitated sex work has mushroomed as a sector of the market, while street prostitution has remained relatively stable over time or has declined in some places.[11]

It is often claimed that prostitution is growing exponentially and that the Internet has driven this increase. These claims may be true, but we lack baseline data (from, say, two decades ago) and have no current, reliable data to compare to a baseline. The Internet has certainly made it easier for sex workers to advertise their services and for clients to locate them, which *might* indeed translate into an increasing number of transactions, but that is only speculative. What about arrest data? In the United States, the number of arrests for prostitution offenses has *declined* over the past three decades, dropping steadily from a peak of 125,600 in 1983 to 56,600 in 2009.[12] We might expect arrests to increase if the number of transactions has increased, but since arrest patterns can be influenced by extraneous factors (such as police department priorities) arrests are a problematic measure of transactions. Surveys asking respondents about their own involvement in prostitution are another measure. As noted earlier, the number of American men saying they have bought sex has been quite stable (15–18 percent) for about twenty years, suggesting that the number of paid sex transactions has not increased significantly during that time.

For the past decade, the adult industry has sponsored annual trade shows in Las Vegas. The four-day event (the Adult Entertainment Expo) attracts about 300 exhibits featuring porn stars and sex-toy and video companies, and the attendees include industry moguls, producers and directors, the media, and thousands of fans. The Expo has many dimensions—the marketing of products and brands, on-site entertainment, networking among industry people, fans lining up for autographs and photographs with porn stars, outreach to the media, and a huge awards show for adult entertainers.[13] Similar conventions have been held in Berlin, Germany (Venus), Vancouver, Canada (Taboo), Moscow, Russia (Eros-Expo Russia), and other cities around the world.

These trends might suggest that the sex industry is steadily becoming normalized, but this conclusion would be premature. Despite its size, profits, numerous customers, and (gradual and partial) mainstreaming, commercial sex continues to be viewed by many people as *deviant and disreputable*. In 1973, 56 percent of Americans felt that pornography leads to "a breakdown in morals," a figure that remained fairly stable over the next two decades, with 61 percent subscribing to this opinion in 1994 (the last year this question was asked).[14] In 2008, fully half the population deemed viewing porn as "sinful behavior."[15] Almost half the American public thinks that pornography is "demeaning towards women" (a quarter disagreed, and the remainder were undecided),[16] and even in liberal New Zealand, only a minority of the public condones viewing porn on the Internet: just 41 percent thought that it was "morally acceptable" for a single person to do so, falling to 21 percent for a married person.[17]

Prostitution is even more taboo. Two-thirds of the British population believes that "paying for sex exploits women," and despite the usual pattern in which young people are more tolerant of vices than are their elders, in this poll young adults were less liberal than were older cohorts: 80 percent of those aged 18–24 subscribed to the exploitation view.[18] A somewhat different question was asked in another British poll: 49 percent believed that "most prostitutes are only in that role because they are victims of exploitation." At the same time, 59 percent thought that "prostitution is a perfectly reasonable choice that women should be free to make."[19] In other words, even if most prostitutes have been exploited, this does not mean that others should be prevented from freely choosing this kind of work. With regard to public policy, 51 percent said that it should be legal for a woman to sell sex. The morality of prostitution is a separate issue, however. Only 39 percent of Britons thought that it was "acceptable" for a man to purchase sex from a woman, and 38 percent felt it was acceptable for a woman to sell sex to a man.[20]

Americans also hold fairly negative views of prostitution, although the number viewing it unfavorably seems to have lessened in recent years. A 1977 poll found that 61 percent thought that the idea of "men spending an evening with a prostitute" was morally wrong.[21] Similarly, in 1981, 64 percent of Americans felt that prostitution can "never be justified."[22] But the proportion taking the "never justified" view has declined in recent years, falling to 47 percent in 1999 and 43 percent in 2006. Still, Americans remain less tolerant of prostitution than most Europeans are (see chapter 4).

Many Americans favor either more controls or a total ban on most types of commercial sex. Prostitution should remain illegal, according to between 45 and 70 percent in the most recent polls (the differences reflect question wording).[23] In 2008, one-third felt that pornography should be banned outright—down only slightly from two decades earlier.[24] Stripping and commercial telephone sex also carry substantial stigma. In 1991, almost half the American public believed that strip clubs should be illegal, while three-quarters thought telephone numbers offering sex talk should be illegal.[25]

What we have, in sum, is a very mixed picture—a lucrative industry that employs many individuals and attracts numerous customers but is regarded by many people as immoral or harmful and in need of either stricter control or total elimination. The sex industry continues to be widely stigmatized. That some individuals buy sex, go to strip clubs, or watch porn precisely *because* it is transgressive or even risky—the "forbidden fruit" dimension—does not detract from the central fact that the sex industry remains socially marginal even where it is legal.

Competing Paradigms

Sex work is just as controversial in academia as it is in the wider society. Three perspectives in academic writings view sex work through radically different prisms.

The Empowerment Paradigm

The empowerment paradigm highlights the ways in which sexual services qualify as work, involve human agency, and may be potentially validating or empowering for workers.[26] This paradigm holds that there is nothing inherent in sex work that would prevent it from being organized for mutual gain to all parties—just as in other economic transactions. This kind of work may enhance a person's socioeconomic status and can offer greater control over one's working conditions than do many traditional jobs. Analysts who adopt this perspective draw parallels to kindred types of service work (physical therapy, massage, psychotherapy) but also emphasize the ways in which the work may benefit the worker. Sex workers can acquire professional expertise, business savvy, proficiency at customer relations, valuable interpersonal skills, and ways of taking control of a situation. It may have other benefits as well: "Many prostitutes emphasize that they engage in sex work not simply out of economic need but out of satisfaction with the control it gives them over their sexual interactions."[27] Empowerment theorists also argue that most of the problems associated with prostitution are traceable to its criminalization and not intrinsic to sexual commerce. They advocate alternatives to criminalization that have the potential to enhance workers' control over working conditions, job satisfaction, and socioeconomic status.

Some writers who adopt the empowerment paradigm go further and make bold claims that romanticize sex work. Wendy Chapkis describes a "sex radical" version of empowerment in which sex workers and other sexual outlaws "embrace a vision of sex freed of the constraints of love, commitment, and convention" and present "a potent symbolic challenge to confining notions of proper womanhood and conventional sexuality."[28] Camille Paglia echoes this view when she argues that the prostitute is the "ultimate liberated woman, who lives on the edge and whose sexuality belongs to no one."[29] Shannon Bell describes her book *Whore Carnival* as "a recognition and commendation of the sexual and political power and knowledge of prostitutes."[30] Sex expert Annie Sprinkle lists "Forty Reasons Why Whores Are My Heroes," which include claims that they "challenge sexual mores," "teach people how to be better lovers," "make lonely people less lonely," are playful, independent, multicultured, creative, and entertaining, and "are rebelling against the absurd, patriarchal, sex-negative laws against their profession."[31] Former prostitute Dolores French proclaims that prostitutes are "the world's most interesting women":

> They are tougher, smarter, quicker, and more resilient than other women. . . . I tried to explain to her [French's mother] that I wasn't doing it for the money. I was doing it because I believed in it, because I didn't think it was dirty or shameful but instead something noble and helpful. I was improving the quality of my clients' lives. I had the opportunity to renew people's self-esteem.[32]

And Camille Paglia takes issue with the very notion that prostitution is an arena of male domination over women: "The feminist analysis of prostitution says that men are using money as power over women. I'd say, yes, that's all that men *have*. The money is a confession of weakness. They have to buy women's attention. It's not a sign of power; it's a sign of weakness."[33]

Empowerment is rare in news-media reports on the sex industry but is represented in some entertainment media, such as the television shows *Cathouse, G-String Divas,* and *Secret Diary of a Call Girl* and some feature films.[34] In academic writings, it is unusual for an author to adopt the empowerment perspective in an unqualified manner—that is, defining sex work as a means of enhancement or upward mobility across the board. Instead, writers describe individuals or groups whose lives changed for the better as a result of sex work. In one of Mexico's legal prostitution zones, for instance, sex work allows women to escape from abusive relationships with their husbands. The zone is a place where "women can live and work without the dependence on male spouses or family that Mexican culture prescribes."[35] Consider Gabriela: "Free of her husband, she was transformed from a quiet, deeply depressed person to a sometimes outspoken, confident, and much happier woman."[36] Cleo Odzer writes in her ethnographic study of Bangkok's red-light district, "Patpong women relished bending *farang* [foreign] men to their wills. They used their sexuality and exotic mystique to maneuver them into compromises."[37] Odzer compares Thai prostitutes favorably to other Thai women: the prostitutes had more independence, were more savvy and enterprising, traveled on their own, learned other languages as a result of their contact with foreign men, and became skilled businesswomen. Moreover, "working Patpong offered adventure, excitement, and romance." While sex work is stigmatized in Thailand, "within Patpong itself, their occupation was not only accepted but glamorized."[38] Another analyst echoes this assessment in comparing Thai prostitutes' independence with that of other Thai women:

> They are women who have the spirit of a fighter—in sexual relations and others. While their middle-class sisters are being repressed by conservative values and the sexual double standards, they seem to have more autonomy in their personal and sexual lives. . . . It is interesting to watch an innocent and obedient young girl turn into a sophisticated and rebellious woman in such a male-dominated society where "good" women are all subservient and respectful to male superiority beyond question.[39]

The empowerment paradigm is particularly evident when we move from mainstream, heterosexual sex work to alternative genres or markets. Research on gay male, lesbian, and transgender sex work highlights the ways in which the work can be not only identity affirming for the workers (and customers) but also capable of making a larger statement about the value of these marginalized populations, thereby presenting a challenge to mainstream heterosexist culture:

- A significant segment of the male prostitute population experiences identity-enhancing outcomes from sex work.[40]
- Pornography historically helped to affirm gay male identity and today holds a fair amount of esteem within the gay community. Joe Thomas describes the "positive value of having one's own sexual identity—rejected and stigmatized by the status quo—validated by seeing it played out in front of one's very eyes. . . . Gay pornography is one of the few venues for seeing gay sexuality presented in a positive light."[41]
- A unique study of strip clubs where both the dancers and customers are African American women found that the clubs facilitated cultural bonding, consciousness raising, and empowerment among the black women involved. These clubs differ radically from the conventional ones where female dancers entertain a male audience.[42]
- A Brazilian study reported that for transgender sex workers, prostitution was the only sphere of life that enhanced their self-image. Prostitution gave them a "sense of personal worth, self-confidence, and self-esteem."[43] They sold sex not only for the money but also for emotional and sexual fulfillment. In focus groups in San Francisco, researchers discovered that "sex work involvement provided many young transgender women of color feelings of community and social support, which they often lacked in their family contexts."

Another advantage was that sex work gave these individuals a "sense of independence and non-reliance on others (i.e., managers, co-workers) who might express discrimination or harassment."[44] Sex work was one of the few arenas in which they could shield themselves from societal rejection.

- Research on pornography made by and for women discovered that female producers are often motivated by loftier goals than are their counterparts in the mainstream porn industry. Instead of simply seeking to make money, many of these female artists are motivated by feminist objectives, sex worker activism, and a desire to create materials that challenge conventional male-centered ideals of sexual relations. The researcher, Jill Bakehorn, shows how this work validates the women who create it and is designed to be empowering for the audience as well.[45]

In each of these cases, we see evidence of how sex work can be embraced and used for either personal validation or as part of a larger identity politics that redefines or inverts the conventional meanings associated with stigmatized vice.

To reiterate, the empowerment paradigm is rarely presented in an absolute way in academic research; few scholars would define sex work solely in terms of empowerment. Instead, researchers identify individuals or populations that have experienced positive outcomes from their participation in or exposure to the sex industry.

The Oppression Paradigm

The oppression paradigm is embraced by a number of academics as well as, not surprisingly, antiprostitution activists. It is grounded in a particular branch of feminist thinking, radical feminism, and differs from the religious right's objections to commercial sex, which centers on the threat it poses to marriage, the family, and society's moral fiber. The oppression paradigm holds that sex work is the quintessential expression of patriarchal gender relations and male domination. Indeed, the very existence of prostitution rests on structural inequalities between men and women: women would not sell sex if they had the same socioeconomic opportunities as men. But prostitution is not only rooted in inequality; it also *perpetuates* inequality both symbolically and instrumentally. Carole Pateman describes the symbolic harm:

The general display of women's bodies and sexual parts, either in representations or as live bodies, is central to the sex industry and continually reminds men—and women—that men exercise the law of male sex-right, that they have patriarchal right of access to women's bodies. . . . [In prostitution] the sex act itself provides acknowledgment of patriarchal right. When women's bodies are on sale as commodities in the capitalist market, . . . the law of male sex-right is publicly affirmed, and men gain public acknowledgment as women's sexual masters—that is what is wrong with prostitution.[46]

Not only does the sex industry objectify and commodify women's bodies; it also gives men the idea that they have a "right" to buy erotic entertainment from women, thus reinforcing women's subordination to men. Oppression theorists argue that this fundamental harm will persist no matter how prostitution, pornography, and stripping are organized; legalizing these practices in an attempt to "improve" them will not alter the gender inequality that is intrinsic to sexual commerce.

The instrumental dimension is reflected in the argument that exploitation, subjugation, and violence are intrinsic to and ineradicable from sex work—transcending historical time period, national context, and type of sexual commerce.[47] As oppression theorists are fond of saying, sex work *is* violence, categorically. The solution is nothing short of the total elimination of prostitution, pornography, strip clubs, and all other commercial sex.

What is striking about the oppression paradigm is its exclusive focus on the *negative*. The leading advocates of this paradigm not only deny that there can be anything positive about sex work but also reject the idea that it can be neutral—revolving around everyday, routine work practices. To concede the latter would be to acknowledge the "work" dimension, which they flatly deny. Another notable feature of oppression writings is the *neglect of male and transgender sex work*, which is jettisoned by the almost exclusive theorizing of prostitution as an institution that victimizes women and girls.

Readers unfamiliar with the sex work literature would be surprised at both the dogmatic tone and the grandiose claims characteristic of the oppression paradigm—a radical departure from conventional scholarly writings. Its advocates frequently offer dramatic sound bites and equate prostitution with practices that are widely condemned:

- "Prostitution is better understood as domestic violence than as a job."[48]
- "Prostitution is rape that's paid for."[49]
- "Prostitution, pornography, and trafficking meet or exceed legal definitions of torture."[50]

Prostitutes are recast as "sex slaves" and "prostituted women," thereby erasing any semblance of human agency. Janice Raymond holds that "prostitution is something that is done to women,"[51] and Sheila Jeffreys expands on this notion: "Anti-prostitution campaigners use the term *prostituted women* instead of *prostitutes*. This is a deliberate political decision and is meant to symbolize the lack of choice women have over being used in prostitution."[52] Melissa Farley describes this powerlessness in absolute terms: "Prostitution dehumanizes, commodifies, and fetishizes women. . . . In prostitution, there is always a power imbalance, where the john has the social and economic power to hire her/him to act like a sexualized puppet. Prostitution excludes any mutuality of privilege or pleasure."[53] This wholesale denial of women's agency in sexual commerce and emphasis on passive victimhood violates a central tenet of feminism, which centers on women's intentionality and empowerment.

If female sex workers are passive victims in the oppression paradigm, male customers are depicted as individuals with full agency—as powerful and violent misogynists:

- They "buy women" rather than sexual services.[54]
- "These men must be viewed as batterers rather than customers."[55]
- "Johns are regularly murderous toward women."[56]
- "These [clients] are not just naughty boys who need their wrists slapped. They could be more accurately described as predators."[57]

One prohibitionist organization has even proposed that all customers be branded "sex offenders" and listed on a sex-offender registry: "This naming is important since it places men who buy sex in the same category as rapists, pedophiles, and other social undesirables."[58]

Oppression writers see animus in men's consumption of sexual services. Donna Hughes writes, "Men who purchase sex acts do not respect women, nor do they want to respect women."[59] Andrea Dworkin goes even further: "When men use women in prostitution, they are expressing a pure hatred for the female body. . . . It is a contempt so deep, so deep, that a whole human life is reduced to a few sexual orifices, and he can do anything he wants."[60] And Farley declares, "The difference between pimps who terrorize women on the street and pimps in business suits who terrorize women in gentlemen's clubs is a difference in class only, not a difference in woman hating."[61]

Sensationalism is abundant in this body of literature. Anecdotal horror stories are a staple of these writings and are clearly designed to arouse readers' indignation. Reports, websites, and journal articles feature quotations from women who have had horrible experiences that are presented as typical. The authors frequently write in a dramatic or alarmist manner, sometimes unwittingly objectifying women themselves. One of Jeffreys's books on the sex industry is titled *The Industrial Vagina*, and Farley writes, "When women are turned into objects that men masturbate into, profound psychological harm results for the person who is acting as receptacle."[62] Similarly objectifying is Farley's assertion, "Her self and those qualities that define her as an individual are removed in prostitution and she acts the part of the thing he wants her to be."[63]

Oppression theorists often make bold claims simply *by fiat*—as self-evident, absolute principles. At times, the reasoning is confusingly circular. Consider this passage from an article entitled "Pornography as Trafficking" by prohibitionist icon Catharine MacKinnon:

> In the resulting materials, these people are then conveyed and sold for a buyer's sexual use. . . . Each time the pornography is commercially exchanged, the trafficking continues as the women and children in it are transported and provided for sex, sold, and bought again. Doing all these things for the purpose of exploiting the prostitution of others—which pornography intrinsically does—makes it trafficking in persons.[64]

The slippage between "materials" and "persons" is striking. Conflation is even more conspicuous in MacKinnon's argument that "the pornography industry, in production, creates demand for prostitution, hence for trafficking, because it is itself a form of prostitution and trafficking."[65] Distinctions are erased in order to render all types of sex work part of the same syndrome of oppression.

While the oppression paradigm is founded on grand ontological characterizations of sex work, some of its proponents also make specific empirical claims that, taken together, present an image of *concentrated, manifold victimization*. Such claims include the following: that *most* prostitutes enter the trade when they are 13–14 years old, were physically or sexually abused as children, were tricked or forced into the trade by pimps or traffickers, are subjected to routine violence while working, use or are addicted to drugs, suffer severe psychological problems, and desperately want to exit the sex trade.[66] When these claims are generalized to "most" sex workers, they are fallacies: they are largely or wholly drawn from nonrandom, unrepresentative, and small samples of the street-based population. In other words, we cannot even say that these generalizations apply to street prostitution, let alone the various types of indoor prostitution. The claims are based on doubly skewed samples.

Moreover, there are studies that challenge each of the aforementioned claims. Regarding age of entry, some studies of street prostitutes find that a majority began selling sex while under age 18, but other street-based research reports that a minority began to sell sex prior to age 18 and an even lower number at age 14.[67] A study of 557 street and indoor prostitutes working in three Dutch cities found that the median age of entry into prostitution was 27 for non-drug-using female workers, 25 for drug-using female workers, and 24 for transgender workers (the entry range was 20–33 years old).[68] Studies based exclusively on indoor workers report diverse findings as well. A survey of 815 prostitutes working in six different types of establishments in Thailand found that only 1.5 percent were under age 18 at the time of the survey, and 9 percent reported that they were under 18 when they first started selling sex; the average age of the study participants was 28.3 years. The researchers attributed the low number of underage workers to vigorous police enforcement. Similarly, very few of these workers had tried drugs.[69] Regarding childhood experiences of abuse, a sample of 127 street and indoor workers in the Netherlands reported that 16 percent of the sample had experienced sexual abuse by relatives and 9 percent by nonrelatives prior to age 16—far fewer than what oppression theorists claim.[70] Regarding the claim that extremely high percentages of prostitutes are assaulted, robbed, raped, and otherwise victimized while working, there is counterevidence reporting much lower rates, especially in studies of indoor prostitution (discussed further in chapter 2). The key point is one of *variation* across studies in the proportion of prostitutes who began working while underage, who use drugs, who have been victimized while working, and so forth. The large research literature on sex work shows that the grand generalizations of oppression theorists are simply fallacies.

Many of the writings in the oppression paradigm feature quotations from a few sex workers, typically the most disturbing stories presented as indicative of intrinsic problems. Gayle Rubin has criticized an earlier generation of oppression writers for cherry picking the "worst available examples" and casting them as representative.[71] If these authors comment at all on findings that they did not expect, they go to great lengths to discredit such findings. Particularly inconvenient are those sex workers whose experiences clash with the author's views. Raymond writes, "There is no doubt that a small number of women *say* they choose to be in prostitution, especially in public contexts orchestrated by the sex industry."[72] But the number is "small," and her emphasis on the word "say" and her use of "orchestrated" casts doubt on the veracity of the women's testimony. Prior to interviewing a few workers in Nevada's legal brothels, Farley stated, "I knew that they would minimize how bad it was."[73] If the respondent did not acknowledge that working in a brothel was "bad," she was in denial, and Farley sought to penetrate this barrier: "We were asking the women to briefly remove a mask that was crucial to their psychological survival."[74] She also asserts that "most" of the women working in the legal brothels had pimps, despite the fact that the women were "reluctant to admit that their boyfriends and husbands were pimping them."[75] And "a surprisingly low percentage" of the women said that they had been sexually abused as a child, which Farley dismisses as being "lower than the likely actual incidence of sexual abuse."[76]

In Farley's study of six countries, she found substantial support for legalization of prostitution: a majority (54 percent) of the prostitutes interviewed across the countries (and 56 percent in Colombia, 74 percent in Canada, and 85 percent in Mexico) said legalizing prostitution would make it safer.[77] These inconvenient figures are presented in a table but are not discussed in the text (Farley simply says that 46 percent of the total did not believe legalization would make prostitution safer). In another article, Farley discounts those who favor legalization: "Like everyone else, our interviewees minimized the harms of prostitution and they sometimes believed industry claims that legalization or decriminalization will somehow make them safer."[78] Workers who want legalization apparently could not have formed this opinion on their own and must have been deceived by advocates.

When oppression writers comment at all on findings from other studies that clash with their paradigm, these findings are discounted, reinterpreted, or inverted.[79] Most of the time, however, these writers simply ignore findings that challenge their claims. Karl Popper, the renowned philosopher of science, described *prescientific reasoning* as conclusions formed in the absence of evidence or lacking in the critical ingredient of falsifiability.[80] As should be abundantly clear by now, the oppression paradigm is first and foremost a prescientific ideology. Its central tenets are not derived from carefully conducted research, which would contradict or radically qualify those very tenets. In short, the oppression paradigm pays little heed to the canons of scientific objectivity, and this is due to its advocates' overriding commitment to abolishing sex work.

Popular in some academic circles, the oppression framework also predominates in the media, in political discourse, and in policymaking in many countries. The mass media are saturated with stories highlighting worst cases, and news reports usually center on themes of violence, pimping, crime, disease, and immorality.[81] Government officials in most of the world view prostitution through the same lens. The oppression paradigm is occasionally questioned, however. In the debates on a legalization bill in the parliament of Western Australia in 2007 and 2008, the ruling Labor Party systematically critiqued the assertions of a prominent oppression writer (Janice Raymond) and voted to legalize prostitution because of its harm-reduction potential.[82] And in a recent successful challenge to the constitutionality of Canada's prostitution laws, the court downgraded the testimony of three antiprostitution witnesses (Melissa Farley, Janice Raymond, and Richard Poulin) because of their biases.[83] These two examples demonstrate that on rare occasions state officials have rejected the dominant oppression frame and the claims of its advocates.

The Polymorphous Paradigm

Both the oppression and empowerment paradigms are one-dimensional and essentialist. While exploitation and empowerment are certainly present in sex work, there is sufficient variation across time, place, and sector to demonstrate that sex work cannot be reduced to one or the other. An alternative, what I call the *polymorphous paradigm*, identifies a constellation of occupational arrangements, power relations, and participants' experiences. Unlike the other two perspectives, polymorphism is sensitive to complexities and to the structural conditions shaping sex work along a continuum of agency and subordination.[84] The policy implications are clear: rather than painting prostitution with a broad brush, we can identify those structural arrangements that have negative effects and bolster those associated with more positive outcomes.

Because the complexities of the polymorphous model cannot be boiled down to sound bites, it rarely appears in the news media, popular culture, political debates, or public discourse. Consequently, the prostitution myths described earlier have become the conventional wisdom. But there are some exceptions in popular culture. In the first episode of the autobiographical Showtime television series *Secret Diary of a Call Girl*, a London escort tells the audience, "There's as many kinds of working girls as there are people. So you can't generalize." And a few movies present prostitution in a richly nuanced or mixed manner rather than stereotypically.[85]

A growing body of research documents tremendous international diversity in how sex work is organized and experienced by workers, clients, and third parties.[86] These studies undermine some deep-rooted myths about

TABLE 1.1
Selected Types of Prostitution

	Location	Prices Charged	Exploitation by Third Parties	Public Visibility	Impact on Community
Independent Call Girl / Escort	Private premises/ hotels	High	None	None	None
Escort Agency Employee	Private premises/ hotels	High	Moderate	None	None
Brothel Employee	Brothel, sauna club, massage parlor	Moderate to high	Moderate	Low	Little or none, if discreet
Window Worker	Window rooms	Moderate to low	Low to moderate	High	Some, depends on number and location
Bar or Casino Worker	Bar/casino contact; sex elsewhere	Moderate to low	Low to moderate	Moderate	Equivalent to impact of bar/casino
Streetwalker	Street contact; sex in cars, alleys, parks, etc.	Low	High	High	Adverse

Table refers to female workers. The indoor workers depicted here do not include those who have been trafficked against their will or otherwise forced into prostitution, whose experiences differ from those who have entered this work voluntarily.

Exploitation by third parties means third-party receipt of at least some of the profits. *Impact on community* refers to effects on the surrounding neighborhood's quality of life. *Public visibility* excludes appearances in advertisements, such as an online website.

Source: Adapted and modified from Richard Symanski, *The Immoral Landscape,* Toronto: Buttersworth, 1981, p. 14.

prostitution and present a challenge to those who embrace monolithic paradigms. Victimization, exploitation, agency, job satisfaction, self-esteem, and other dimensions should be treated as *variables* (not constants) that differ between types of sex work, geographical locations, and other structural conditions. In the remainder of this chapter and in chapter 2, I present evidence in support of the polymorphous paradigm by contrasting different types of prostitution.

Many historical studies of prostitution excel at describing hierarchies, as well as changes in sexual commerce over time.[87] Such historical diversity and change offers abundant counterevidence to grand claims about the "intrinsic" nature of commercial sex. Today, no less than in the past, prostitution is stratified. Prostitutes vary tremendously in their reasons for entry, risk of violence, dependence on or exploitation by third parties, experiences with the authorities, public visibility, number and type of clients, relationships with co-workers, and impact on the surrounding community. Age, appearance, and ethnicity also figure into the hierarchy, shaping workers' earning power. And location is a key variable—with important distinctions between sex work conducted on the streets, indoors in a hotel or residence after an initial contact is made elsewhere (e.g., in a bar, karaoke club, restaurant, casino), and in indoor settings where both the initial contact and sex occur in the same place (e.g., brothels, massage parlors, saunas, hair salons, clubs). A hybrid type is window prostitution, in which workers operate indoors but are observable from outside. They are much more visible than are other indoor workers, but they are shielded from the street by their rooms. Window prostitution exists in two of the cities examined later in this book, Amsterdam and Antwerp, as well as in several other cities around the world.

Table 1.1 presents a typology of prostitution. In street prostitution, the initial transaction occurs in a public place (a sidewalk, park, truck stop), and the sex act takes place either in public or in a private setting (alley, park, vehicle, hotel, etc.). Many underage street prostitutes are runaways who end up in a new locale with no resources and little recourse but to engage in some kind of criminal activity—whether theft, drug dealing, or selling sex. They sell sex out of dire necessity ("survival sex") or to support a drug habit. The process typically begins with bartering sex for food, drugs, or a place to stay and evolves into more routine sex-for-money exchanges. Some do this independently, but many underage prostitutes quickly become involved with pimps.[88]

Street prostitution is associated with myriad problems. Many street workers use addictive drugs, work in crime-ridden areas, are socially isolated and disconnected from support services, engage in risky sex, are exploited and abused by pimps, and are vulnerable to being assaulted, robbed, raped, or killed on the streets. By standing on the sidewalk, they are accessible to predators who seek to rob or attack them, as well as to voyeurs who shout insults and obscenities at them. Friction with local residents is also common. Those street sellers who are free of drugs and pimps have greater control of their work but still confront the occupational hazards just described.[89]

The types presented in table 1.1 are not rigid. An individual may fit into more than one category. For instance, independent call girls may also accept occasional appointments from an escort agency, and massage parlor or brothel workers sometimes moonlight by meeting customers in private and keeping the earnings for themselves. But it is rare for workers to experience substantial upward or downward mobility. As a rule, "the level at which the woman begins work in the prostitution world determines her general position in the occupation for much of her career as a prostitute. Changing levels requires contacts and a new set of work techniques and attitudes,"[90] and moving up often requires a level of health and attractiveness that many street workers lack. If a move takes place, it is usually lateral, such as from the street to a down-market peep show, from a massage parlor to an escort agency, or from an escort agency to independent work. Occasionally, an upper– or middle-tier worker whose life situation changes (e.g., because of aging or drug addiction) is no longer able to work in that stratum and gravitates to the street, and police crackdowns on indoor businesses can force some of these workers to the streets. But in general, indoor workers are not inclined to consider street work as an option.[91] Likewise, transitioning from street work to escorting or a brothel is quite rare. Most street workers lack the education and skills required for indoor work, insofar as it requires prolonged social interaction with clients; many would be rejected on appearance grounds by an indoor operator; and many street prostitutes would dislike working indoors because they would not see the "action" that they are accustomed to on the streets or because they would have trouble conforming to the myriad rules imposed on them by house managers.[92]

What about the clients of sex workers? Earlier in the chapter, we saw how oppression-paradigm writers demonize "johns." Yet the evidence shows that customers vary tremendously—in age, race, and social class; in their reasons for buying sex; and in their experiences during paid sex encounters.[93] Most do not fit the stereotype of the violent misogynist.[94] Sociologist Martin Monto concludes that there is "no evidence to suggest that more than a minority of customers assault prostitutes" and that "most clients do not hold views that justify violence against prostitutes."[95] Only a fraction of arrested customers have a previous conviction for a violent or sexual offense.[96] Some are indeed predators intent on acting violently, while others seek out the most vulnerable prostitutes because they feel they are easily controlled. But other clients are "repulsed at the idea of buying sex from prostitutes who are desperate, vulnerable, or coerced into prostitution" and say that if they met a trafficked victim, they would try to help her escape or contact the police.[97] On websites where clients recount their experiences and share information with others, it is "not uncommon for these writers to complain about violence against prostitutes or to encourage others to treat prostitutes with respect."[98] Interestingly, the largest study of client interactions with call girls reported that in half these encounters the men played the subordinate role: they "enjoyed relaxing and letting the call girl direct the love play."[99] Clients use their economic power to buy sex, but they do not necessarily enact domination in the course of their sexual interactions.

Customers patronize prostitutes for diverse reasons. One popular reason is the notion of physical "needs." The director of a clients' organization in the Netherlands expressed this view: "I think the value of prostitution has to be made clear. The value of prostitution is that men who are in need, or even *very urgent* need, can find relief. It's as simple as that. People are justified to seek outlets for, in many cases, a very burdensome frustration."[100] These needs are socially constructed rather than biological—an "ideology of male sexual needs," according to Mary McIntosh—but they are nevertheless part of the vocabulary of motives for buying sex.[101] There are plenty of other factors involved. Some individuals buy sex opportunistically when they encounter a sex worker in a bar or on the street, whereas others plan a liaison ahead of time based on one or more of the following motives:

- Some seek to exert physical or emotional control over another person: they target sex workers because they are more accessible and vulnerable than ordinary individuals and less likely to report victimization to the police.
- Some have difficulty finding a partner for a conventional relationship.
- If they currently have a partner, some are unsatisfied with the partner's sexual behavior.
- Some are looking to fulfill a fantasy by having sex with a person with a desired physical appearance (e.g., physique, ethnicity), someone who will engage in desired activities (such as role playing or sadomasochism), someone who will teach them new sexual techniques, or someone of a different sexual orientation (e.g., heterosexual men who wish to experiment with a gay male or transgender provider, or heterosexual women seeking a lesbian experience).

- Some find this transgressive conduct risky, thrilling, or sporting (clients in online chat rooms refer to themselves as "hobbyists" or "mongers").
- Some wish to avoid the long-term obligations or emotional attachment involved in a conventional relationship.
- Some seek a limited, quasi-romantic emotional connection in addition to or instead of sex.[102]

Comparing the last two motives, we can see that some men pay for sex to *avoid* intimacy, whereas others are consciously *seeking* intimacy and companionship. What do clients consider when making a decision to buy sex? One study reported that they place a premium on avoiding arrest (79 percent), personal safety (77 percent), and privacy (77 percent) and want the provider to be sexually healthy (90 percent); less than half (43 percent) said that cost was an important factor.[103] These considerations influence, but do not dictate, the decision to buy sex in one venue as opposed to in others. Streetwalkers may be attractive because of easy access, low prices, or the excitement of cruising for sex. Other clients avoid the streets because they view them as dangerous places (risks to health, safety, and arrest) or because they view street workers as more vulnerable, desperate, or exploited by pimps.[104] They prefer indoor establishments because they are viewed as being safer, less sordid, more discreet, and more relaxing.

In sum, along several key axes, clients vary as much as sex workers do. Research on both populations overwhelmingly supports the polymorphous paradigm.

The polymorphous perspective stands in stark contrast to the other two paradigms discussed in this chapter—oppression and empowerment—both of which are simplistic and monolithic. By recognizing and sociologically accounting for diversity in the world of prostitution—a diversity that includes empowerment of some workers, oppression of others, and shades of gray in between—polymorphism offers a rich and more sophisticated template than do the other two frameworks. Chapter 2 extends the analysis with a more detailed account of indoor prostitution, as a prelude to the examination of legal prostitution systems in chapters 4–6 in places where the legal sector is usually restricted to indoor work.

2

Indoor Prostitution

What Makes It Special?

Many writers who generalize about prostitution base their ideas on images of street prostitution, which accounts for most of what we "know" about this world. Yet there is another type—indoor prostitution—that deserves much more attention, for several reasons: (1) in many countries, paid sexual transactions are far more common indoors than on the streets. In Thailand, for example, almost all prostitutes work indoors, while in the United States and Britain about four-fifths do so;[1] (2) the street and indoor markets differ substantively, with indoor work presenting the clearest evidence challenging popular images of degradation and oppression; and (3) most of the nations that have legalized prostitution have done so only with regard to indoor settings. Thus, it is crucial to explore the dimensions of indoor sex work before proceeding to my examination of legal prostitution later in the book.

Conditions Shaping Indoor Prostitution

Indoor prostitution takes place in brothels, massage parlors, bars, hotels, saunas, private premises, dance halls, and on boats docked in harbors. It can be found in back rooms of tanning salons, beauty shops, barbershops, cafes, and other conventional businesses. Insofar as *indoor prostitution* is an omnibus concept covering such a large variety of settings, we must be careful not to reify it as a monolithic category. There is plenty of variety within the indoor sector, but at the same time it is important to make some general distinctions between indoor and street work. It is not the mere fact of being indoors that distinguishes indoor from street prostitution but rather that *certain characteristics of indoor settings are preconditions for a work environment that can be superior to the streets.* These characteristics include the following:

- Indoor workers are less accessible and hence less vulnerable to street predators.
- Meeting a client indoors allows for more thorough screening than what is usually possible on the street.
- If one works indoors with a manager, receptionist, or other providers, they are available to intervene in the event that a client becomes abusive.
- Working indoors shields one from the elements, which can pay dividends for one's comfort and health.
- If conducted discreetly, indoor work does not present a public nuisance, whereas street commerce is often associated with public disturbance and generates complaints from nearby residents and merchants.

These features mean that indoor prostitution offers some important *potential* advantages over street prostitution. But other structural conditions are also crucial. These factors include one's economic situation prior to entering sex work, drug dependency, immigration status, adequacy of procedures for screening clients, relationships with third parties, whether workers are employees or independent operators, and whether selling sex is legal or illegal. Regarding the first variable, prostitutes who work indoors generally come from more advantaged socioeconomic backgrounds than do those who work on the streets.

Societal context is crucial, with indoor work in developing countries more likely to exist under harsher conditions than in developed countries.[2] Developing countries may have quite a few rudimentary brothels where the work is low paying and hazardous. At the same time, a developing nation may also have an elite sector. In Pakistan, for example, wealthy men have sexual liaisons with high-class courtesans, who "are able to enjoy a degree of economic independence and exercise an agency that is unknown to all but the most highly educated women in mainstream society."[3] They accompany men to parties and other events and provide men with a fantasy relationship, much like elite escorts in Western countries, except that the Pakistanis also perform traditional *kathak* dances in private for their clients. Vietnam has plenty of low-tier commercial sex but also a distinct upscale market for rich men who "are paying for beautiful and desirable women who spend more time talking with them in restaurants and cafes than engaging in the performance of sex."[4] The women receive expensive gifts rather than money; spend a great deal of time engaging in "romantic" emotional labor; and are very selective in their choice of clients, which only increases their desirability. And some developing nations have an

TABLE 2.1

Victimization Rates, Street and Indoor Prostitutes

Robbed Street	*Robbed Indoor*	*Assaulted Street*	*Assaulted Indoor*	*Raped Street*	*Raped Indoor*
37	10	47[1]	14	22	2
37	9	39	14	37	9[2]
42	25	41	21	27	8

Respondents were asked whether they had ever experienced, while working, any of these crimes.

1. Slapped, punched, or kicked. A separate category is "beaten"—reported by 27% of street workers and 1% of indoor workers.

2. Sexual assault, includes rape.

Sources (first row): Stephanie Church et al. (2001), N = 115 street and 125 indoor prostitutes (in saunas or as escorts) in Britain; (second row): John Lowman and Laura Fraser (1995), N = 62 street and 22 indoor workers in Canada. 10% of street and 0% of indoors reported experiencing attempted murder; (third row): Libby Plumridge and Gillian Abel (2001), N = 78 street and 225 indoor workers (escorts and massage parlors) in New Zealand.

even wider array of sex for sale. A recent survey of 815 sex workers in Thailand found significant differences between those who worked in brothels, karaoke clubs, go-go bars, massage parlors, or beer bars, or as freelancers.[5] Cleo Odzer's ethnography describes the hierarchy in sexually oriented bars in Bangkok and Pattaya:

> Working in a blow job bar or performing in Fucking Shows was at the bottom. Next came dancing nude and performing trick shows. . . . Bikini dancing in ground-floor establishments was high status, but working in evening clothes without having to dance, like Hoi, was higher. . . . At the top of the status hierarchy were the beauties who didn't work for a bar at all but came and went on their own time. Some of the larger establishments allowed these women to mix with their clientele.[6]

Societal context is an important variable, with the harshest working conditions more prevalent in poor and developing nations, but even there sex work may be highly stratified and include an elite echelon. It is important to recognize both cross-national and intrasocietal differences.

Third Parties

Much depends on the balance of power between sex workers and third parties. Many workers operate independently; others employ another person to serve as a middleman or a receptionist/gatekeeper, while others work for a manager who exercises at least some control and extracts some or all of the profit. Third parties play various roles—recruiting workers, screening clients, mediating disputes, dictating and enforcing conduct norms, and providing security. As in most other kinds of work, managers generally treat sex workers as subordinates and seek to limit their job autonomy.[7] What varies is whether they engage in unfair managerial practices or otherwise abuse their workers. On the streets, pimps range from the stereotypical parasite who exercises total and highly abusive control to pimps who behave less oppressively and treat their workers more as business partners than as exploitees.[8] The managers and owners of indoor establishments also differ. Some provide the bare minimum of amenities, are lax about health and safety, favor certain employees over others, or treat all of their workers poorly; others have collegial relations with their employees, rigorously screen customers, and provide safe and healthy working conditions.[9] Another third party is the middleman who connects sex workers with clients. The middleman's services can be crucial to transactions in which direct client access to workers is hampered, such as for long-distance truck drivers unfamiliar with a particular town on their route.[10] And finally, some sex workers employ receptionists or maids who screen clients and otherwise assist the provider; those who remain on-site during transactions are available to intervene in the event of problems with a customer. Research shows that the presence of such gatekeepers reduces the risks associated with working alone.[11]

When prostitution is legal and regulated by the authorities, much of the regulation is designed to control third parties who run brothels and other indoor businesses, forcing them to improve working conditions and, more generally, empowering workers vis-à-vis managers and owners.

Victimization

In general, indoor sex workers in developed countries are much less likely than street workers to have a background of childhood abuse (neglect, violence, incest), to enter sex work at a young age, to engage in risky behavior (e.g., use of addictive drugs, engaging in unprotected sex), or to be victimized. Off-street workers who have not been coerced into prostitution are much less likely to experience assault, robbery, rape, threats of violence, or murder. In addition to differences in *ever* having been victimized, street workers are more likely to experience *more frequent* and *more severe* victimization over time. Some studies report high percentages of indoor providers who have *never* experienced violence on the job. This was the case for 78 percent of indoor workers in a British study and 77 percent in Belgium.[12] And research in the Netherlands in the early 1990s reported that two-thirds of a sample of 127 prostitutes had never experienced physical violence and 61 percent had never experienced sexual violence on the job (most of the remainder had experienced violence infrequently).[13] This sample included both street and indoor workers (in brothels, clubs, and windows) and presented figures for all types combined, so it is likely that the number experiencing violence would be even lower if the sample was restricted to the indoor workers.

Some comparative data are presented in table 2.1. The figures are drawn from a selection of studies that illustrate the general pattern that "street workers are significantly more at risk of more violence and more serious violence than indoor workers."[14] Although random sampling was not possible in the studies that have documented these differences, the fact that they consistently find significant street-indoor disparities lends credence to the general conclusion.[15]

Each type of setting has advantages and disadvantages for the actors involved. Those who work in group settings—in brothels, massage parlors, saunas, and bars—benefit from the presence of gatekeepers and colleagues from whom they can learn the trade and who also can intervene in the event of an unruly customer. Brothels and massage parlors often have screening mechanisms, video surveillance, and alarm systems. In bars and dance clubs, workers have time to screen prospective customers; conversing over drinks allows them to assess the client's temperament. The presence of co-workers not only increases safety but can also increase job satisfaction, because workers can share experiences and support one another. This is especially likely when the workers hail from similar backgrounds. For example, many of those who work at a particular bar in Thailand have chain migrated from the same cluster of rural villages and have similar experiences prior to moving to the cities. At the same time, the presence of co-workers can foster competition and altercations—to be expected when people work in close proximity and perhaps live on the premises as well.

Call girls and escorts are vulnerable because they work in isolation at their own residence or at the client's hotel or residence. A greater proportion of their clients are low-risk regulars, however.[16] And these workers employ their own safeguards. Call girls blacklist and alert other providers about abusive clients. If one works for an agency, it is now common practice for the gatekeepers to conduct a background check on every first-time client (including his place of work, phone numbers, home address, Social Security number), verifying this information with a Google search and return phone calls. Independents use the same screening methods and may also require a reference from another provider and proof of employment (to thwart police stings). A study of call girls noted that they develop "a sensitivity to detecting potential danger in the caller's attitudes, manners, tone of voice, or nature of the conversation."[17] And they routinely check in by phone with the agent or a friend at a designated time before and after a visit, using code words if they sense trouble.[18] "The girls call to check in when they first get to an appointment," one agency booker stated. "We had code words, like 'Red Bull.' If I heard her say she needed a Red Bull, I'd try to distract the guy on the phone so she could get out of there."[19] These procedures are not infallible, but they do help to decrease risks. As one escort writes, "It's a good idea to stay suspicious, in my experience. . . . No one has ever taken advantage and I want to ensure it never does happen. That's part of why I work through an agency."[20]

Well-Being

Many indoor sex workers in developed countries are similar to nonprostitutes in measures of mental health and self-esteem. One study of the mental health of 187 prostitutes found that those who worked independently and at the high end of the pay scale were most likely to score in the top quartile on measures of emotional well-being, whereas those whose work was low paying, on the street, or in brothels with poor working conditions scored in the lowest quartile on well-being.[21] Other research, comparing indoor prostitutes with an age-matched sample of nonprostitute women, found no differences in their physical and mental health, self-esteem, or the quality of their social networks.[22] This contrasts with street workers, who face ongoing danger and stress at work, contributing to psychological problems that are only exacerbated by drug addiction, health problems, and social isolation. A third study reported that streetwalkers exhibited significant psychological problems, whereas call girls and brothel workers generally were "handling themselves well, manifesting good emotional controls, being well aware of conventionality, and doing well in the occupation of their choice."[23] Similarly, research on call girls conducted by Ann Lucas concluded that they tended to have the "financial, social, and emotional wherewithal to structure their work largely in ways that suited them and provided . . . the ability to maintain healthy self-images."[24] Having engaged in other kinds of work in the past, the call girls interviewed by Lucas "expressed a clear preference for prostitution. . . . [They] entered their vocation voluntarily and valued the independence, autonomy, and control it offered."[25]

Indoor workers generally report more job satisfaction than street workers do. An Australian study found that half of call girls and brothel workers felt that their work was a "major source of satisfaction" in their lives, and seven out of ten said they would "definitely choose" this work if they had it to do over again.[26] A prostitute working in one of Nevada's legal brothels remarked, "I've always been a sexual person. I enjoy doing it. I mean, the money's wonderful but, hey, I enjoy what I do for a living too. I love the people, it's safe, it's clean."[27] Another Nevada provider elaborated: "Prostitution doesn't need to be demeaning, done without self-respect. It's a very intimate, service-oriented, people-oriented profession. I feel what I do, I do good."[28] A majority of indoor workers in several other studies similarly report that they enjoy the job, feel that their work has at least some positive effect on their lives, or believe that they provide a valuable service.[29] Again, these findings hardly apply to all indoor workers; instead, what these studies tell us is that positive outcomes are *more prevalent* in the indoor arena than on the streets.

Surprising as it may seem, indoor prostitutes' self-image can *improve* over time as a result of their work experiences. Diana Prince's comparative study of 75 streetwalkers and 75 call girls in California and 150 legal brothel workers in Nevada found that almost all of the call girls (97 percent) reported an increase in self-esteem after they began working in prostitution, compared with 50 percent of the brothel workers but only 8 percent of the streetwalkers.[30] Similarly, in another study, three-quarters of indoor prostitutes (most of whom worked in bars) felt that their life had improved after entering prostitution (the remainder reported no change; none said it was worse than before).[31] Male sex workers can experience the same ego enhancement over time. Interviews with 46 male escorts found that they felt desired, attractive, empowered, and important as a result of being generously paid for sex; they also experienced increased self-confidence and more favorable body images over time.[32] Their work experiences conditioned them to become more assertive and self-assured. Similarly, bar prostitutes in Thailand can be "immediately recognized . . . [by] the way they interacted with others—more forthright and confident, more demanding and outgoing" than typical Thai women.[33] And their counterparts in Cambodia "knew they were physically and sexually desirable and they flaunted their ability of possessing degrees of control over the men they met. They felt empowered by their linguistic ability, their sexuality, and their interpersonal talents."[34]

Why would self-esteem be high or increase among those who work in the upper echelons? Psychosocial well-being is associated with a range of structural factors, including education, income, control over working conditions, relations with third parties, and client base. The following features stand out:

- Income is a major source of self-esteem. While middle-range call girls earn $200–$500 per hour, top-tier workers charge much more ($1,000–$10,000 per hour or per session), and they are also lavished with fringe benefits, such as expensive gifts and paid travel to meet clients.[35] Escort agency, brothel, and massage parlor employees make considerably less because a large share (30–50 percent) goes to the business owner.
- Indoor workers, and especially those at the high end, develop a professional skill set over time. The skills include techniques for managing customers during intimate, hands-on activities; displaying self-confidence in setting terms and negotiating boundaries; adoption of safety precautions; and becoming "savvy businesswomen."[36]
- Acquiring new cultural capital is another benefit for many upscale sex workers. By associating with highly educated, cosmopolitan, jet-setting, or foreign clients, they are able to expand their cognitive horizons in valuable ways. Many in this echelon enjoy intangible rewards in addition to the income: adventure, excitement, mystery, fine dining, entertainment, and sightseeing.
- Another source of job satisfaction is revealed by indoor workers who describe "feeling 'sexy,' 'beautiful,' and 'powerful' only after they had begun to engage in sexual labor and were receiving consistent praise from their clients."[37] A large study of call girls reported that they "were proud of their bodies, of the way in which their bodies aroused men."[38] Former sex worker Dolores French captures this feeling eloquently: "If you take care of your body, and if men are constantly telling you how beautiful and desirable you are, you begin to love yourself deeply, even if you didn't to start with. Being a courtesan, for me, brought about a whole new feeling of self-esteem and self-worth."[39] In other words, in addition to the material rewards of high-end sex work, positive reinforcement and other good experiences may help enhance workers' self-image. Some derive pleasure from the sex itself, at least some of the time. As one brothel worker remarked, "With as much sex as we have, how could a woman not enjoy it occasionally?"[40] For some, getting paid

for sex is an added turn-on, magnifying the physical pleasure. And the same applies to male and transgender prostitutes who report frequently enjoying sex with their clients.[41]

High self-esteem is hardly universal, even in the top echelon, but the evidence just cited certainly contradicts the oppression paradigm's claim that sex workers at all levels are psychologically traumatized and suffer long-term emotional damage because of their work.[42]

At the same time, it is important to recognize that social stigma colors all sex work. Stigma is reflected in opinion polls, testimony from the workers themselves, and the inevitable censure of public figures who become involved in sex scandals. The intensity of stigma appears to be less for workers in the upper echelons and for male workers than for women, but it remains an occupational hazard for all sex workers, one that they grapple with in different ways.[43] A study of male and female escorts found that some of them "rejected the stigma attached to prostitution" and "expressed pride in the services they provided to clients"; the researchers characterized these escorts as embracing a "positive marginality" that redefined the meanings typically associated with their marginalized status.[44] For other escorts, the stigma is harder to overcome, resulting in certain protective strategies, for example, compartmentalizing their deviant work persona from their "real identity"; concealing their work from family, friends, neighbors, and strangers; distancing themselves from clients; using neutral or professional terms to describe their jobs ("working woman," "provider"); and viewing their work as a valuable service (providing pleasure or sex therapy, comforting lonely men, keeping marriages intact). The deep-rooted "whore stigma" is an ongoing source of stress in sex workers' lives and leads them to engage in coping strategies that are themselves stressful or socially isolating.

In sum, each type of indoor sex work can be distinguished from the others along various axes, but indoor work also has some important general dimensions that differentiate it from street prostitution. This point is developed further in the remainder of this chapter.

The Attractions of Indoor Prostitution

Chapter 1 noted that the customers of sex workers vary tremendously and cannot be lumped into a single category. It is equally the case that clients of indoor prostitutes differ from those who buy sex on the street:

- First, they differ demographically. Street clients come from all walks of life—ranging from poor to upper-class men.[45] By contrast, clients of indoor workers and especially upscale providers are less diverse—typically more affluent, white collar, and well educated.
- Second, many indoor clients seek a different kind of experience than what they would have on the street. As discussed later in this chapter, indoor clients typically spend much more time with a provider, almost guaranteeing that social as well as sexual intercourse will take place. These men are attracted to indoor providers precisely because they offer a range of services in addition to sex. (Of course, not all indoor settings are the same. In the window prostitution districts in Europe, the encounters typically take 15–20 minutes, allowing for only truncated conversation and nonsexual intimacy. The indoor patterns described in this chapter are more characteristic of settings where the encounter is longer and thus potentially variegated.)
- Third, some indoor sex venues feature a variety of recreation and entertainment. Many brothels offer an array of activities—a bar, pool table, Jacuzzi, sauna, sitting room with sofas, poll dancing, and so on. At least some of the clients patronize these places for their party atmosphere, similar to what many regular clients of strip clubs value about them.[46]
- Fourth, for the reasons just mentioned, indoor clients are more likely to seek and experience rapport, trust, and intimacy with providers. This is especially true for those who are regular clients, but even for nonregulars the indoor experience can be radically different from what is possible on the streets.[47]

Let us explore in more depth the experiential dimensions of indoor prostitution.

Though it is not widely known, indoor and street prostitution can offer very different kinds of experiences for clients and providers alike. Street encounters are fleeting: as a rule, conversation is minimal, and the two parties quickly proceed to sex. Conditions on the street—including police surveillance, the furtiveness of the action, and the often cramped settings in which sex occurs—all operate against anything more than a brief and impersonal encounter. Because so little time is spent with customers, the amount and quality of both physical and social contact is truncated. Street workers "depersonalize their contacts with clients," and even their regular clients are viewed instrumentally, as purely economic assets.[48]

Indoors, social and physical exchanges are potentially more varied, more mutual, and more "romantic." The sessions are longer than they are on the street, and compared to the front seat of a car or a dark alley, indoor settings themselves are much more conducive to prolonged and multifaceted activities. Not only is the customer offered a greater variety of physical pleasures, but the indoor worker is as well. They are more likely than street workers to be caressed, kissed, massaged, or hugged *by* their clients and to *receive* oral sex or manual stimulation from them.[49] When call girls in Los Angeles were asked what kinds of activities they had engaged in with their last client, 26 percent of them reported that the man had massaged their genitals and 17 percent had received oral sex from him.[50] Decades earlier, a four-year study of more than 1,200 encounters between 64 call girls and their clients in New York reported that in one-quarter of all the sessions the client massaged the woman's genitals, and in fully 43 percent of the sessions the man engaged in cunnilingus.[51] In Queensland, Australia, 68 percent of a sample of 103 legal brothel workers and 83 percent of 102 call girls interviewed stated that they had received oral sex from a customer at some time, and 57 percent of clients (N = 160) stated that they had provided oral sex to a brothel or private provider.[52] In their online reviews of escorts on the British website Punternet, clients spend more time writing about their efforts to please the woman than about their own sexual satisfaction; their accounts often describe cues that suggest that the woman had an orgasm.[53] Indeed, in at least some indoor venues, the workers *expect and request* such reciprocal behavior from clients as a routine part of the encounter.

Similarly, social interaction is more multifaceted indoors than it is on the street. Encounters between call girls and their clients involve a complex and "elaborate interplay of social, sexual, and psychological behavior."[54] Most of the 75 call girls and 150 brothel workers interviewed by Diana Prince believed that "the average customer wants affection or love as well as sex,"[55] and another study of call girls discovered that "for many men, sex is the pretext for the visit, and the real need is emotional."[56] In these cases, social intercourse is at least as important as sexual intercourse is. This multifaceted "connection" has now become known as the "girlfriend experience" (GFE) and the analogous "boyfriend experience" (BFE) offered by men to women or to other men. This GFE/BFE is especially likely when a regular client gets to know a provider over the long term, but it is also available in more short-term engagements. When clients in one study were asked about their motivations for buying sex in an indoor venue, a majority selected "like sex workers' company" (60 percent of clients in brothels, 78 percent of clients of call girls), and similar majorities selected "able to talk frankly with sex workers" as one of their reasons for visiting brothel workers (62 percent of their clients) or call girls (69 percent of their clients).[57] Christine Milrod asked a sample of 567 clients who had accessed sex workers through the Internet about the desired characteristics of a GFE service provider: 76 percent wanted someone who was "romantic and tender toward the client," 73 percent said she should have a "happy and cheerful personality," and 64 percent valued "enthusiasm in trying a variety of sexual activities."[58]

Unlike the streets, therefore, indoor encounters can offer a semblance of romance, friendship, or companionship—better thought of as *paid dates* than paid sex. The fact that some indoor workers (escorts) go out to dinner with, receive gifts from, and travel with clients—unheard of on the street—also symbolizes a radically different kind of relationship than one reducible to sheer monetary exchange.

The GFE concept has now gained legendary status. In 2009, the motion picture *The Girlfriend Experience* appeared, directed by mainstream movie director Steven Soderbergh and featuring adult-film star Sasha Grey in the lead, escort role. Escort agencies and independent call girls increasingly advertise nonsexual services, with many websites now trumpeting providers' expertise in delivering a GFE. Some escort agencies even include a code of etiquette in their contracts, instructing employees, for example, to cuddle and to avoid rushing the client.[59] In a sense, the customer buys a kind of *relationship* with an escort rather than just sex—one that may evolve over time into a genuine emotional connection, albeit one that is paid for.[60] And this kind of relationship occurs among male escorts and some of their clients as well.[61] For agencies, providers, and clients, the GFE—both its marketing and its enactment—may help to partially normalize the profession and mitigate the stigma of prostitution insofar as it can be associated with valued emotional dividends. The Emperor's Club escort agency, for instance, billed itself on its website as offering a GFE that would make life "more peaceful, balanced, beautiful, and meaningful."

Elizabeth Bernstein argues that the GFE has expanded from its previous niche market to prostitution in general and that customers are increasingly seeking this kind of experience. She claims that paid intimacy and other nonsexual services are "historically unprecedented" and "unique" to the present era,[62] but the evidence for this is thin. Historical studies show that brothels in the past offered more than just sex and thrived on a variety of entertainments and leisure activities. For instance, in 19th-century America, top-tier brothels offered patrons musical entertainment, drinking, and casual mingling with women in the parlor prior to bedroom activities. In China at the same time, men visited brothels "to listen to music and join in socializing; sexual intercourse, although available, was not yet the major focus of activity and was portrayed as part of a romantic encounter rather than as a thoroughly commodified activity."[63] Sex with a courtesan was possible only after a protracted period of courting her and building an emotional bond.[64] Similarly, the clients of 20th-century call girls have long sought emotional intimacy. A large study of call girls and their customers four decades ago provides plenty of evidence of affective bonding at that time. As the researcher, Martha Stein, writes, "For many of the regular clients, talking about their problems or confessing secret worries was a crucial part of the transaction. . . . The call girls were skilled at sensing just how the client wanted to be treated and at encouraging him to express his real needs."[65] In short, the desire for companionship, nonsexual intimacy, and a semblance of romance is hardly new to sex work. What has changed is the *marketing* of this kind of experience and the creation of a new *label* for it. Its apparent novelty is simply a function of greater documentation with the advent of the Internet and website postings. And it is also important to note that some indoor liaisons lack the GFE entirely. Some clients are seeking a fantasy sexual tryst with a "bombshell" or a succession of partners who are valued for their physical attributes and sexual techniques rather than for anything nonsexual.

Data from websites shed light on what happens indoors. In addition to those sites on which workers advertise (listing services and prices, biographical sketches, and photos), other sites contain message boards for clients and providers.[66] These sites offer a forum where novices can learn from seasoned clients and find information on what to expect regarding prices and services; reviews of a specific worker (appearance, demeanor, performance); location of establishments; and information on local police activity. The sites provide unique insight into customer beliefs, justifications, expectations, and behavioral norms—dimensions addressed only partially in previous studies based on interviews and surveys. Reviews of individual providers range from derogatory to lukewarm to those that lavish praise and offer enthusiastic recommendations to other clients. Many of the cyber exchanges also discuss appropriate and inappropriate behavior toward sex workers—chiding misogynists, those seeking underage workers or unsafe sex, and other wayward individuals. We are witnessing, in other words, an emergent subculture with its own etiquette and code of ethics.

Reviews of postings on these websites coupled with interview data indicate that many clients of indoor workers seek much more than sex.[67] They place a premium on the provider's being friendly, affectionate, attentive, and generous with time; having good communication skills and rich life experience; and being willing to engage in cuddling, kissing, and sensual massage. These desires are not confined to a few men: they were pervasive themes in an analysis of more than 5,000 client reviews of 2,661 escorts in Britain, where customers' online entries focused more on the GFE and the workers' personalities than on their physical attributes or sexual performances.[68] This is confirmed in Milrod's survey of clients sampled from The Erotic Review website: when asked to select from a list of "the most attractive characteristics" of an Internet sexual-service provider, 70 percent of the men chose "they act like girlfriends and not like prostitutes at all," 81 percent selected "happy and cheerful personality," 62 percent liked them because they are "romantic and tender toward client," while 76 percent also valued the physical dimension, selecting their "beautiful and healthy appearance."[69] Interviews with the clients of indoor workers highlight the premium they place on an encounter that offers intimacy, a desire for "rapport, chemistry, passion, connection."[70] Frequently, the men wax affectionate, recounting being treated "lovingly" or calling the companion endearing names such as "honey" or "sweetie," just as a boyfriend or husband might do. Of course, not all clients are seeking intimacy, but many "do not separate sex from emotional connectivity with sex workers."[71] This is especially true for regulars, who visit the same provider multiple times.

Sex workers echo these sentiments. As Ann Lucas concluded from her interviews with escorts, "for many men, sex is the pretext for the visit, and the real need is emotional."[72] For these men, the encounters are much more therapeutic than carnal. One escort says, "Most of them are looking for someone who will listen to them and who makes them just feel special. . . . They just want companionship . . . to spend time with a woman." When she embraced one client, he broke into tears and told her it had been a year since anyone had hugged him.[73] As police detective Angel Batista on the Showtime television series *Dexter* remarked after being caught trying to buy sex from an escort, "I'm a divorced cop, a divorced alcoholic cop. And I needed to fight that loneliness. So I found affection any way I could. I needed to connect with someone, anyone who wouldn't hurt me back no more."[74] Whereas a conventional date may result in rejection or other kinds of "hurt," Angel viewed the paid encounter as less emotionally hazardous.

For some clients, a GFE/BFE has a limited, strictly sexual connotation and involves French kissing, mutual oral sex, unlimited touching, and sex without a condom—all of which may help them forget that they are paying for sex. But generally the concept has a broader meaning, centered on an emotional connection or romantic sex. Consider this client's online posting:

This was the single most amazing session I have ever had with an escort. For some reason, and I'm not sure how she pulls it off, it felt completely— at every level, emotionally and physically—as though I were with a girl- friend who knew my every quirk, like, and dislike. It didn't feel like sex. It felt like making love. Even leaving, I didn't feel as though I had visited an escort. This lady works magic.[75]

For these men, emotionless sex is defined as "bad sex." Revealingly, one of the rating options available to clients who review escorts on The Erotic Review website is "I Forgot It Was a Service"—illustrating again how the GFE may trump the economic dimension and decommodify the encounter from the client's perspective. It is significant that many indoor clients talk about "making love" instead of "having sex" with their provider.[76] And a pro- vider's willingness to kiss, to receive oral sex or manual stimulation, and to engage in mutual fondling and cuddling are some of the "indicators" clients use in constructing their experience as lovemaking. Such reciprocal acts help to convince the man that the sexual encounter is an authentic one, going beyond a commodified transaction. A man who performs oral sex on a sex worker can construe this as a genuine act of "giving back" rather than simply "using" the provider's services. Of course, this does not mean that the sex worker necessarily experiences such client behavior as pleasurable; this natu- rally varies across providers.

Clients who seek emotional intimacy and companionship present a chal- lenge to the notion that commercial sex necessarily involves cold objectifica- tion. A study of call girls and their clients conducted decades ago concluded, "It would be an oversimplification to say that the men saw the call girl sim- ply as a sex object. They wanted not a sex object, but a sex partner. . . . It was extremely important to them to like the woman they were with and to feel that she liked them."[77] When 438 clients in another study were asked if they would marry a prostitute, half said they would, which suggests that these men view at least some sex workers as more than sex objects.[78] And a British study concurs: indoor clients were "respectful of sex workers as women and as workers rather than simplifying their identities as Others"; sex workers were not viewed "simply as bodies" or as "targets of sexual conquest" but instead as persons with whom one could have a meaningful personal connection.[79] The men also sought providers who were independent entrepreneurs and had control over their work, and they avoided those who they sensed might be subject to third-party exploitation.[80] This evidence clashes with the oppression paradigm's depiction of all customers as callous or predatory misogynists.

Clients' testimonials indicate that some of them, and perhaps large numbers, have had very good experiences with sex workers and feel that such activities have enhanced their lives. On The Erotic Review website, where clients rate their providers on a scale of 1 to 10, most of the ratings are at the high end: 8–10. This offers some quantitative evidence of the frequency of satisfaction, at least among patrons of the escorts who advertise on this site. But given that paid sex is both culturally transgressive and personally intimate, clients can and do experience it negatively. Some harbor fear of discovery, shame for engaging in disreputable behavior, guilt for betraying their wives or girlfriends, or dissatisfaction with the encounter itself (e.g., the sex was rushed or impersonal, performance problems for one or both parties, feeling manipulated or economically exploited).[81] They complain that a particular sex worker engaged in the bare minimum of conversation, watched the clock, did not look at them during sex, became argumentative, or otherwise detracted from the experience. Some say that they were victims of false advertising, that is, that the provider they met did not look or behave as advertised. Yet others fear contracting a disease, feel embarrassed about paying for sex, regret spending time cruising online advertisements or prowling the streets, or feel they have "cheated" themselves by not pursuing a conventional relationship.[82] Negative experiences are more common among first-time clients than among regulars; for the novice, engaging in this stigmatized activity can produce feelings of anxiety, embarrassment, nervousness, and disappointment.[83] From the client's perspective, therefore, a lot of things can "go wrong" physically or emotionally in a paid sex encounter, whether on the street or indoors. But it can also be a very satisfying experience.

For the workers, providing a comprehensive GFE has both advantages and disadvantages. One benefit is that time spent in nonsexual pursuits reduces wear and tear on the body, but the downside is that one has to feign intimacy with some clients who are not especially likable. The GFE can be quite draining for the provider, who must work hard to ensure that customers are comfortable, relaxed, and happy and to remain pleasant, witty, and attentive—while at the same time working to maintain behavioral rules and emotional boundaries. This tall order makes enacting the GFE "extraordinarily stressful work. . . . It calls for emotional labor of a type and on a scale which is probably unparalleled in any other job."[84] "Part of the art of prostitution is using sex to create a feeling of trust and intimacy, to bring people in touch with their own self worth," writes Dolores French. "Regulars are sometimes hard to do because each time you see them you have to go deeper, you have to give more."[85] As one famous provider quips, "There's a lot of talk in escort circles of the Girlfriend Experience. That's because it is by far the most requested thing we offer. I have been cuddled to within an inch of my life by well-meaning chaps whose only previous acquaintance with me was via a website."[86] Stress is amplified when a client violates the provider's expressed boundaries, reveals unpleasant or troubling details about his personal life, begins to expect free sex, wants a date on demand, becomes obsessed, or falls in love.[87] Street workers are largely free of these strains and are clearly not interested or equipped to engage in such extended emotion work, which is disdainfully called "honeymooning" by those on the street.[88]

Indoor providers' views of their clients are predictably mixed—just as for any service occupation whose workers spend an extended amount of time with clients. Martha Stein's research found that clients ranged from individuals who were disliked to those who were beloved.[89] While some customers are demanding, disputatious, or hard to please, this does not appear to be the norm among clients of upscale sex workers. The call girls in Stein's study liked most of their clients,[90] and the researchers in an Australian study found that "most call girls have not had bad experiences, and more often than not they have positive things to say about their customers."[91] One British escort writes, "Compared to real relationships, these men [clients] are absolute pussycats, and easily pleased pussycats at that."[92] Natalie McLennan, who worked for the now-defunct NY Confidential escort service, states that most of her clients were looking for companionship and were "well-groomed, very well-mannered, well-educated" lawyers and businessmen who "work really, really hard and don't necessarily have the free time to go out on dates. I didn't hold back from finding things about my clients that were really attractive and really endearing to me. As a result, I definitely developed feelings for them."[93] Providers become quite fond of some of their regular customers, as two escorts confide:

The only way I can sustain regulars is if I actually like them and I may like them for different reasons. . . . Most of my regulars know who I am, so I can be myself, and I try to enjoy myself sexually too because I really hate wasting time doing things that I don't want to do. . . . A number of my clients are intelligent men who are well informed and can carry on a stimulating conversation.[94]

To me they're friends and I've never talked about them as "johns" or "jobs." . . . I get as much pleasure from them as I like to think they get from me, and I'm not just talking about the sex but [also] building up a real rapport with them. . . . I treat them as I would a boyfriend.[95]

If the GFE is nothing more for some providers than "counterfeit intimacy"—a manufactured emotional connection with a client—other sex workers, like those just quoted, develop "authentic (if fleeting) libidinal and emotional ties with clients, endowing them with a sense of desirability, esteem, or even love."[96] The GFE may be precisely what the buyer desires—a brief but rewarding human connection free of the strains of a conventional relationship.

The GFE experience is most emblematic of the work of call girls and escorts and somewhat less common or elaborate in brothels or massage parlors. For the former, "a show of affection is offered their clients because the nature of their business depends on a 'love nest' scenario to attract clients, in contrast to the more obviously mercenary sexual services found in most brothels" and the limitations imposed by their managers.[97] Nevertheless, the GFE is not monopolized by escorts; emotional bonds can grow between the regular patrons of a favorite masseuse or brothel worker as well. Another example is the sex workers that tourists meet at vacation spots, especially when the two parties end up spending days or weeks together, as discussed in the following section.

Indoor Commercial Sex Away from Home

People buy sex when they travel abroad, including those who make special plans to visit a particular red-light district that caters to tourists. Some of these settings offer the possibility of a protracted engagement between the parties rather than a single, brief encounter. In many bars in Thailand, the Philippines, and the Dominican Republic, for example, men pay a bar fee to leave the club with a dancer or hostess and spend a night or several days together, perhaps visiting tourist sights, during which the man pays all expenses. Bar workers see these longer engagements as a means of securing upward mobility; hence, the sex trade is "a way not just to solve short-term economic problems but to change their lives."[98] But such relationships are not limited to material benefits; in Thailand, for instance, they also confer *status* on the women (from their peers) because foreign men are perceived as being more respectful toward women than traditional Thai men are.[99] A minority of the foreign men become boyfriends and enter into long-term or serial relationships—sending email, gifts, and money from overseas and reuniting on return visits. Many of the women and some of the men are consciously seeking a long-term relationship, and some end up marrying.[100] In this context, prostitution can be a precursor to prolonged and possibly permanent attachments.

Data are lacking on the number of male tourists who become involved in this open-ended kind of arrangement with a sex worker, but one study compared male tourists' relations with prostitutes to their activities in their home country. Researchers interviewed 530 clients of prostitutes in Germany and 661 German sex tourists in Thailand, the Philippines, Brazil, Kenya, and the Dominican Republic. The length of the sexual encounter was a few hours or less at home in Germany (79 percent less than one hour, 21 percent one to two hours), whereas the sex tourists spent extended periods of time with a prostitute away from home (21 percent spent two or more hours but less than an entire day, 13 percent an entire day, 45 percent several days).[101] Such protracted, noncontractual relationships—coupled with the indirect material compensation given to the women (rather than payment per sex act)—allow the men to view themselves as boyfriends rather than as clients and allow the women to view themselves as "having a string of individual relationships with men who just happen to pay her bills and support her family."[102]

A similar dynamic occurs among gay tourists and male sex workers, for whom the contact begins as paid sex but can evolve into a romantic relationship. This dynamic is nicely illustrated in anthropologist Mark Padilla's three-year study of the Dominican Republic.[103] While some of the sex workers in the study wanted only short-term encounters, to avoid potential emotional complications, others were looking for more lasting associations because they are more lucrative, including gifts sent by the tourist after he returns home. Only about a third of Padilla's Dominican respondents believed that they could fall in love with a foreign client, yet many did so, especially with clients who offered the greatest material support. Many clients were looking not just for sex but also for an authentic emotional relationship with a local man, and most of them held eroticized fantasies about "exotic" Caribbean men. Their racial and sexual stereotypes of the Other mirror the way many heterosexual male tourists view female sex workers in the Caribbean and Southeast Asia. The women are stereotyped (and market themselves) as more compliant and nurturing than "demanding," liberated women back home.[104]

The bonding phenomenon also has been documented in other places where foreigners have extended contact with local sex workers. Such settings include mining towns, military bases, and the harbors where foreign sailors spend rest-and-relaxation time. Many of the workers in waterfront bars develop multifaceted relationships with the sailors whose ships dock there and later revisit the place. Henry Trotter's ethnographic study of nightclubs in the harbors of two South African cities explores this distinctive dockside bar prostitution.[105] For sailors who are interested in sex, it not *just* sex that attracts them to the bars: the bars also offer opportunities for binge drinking, playing pool, singing karaoke songs, watching TV, and dancing. Having been denied contact with women for so long at sea, the men seek their companionship through prolonged conversations and flirtation, while others are looking for sex as well. The women use the conversations to make the men care about them, holding out the hope of forging a serial relationship with a man or (even more prized) marrying and relocating to his country, which a few succeed in doing. The bars are rich geocultural intersections that broaden the workers' horizons: "Through their continual interactions with foreign seamen, [the women] become major traffickers in culture, ideas, languages, styles, goods, currencies, genes, and diseases."[106] What is remarkable about these sites is the extent to which the women adopt multiple cultural toolkits and learn foreign languages, which they acquire through numerous conversations with the men. They are adept at using their international cultural capital to present themselves in a way that other local women cannot. Similarly, for bar workers in Thailand,

> the work develops the emotional and practical knowledge and practices necessary to function in a variety of settings in a foreign language with foreign customers of higher status. . . . [When the sex worker spends days] accompanying foreign tourists, the sex worker sees a wider array of middle-class venues and tourist sites and partakes more often in leisure and consumption practices of the relatively well-to-do than do middle-class Thai women, let alone fellow villagers working in factories or private homes.[107]

The same dynamic is evident in bars and clubs frequented by tourists in other Asian countries as well as near foreign military bases, where local women sell intimacy and acquire a repertoire of cultural capital—valuable language skills and knowledge of other societies—that enhances their status relative to other local women.[108]

Each party can develop an emotional bond to the other, albeit for different reasons. A survey of 466 Thai bar prostitutes found that more than 80 percent of them had experienced "a relationship with a customer in which they had developed strong feelings for him," and about half of the 141 clients interviewed said that they had developed feelings for the woman as well.[109] The women's relationships with foreign men, if they lasted more than a night, were often experienced as "more authentic, intimate, esteemed, and more critical to women's sense of their own identity."[110] In order to distinguish such relationships from those in which the sexual encounter is brief and superficial, Heidi Hoefinger coined the term *professional girlfriend*. Hoefinger interviewed women in Cambodia and discovered that "the work that they do is far more complex than merely providing sexual services, and it was common for the women to stop viewing the relationships as 'work' soon after they began developing feelings for the men."[111] These women exchange sex for material benefits but only as part of their larger role as professional girlfriends. If the relationship lasts a week, a month, or longer, the girlfriend aspect can become much more genuine than what is typical of the truncated GFE offered by escorts who see a client once or periodically.

I have already noted a similar pattern for gay male tourists and local men, and there is a parallel for some female tourists as well. This occurs when affluent Western women meet young local men at clubs and beaches. Male and female sex tourism is similar in certain respects. Economic inequality between buyer and seller is pronounced in both cases, giving the buyer a similar measure of control over the worker. Female sex tourists, like their male counterparts, capitalize on their economic resources in relations with local men. Economic inequality can translate into unequal power between the parties, with some women "expressing a preference for keeping a man dependent on them" so that he will be "fully available to meet her needs."[112] One study in the Caribbean highlighted the dominant position of female sex tourists: "The kind of control exercised in their relationships with local men is actually very similar to that exercised by male sex tourists in sexual economic relationships with local women. . . . They are able to use their economic power to limit the risk of being challenged or subjugated."[113]

There are differences between male and female sex tourism as well. A unique comparative study of male and female tourists and sex workers in the Dominican Republic reported that (1) the male prostitutes (known as "beach boys") were motivated by both material interests and a desire for sexual conquest of a Western woman, whereas the female sex workers had largely economic goals; (2) the beach boys felt free to be seen in public (relaxing, partying) with female tourists, which only enhanced their reputation among other men, whereas female sex workers used public space only to solicit men and not for fraternization; (3) the beach boys sold sex and intimacy only to tourists, whereas the female workers sold sex to both local and foreign men; (4) the women were dependent on prostitution for their livelihood, whereas the beach boys had other jobs; (5) "the female sex workers were stigmatized far more than were the beach boys by the local population"; and (6) female tourists were more likely than their male counterparts to have relationships with sex workers lasting for an extended period of time (several days).[114]

Like male tourists, some women become long-term companions or benefactors to a local man, occasionally leading to marriage.[115] But female tourists are more likely than their male counterparts to enter into a sexual exchange with a local person situationally: a minority of women plan it ahead of time, whereas many male sex tourists do.[116] Typically, female sex tourists reject the notion that they are "customers" buying sex from local men. Instead, they construct the encounters as a "holiday romance" or "real love," not as purely physical.[117] Likewise, the local men do not see themselves as prostitutes. For both parties, the encounters are constructed as "romance tourism" rather than as sex tourism.[118] Still, the men do receive material rewards for the time they spend with foreign women, including meals, lodging, gifts, and money. According to Jacqueline Sanchez Taylor, these relationships have all the hallmarks of sex tourism, whether they are short or long term and whether or not money is exchanged, provided that the man receives at least some material benefits.[119] Similarly, Joan Phillips argues that these transactions can be "easily fitted under the umbrella of prostitution," even if the two parties view it differently.[120] Still, these relationships appear to be more complicated than what we find in male sex tourism and deserve to be more fully researched.[121]

Male sex workers also transact with women in clubs and bars at home and abroad. Similar to hostess clubs where women entertain male customers, Japanese *host clubs* are bars where women go to enjoy themselves in the company of attractive male hosts. Such bars have flourished in the past decade, with approximately 200 in Tokyo alone. Male hosts, like their female counterparts in hostess clubs, are trained to be "good listeners, express sympathy and concern about their clients' everyday complaints, and take time to comfort them"; in addition to these supportive practices, they have physical contact (kissing, fondling) with many of their female customers and sex with at least some of them.[122] The hosts serve exorbitantly expensive drinks to their clients and lavish praise and compliments on the women they attach themselves to. The nature of this phenomenon is captured in Akiko Takeyama's concept of "commodified romance." Her ethnographic study of host clubs in Tokyo examines club dynamics and the reasons women seek these paid encounters with men. She reports that "customers claim that there are few other places in Japan's male-centered entertainment world where women can safely enjoy romantic excitement."[123] The hosts treat them like queens, in stark contrast to how most men treat them in the wider society. According to this study and a documentary (*The Great Happiness Space*, featuring a host club in Osaka, Japan),[124] the vast majority of hosts have had sex with at least some of their customers, although they prefer to delay sexual intercourse in order to keep the woman coming back to the club and paying the high prices, of which the host gets a commission.

The sexual socialization of girls, throughout the world, deters many women from becoming clients. But some clearly buy sex, and we need much more research on female clients of male providers and of female providers as well. Further research on female customers will help to clarify the impact of gender on the dynamics of paid sex transactions.[125]

The material presented in this chapter is just a sample of the wide variety of types and settings of indoor prostitution throughout the world. We have seen that the indoor market is hardly monolithic. At the same time, indoor prostitution can differ radically—in its social organization and in the activities and experiences of workers and customers—from what is typical in street prostitution.

Having explored aspects of indoor prostitution, I turn to selected policy issues in Part II of the book and then to case studies in Part III of three settings where legal prostitution is primarily or exclusively confined to indoor venues. The differences between street and indoor prostitution, documented in this chapter, help to explain why most states have not decriminalized street prostitution. When considering legal reform, legislators are often cognizant of the problems associated with street prostitution, including public visibility, disorder, and nuisance as well as the elevated level of danger and risks to public health. This translates into a reluctance to decriminalize street prostitution and a preference for indoor settings instead.

PART II

Policies

America and Beyond

3

American Policies and Trends

Sex is legal. Selling is legal. Why is selling sex illegal?
—George Carlin

For as long as people have traded sex for money, there have been conflicts over such exchanges. The intensity of the conflict varies over time and place, but the sale of sex rarely goes uncontested by those who are fiercely opposed to it. Legalization of vice does not put an end to the matter, even when it can be shown that reform has certain benefits, as in the case of medical marijuana. Yet George Carlin's question in the epigraph above remains apt. Few activities, apart from prostitution, are criminalized just because money is exchanged.

Over the past generation, the United States has grown increasingly tolerant of certain vices. John Dombrink and Daniel Hillyard's book *Sin No More* traces the evolution of public opinion and legal norms on abortion, gambling, gay rights, and assisted suicide but also documents resistance from social forces opposed to any liberalization in these areas—the net effect of which Dombrink and Hillyard call "problematic normalization." They describe a "rising floor" of tolerance but one that has stopped short of full liberalization.[1]

A similar dynamic can be seen in marijuana policy in the United States, marked by noticeable changes over the past decade. Medical marijuana is now permitted in 15 states, and polls show that four-fifths of Americans support this policy.[2] Regarding recreational marijuana, a remarkable event occurred in November 2008, when two-thirds of voters in Massachusetts approved a ballot measure decriminalizing possession of up to one ounce of marijuana.[3] This may be a harbinger of things to come because of the growing number of Americans who support decriminalization not only of medical marijuana but also of recreational marijuana, with the legitimacy of the former apparently spilling over to the latter.[4] The level of support has steadily risen over the past four decades, from 12 percent of Americans in 1969 to

25 percent in 1979 to 36 percent in 2006 agreeing that the "use of marijuana should be made legal."[5] Two 2009 polls reported that a slim *majority* of Americans now support legalization.[6] This does not mean that change is imminent (a legalization measure was rejected by California voters in 2010), but the opinion-poll trends seem to auger well for legal reform in the future.

There is no such liberalizing trend in American prostitution policy. Although some observers have documented a growing "mainstreaming" of the sex industry—especially pornography and stripping, where there has been some spillover into mainstream media and proliferation on the Internet[7]—prostitution remains beyond the pale in the United States. The dominant trend has been in the direction of greater criminalization, not less. One difference between legalization of marijuana and prostitution is that activists are better able to identify victims in prostitution. Another difference is the sheer number of individuals who are current consumers and, as such, potential supporters of decriminalization. About four in ten Americans have smoked marijuana, which is much higher than the number who say that they have paid for sex or been paid for sex (9 percent of total population, 16 percent of men in 2008).[8] And there is far less stigma attached to marijuana consumption.

This chapter describes prostitution policies and trends in the United States as a prelude to my analysis of several other nations in the remainder of the book.

Criminalization

In the United States, prostitution legislation is largely devolved to the states. Federal law bans interstate transportation of prostitutes (under the 1910 Mann Act), and sex trafficking is outlawed under the 2000 Trafficking Victims Protection Act. But otherwise prostitution law is determined by each state. Almost all states prohibit solicitation for prostitution as well as pimping, procuring, operating a brothel, and running any other business that offers or allows sex for sale. There are two exceptions: Nevada permits counties to license and regulate brothels, and Rhode Island had no prostitution law until 2009, discussed later in this chapter.

Approximately 60,000 Americans were arrested in 2009 for violation of prostitution laws.[9] Most arrests involve the street trade, though indoor workers are targeted in some cities. Arrests are sporadic and selective in most cities; in some jurisdictions they are more sustained and may result in displacing street prostitution to another locale.[10]

Criminalization has several consequences. First, arrests and fines have little deterrent effect on the sellers, who quickly return to selling sex. Yet arrest and punishment can be considered harmful because of the stigma of a criminal record. Second, at least some of those arrested present no harm to the public, insofar as their activities occur in discreet private settings between willing sellers and buyers. Third, criminalization is costly to the criminal justice system, expenditures that could be reallocated to other priorities. Fourth, criminalization jeopardizes sex workers insofar as they fear reporting victimization to the police. Many prostitutes are reluctant to report rape, robbery, and assault because they want to conceal their illegal activities or because they believe the police will not take their reports seriously. These are not irrational concerns. American police have a long history of routinely discounting this victimization, seeing prostitutes as somehow deserving of their fate, or exploiting individual workers by demanding sex in lieu of an arrest.[11]

Decriminalization and legalization, to which we now turn, are alternatives to criminalization.

Decriminalization and Legalization

Legalization and decriminalization are examined in depth in chapter 4 and in selected nations in later chapters. In this chapter, I restrict the discussion of these policies to how they have been viewed in the United States, and I describe a third alternative: a two-track policy.

There are three types of decriminalization. *Full decriminalization* removes all criminal penalties and leaves prostitution unregulated, albeit subject to conventional laws against nuisances, sex in public, disorderly conduct, or coercion. Under full decriminalization, prostitution could exist in any locale, so long as the parties do not disturb the peace or violate other ordinances. *Partial decriminalization* would reduce but not eliminate penalties—the charge may be reduced from a felony to a misdemeanor or violation, and the penalty might be a fine instead of incarceration. A third option is *de facto decriminalization*, which means the offense remains in the penal code, but the law is not enforced. Decriminalization may or may not be a precursor to legalization (government regulation).

Proposals for full decriminalization run up against a wall of opposition. A 1983 poll found that only 7 percent of Americans thought that there should be "no laws against prostitution," and in 1990, just 22 percent felt that prostitution should be "left to the individual," while a greater number thought that it should either be "regulated by law" (31 percent) or "forbidden by law"

(46 percent).[12] American policymakers are almost universally opposed to the idea, making it a nonstarter in any serious discussion of policy alternatives. Advocates sometimes manage to get it placed on the public agenda, however. In 1994, a task force in San Francisco explored alternatives to existing prostitution policy. After months of meetings, a majority of the members voted to recommend decriminalization, but the city's Board of Supervisors rejected the idea.[13]

In November 2008, San Francisco residents voted on a ballot measure that would have de facto decriminalized prostitution in the city. The measure stipulated that the police would discontinue enforcing the law against prostitution. The measure failed but was endorsed by a sizeable minority of voters: 42 percent. Four years earlier, Berkeley, California, voters were presented with a similar proposal, and 36 percent supported it.[14] As this chapter shows, the San Francisco and Berkeley cases are exceptional in contemporary America, where liberalization is rarely voted on by the public or even discussed by political leaders. As a task force in Buffalo, New York, reasoned, "Since it is unlikely that city or state officials could ever be convinced to decriminalize or legalize prostitution in Buffalo, there is nothing to be gained by debating the merits of either."[15] Decriminalization is thus the untouchable third rail of prostitution policy in the United States.

Legalization couples decriminalization with some kind of official regulation. In other words, removal of criminal penalties is linked to other controls—such as vetting and licensing business owners, registering workers, zoning street prostitution into a designated area, mandating medical exams, instituting special business fees (a "sin tax"), or periodically inspecting legal establishments. Because legalization involves official regulation, citizens are more inclined to support it than laissez-faire decriminalization. Five polls in table 3.1 show support for legalization ranging between one-quarter to nearly half of Americans. None of these polls specifies the *kind* of regulation, however, so we lack information on the specific restrictions favored by the public. Still, it is noteworthy that such a sizeable minority favors legalization in principle.

In the United States, only Nevada has state-regulated prostitution. Nevada's 30 legal brothels are relegated to rural areas and prohibited in Las Vegas and Reno, due largely to opposition from the gaming industry. A slight majority of the Nevada population favors retaining legal brothels (52 percent, in table 3.1), though the system is more popular in rural counties that already have legal brothels. But this rural-only model is remote, both geographically and cognitively, from urban areas. Illegal prostitution flourishes in Las Vegas

TABLE 3.1

Attitudes toward Prostitution Policies, United States

	Agree (%)
Legalization (1978)[1]	24
Legalization (1983)[2]	46
Legalization (1990)[3]	31
Legalization (1991)[4]	40
Legalization (1996)[5]	26
Legalization (1996)[6]	45
Decriminalization, Berkeley, CA (2004)[7]	36
Decriminalization, San Francisco, CA (2008)[8]	42
Prostitution does not hurt Nevada's tourism industry (1988)[9]	71
Retain legal brothels in Nevada (2002)[10]	52
Legalize prostitution in limited area if downtown Las Vegas (2003)[11]	35

Sources:

1. Louis Harris poll, 1978, N = 1,513. "Engaging in prostitution" should be "regulated by law."

2. Merit Audits and Surveys, Merit Report, October 1983, N = 1,200. Prostitution should be "legal under certain restrictions."

3. Louis Harris poll, 1990, N = 2,254. "Engaging in prostitution" should be "regulated by law."

4. Gallup poll, 1991, N = 1,216. To "help reduce the spread of AIDS, prostitution should be made legal and regulated by the government."

5. Gallup poll, 1996, N = 1,019. "Prostitution involving adults 18 years of age and older should be legal." Question wording does not stipulate restrictions or regulation, unlike the earlier polls, which might explain the lower approval level compared to all but one of the earlier polls.

6. General Social Survey, 1996, N = 1,444. "How much do you agree or disagree with the following statement? There is nothing inherently wrong with prostitution, so long as the health risks can be minimized. If consenting adults agree to exchange money for sex, that is their business." The figure combines the responses "agree strongly" and "agree somewhat."

7. November, 2004, ballot measure (Measure Q), instructing Berkeley police to treat enforcement of prostitution law as the "lowest priority."

8. November, 2008, ballot measure (Measure K), instructing San Francisco police to discontinue all prostitution arrests and defunding the city's john school.

9. Nevada poll, N=1,213, conducted November 1988 by the Center for Survey Research at the University of Nevada, Las Vegas. 22% thought that prostitution "hurts the state's tourism industry."

10. Poll of Nevada residents, N=600, Law Vegas Review-Journal, September 17, 2002. Poll conducted by Research 2000. 31% were opposed to legal brothels and 17% were undecided or had no opinion.

11. Poll of Nevada residents, N=601, Las Vegas Review-Journal, October 30, 2003. "Do you support the legalization of prostitution in a limited area of downtown Las Vegas?" Poll conducted by Magellan Research. 59% were opposed to the idea and 6% had no opinion.

and Reno, despite the existence of legal brothels in adjacent counties. Only a minority of Nevadans want to see legalization extended to Las Vegas: 35 percent favor the "legalization of prostitution in a limited area of downtown Las Vegas," while 59 percent oppose the idea (table 3.1).[16]

Since Nevada legalized brothels in 1971, no other state has seriously considered legalization. Legislators fear being branded as "condoning" prostitution and see no political advantages in any kind of liberalization. On those rare occasions when the idea has been floated, it has had a short life. The San Francisco and Berkeley decriminalization ballot measures, mentioned earlier, were rejected by a majority of voters. Still, it is noteworthy that 42 percent of San Franciscans voted for full decriminalization in 2008, suggesting that this kind of policy shift remains a distinct possibility in the future, at least in this city.

How is legal reform viewed by sex workers themselves? National data in the United States are lacking on this question, but a survey of 247 (mostly street) prostitutes working in San Francisco found that 71 percent supported decriminalization ("get rid of laws that make sex work illegal"), and 79 percent said that sex workers "should determine their own working conditions without being taxed or regulated by government," whereas 83 percent agreed that sex workers should be "required to undergo health screenings to be able to do sex work" even as they roundly rejected other types of regulation.[17] The figures thus show support for general decriminalization plus one kind of regulation. What about clients' views? A survey of 1,342 arrested clients reported that 74 percent of them thought that prostitution should be legalized.[18] Neither survey was based on a random sample, but they are suggestive of high levels of support for liberalizing the law among both providers and their clients.

A Two-Track Policy

If neither formal decriminalization nor legalization is a viable policy in the United States at present, is there any other alternative to blanket criminalization? Since prostitution manifests itself in fundamentally different ways on the street and in indoor venues, it seems sensible to treat the two differently. In fact, most of the nations that have decriminalized prostitution have done so only for indoor venues, not street prostitution. As one assessment concluded, "Street-based sex work is problematic everywhere. . . . Street sex workers comprise the most vulnerable and traumatized section of the sex industry." The authors advocated reducing the street sector by "ensuring an adequate supply of indoor alternatives."[19]

More than 50 years ago, the landmark Wolfenden Committee in Britain produced a report advocating a dualistic approach to prostitution. Street prostitution was defined as a public nuisance and as offensive to the public. As the committee put it, legal penalties should apply to "the manner in which the activities of prostitutes and those associated with them offend against public order and decency, expose ordinary citizens to what is offensive and injurious, or involve the exploitation of others."[20] Because street prostitution was deemed an offense against public order and decency, the Wolfenden Committee recommended harsher penalties for prostitutes who operate outdoors (replacing the existing petty fines) and amplified penalties for repeat offenders. Indoor prostitution was a different matter altogether: "It is not, in our view, the function of the law to intervene in the private lives of citizens."[21] The committee argued that prostitution should be tolerated in workers' private premises but stopped short of advocating licensed brothels because this might encourage men to avail themselves of services if they became so readily available. Thus, only the most hidden and small-scale indoor prostitution was to be allowed. The committee recognized that such a policy could lead to an increase in indoor prostitution but considered this "less injurious than the presence of prostitutes in the streets."[22]

These recommendations were incorporated into legislation two years after publication of the Wolfenden report. The 1959 Street Offenses Act provided enhanced penalties for street soliciting (fines, incarceration) and left indoor prostitution untouched (except for retaining the prohibition on persons living off the earnings of a sex worker). This dualistic policy remained in effect for decades, along with some amendments on the street prostitution side: incarceration was abolished in 1983 for those convicted of solicitation on the streets, relying on fines instead, and a new offense of persistent "kerb crawling" was created in 1985, allowing for the arrest of clients who repeatedly cruise for prostitutes on the streets. The Policing and Crime Act of 2009 takes client culpability a step further, by making it illegal for someone to pay for sex with a person who has been subjected by a third party to force, threats, or deception—regardless of whether the client is aware of the coercion.[23]

The policy framework that I present below is inspired by the Wolfenden report while departing from it in some respects. This *two-track policy* would (1) target resources toward the reduction of street prostitution and (2) relax enforcement against indoor actors who are operating consensually.[24] I am not advocating this policy as a universal solution worldwide, but I do think it has promise in the United States—given that blanket criminalization is problematic, while the more radical proposals of de jure decriminalization or legalization are extremely unlikely in the foreseeable future.

Track One: Indoor Prostitution

Some jurisdictions in the United States, Britain, and many other nations have adopted an informal policy of de facto decriminalization of indoor prostitution—essentially ignoring escorts, brothels, and massage parlors unless a complaint is made.[25] Elsewhere, however, police devote substantial time and resources to this side of the sex trade, accounting for as much as half the prostitution arrests.[26] Law enforcement policies can differ dramatically even between adjacent areas. In Riverside County in California, police have regularly arrested indoor sex workers and their clients, whereas this is not the practice next door in San Bernardino County.[27]

Efforts against indoor operations typically involve considerable planning and resources, and large-scale operations can last months or years. In one case, federal agents raided more than 40 upscale escort agencies in 23 cities—the culmination of a two-year investigation costing $2.5 million.[28] Seattle police recently launched an elaborate sting operation in which officers placed ads and photos on Craigslist and made appointments with men who responded to the ads; a total of 104 men were arrested after they appeared at an expensive condo rented by the police department and were observed discussing a price with the female vice cop.[29] In another case, a vice squad officer in Omaha, Nebraska, posing as a visiting businessman, arranged a date with an escort he met online and had a limo pick her up and deliver her to a hotel, where the two drank wine, only to end in an arrest. A taxpayers' group accused the Omaha police of wasting resources in the operation. The group's president complained that the police "were not good stewards with the taxpayers' dollars in spending the resources that were spent to have her arrested on a misdemeanor charge."[30]

Indoor investigations can be faulted not only for misusing resources that could be devoted to street prostitution but also for sometimes crossing the line of propriety:

- On more than one occasion, vice officers in Lynnwood, Washington, allowed prostitutes to masturbate them before making an arrest. When questioned about this, Police Chief Paul Watkins stated, "The officers didn't cross that line of engaging in intercourse or oral sex. I advised them no oral sex, no intercourse, that's not going to happen. That's the understood policy." Neighboring counties prohibit masturbation. A King County sheriff's department sergeant stated, "I can tell you personally, as a vice cop . . . I never accepted an offer, nor did anyone I know of that I worked with then. I also have no knowledge of any of our vice officers agreeing to sex during investigations. The prostitution law is you make an offer and they agree, sex for money, . . . and you can make an arrest."[31]

- In 2001, two troopers in the Pennsylvania State Police received oral sex from a masseuse before busting a massage parlor in Duncansville. The officers claimed they needed this lip service in order to gather enough evidence for an arrest. The local district attorney said that his office did not look favorably on the "extra steps they took" but also claimed, dubiously, that their actions were no worse than when an undercover cop buys drugs. The officers were not disciplined for their actions, and prosecutors declined to charge the massage parlor's owner.[32]

- For at least a decade, vice cops in Louisville, Kentucky, have had sexual contact with women in massage parlors prior to arresting them. In fully half of the arrests, officers' reports mentioned that a masseuse had fondled their genitals or provided oral sex.[33] Under Kentucky law, police only need a verbal agreement of sex for pay to make an arrest. When the story broke in the city's newspaper in 2004, the police chief claimed that he was unaware of the practice, but the county prosecutor revealed that he had sent a memo to the police in 2002 insisting that the practice be discontinued. The head of the vice unit tried to justify it on the grounds that the women had become savvy in spotting undercover officers partly by initiating sexual contact to see if the man recoils.

- The same practice is followed in Spotsylvania County, Virginia, but there only unmarried officers are involved in massage-parlor busts. The chairperson of the county's Board of Supervisors questioned the tactic and said that officers should be focusing on violent crimes rather than "pursuing pleasurable acts."[34]

- In Allentown, Pennsylvania, the state police paid an informant on four occasions to have sex with women at a spa in 2006 (he received $180 for his time and $360 to pay the women for sex). State police policy prohibits officers from engaging in such tactics, explaining why they use informants instead. Dismissing the charges against the spa owner, a judge expressed his displeasure at the practice: "No adequate supervisory guidance was provided, no standards existed for this type of investigation, and some of the behavior by the participants was sophomoric. We expect more from the police, and demand that they conduct their investigations and utilize their resources without resorting to such embarrassing investigative techniques."[35]

- Confidential informants also engaged in sexual acts in Nashville, Tennessee, and were paid $100 per bust. Police policy prohibits officers from disrobing during an investigation,[36] but the district attorney argued that a recorded agreement on a price should be sufficient to make an arrest (as it is in most other jurisdictions) and added that it was "contradictory letting the confidential informant engage in the very act you're trying to stamp out." In response, the head of the vice unit defended the practice: "What's the greater good? It may be distasteful to some people, but it's better that we have those places shut down." In 2002–2004, a total of $120,000 was spent on such encounters, with informants receiving more than $70,000.[37]

These are just a few of many instances that raise questions about the ways in which scarce resources are being used and the propriety of some of these investigations. But there are other costs as well. Crackdowns on indoor prostitution can have the unintended result of increasing the number of streetwalkers, thus exacerbating the most problematic side of the prostitution trade. Closures of massage parlors and other indoor venues have had precisely this effect in some cities.[38] As a New Orleans vice officer observed, "Whenever we focus on indoor investigations, the street scene gets insane."[39] When I accompanied Washington, DC, vice officers as they arrested clients on the street, the officers told me that "most cops think prostitution should be allowed in hotels but not on the street."[40] Whether or not this is a widely held view among police officers, under the two-track policy resources would be redirected toward street prostitution.

The success of a policy of nonenforcement toward indoor prostitution would require that it be implemented without fanfare in the United States. A public announcement that a city had decided to take a "hands off" approach to this variety of sex work might serve as a magnet drawing outside workers and clients into the locale. But in cities where it is not already standard practice, an unwritten policy of nonenforcement might be a sensible innovation. It would free up resources for the more pressing problems on the street and might have the effect of pushing at least some streetwalkers indoors, as one official commission reasoned: "Keeping prostitutes off the streets may be aided by tolerating them off the streets."[41]

Does the two-track approach unfairly target the street market? Inherent in any two-track approach are disparate effects on actors associated with each track, and with respect to prostitution there are legitimate grounds for differential treatment: (1) certain other types of commercial enterprise and individual behavior (e.g., nudity, urination, being drunk and disorderly) are prohibited on the streets but not indoors and (2) "this kind of policy may not be considered too inequitable if the costs inflicted on society by the street prostitutes are greater . . . than from those working in hotels" and other indoor venues.[42] The legal principle on which this proposal rests is that the criminal law should not interfere with the conduct of consenting adults, provided that this conduct does not threaten the legally protected interests of others. Whereas street prostitution is associated with a variety of harms to workers and to host communities, indoor prostitution is in accord with the harm-reduction principle.[43] This was the position taken by the Wolfenden Committee as well as a San Francisco commission, which concluded that "continued criminalization of private, non-visible prostitution cannot be warranted by fear of associated crime, drug abuse, venereal disease, or protection of minors."[44] More recently, a Canadian government commission declared, "The concern with the law is not what takes place in private, but the public manifestation of prostitution,"[45] and a second Canadian commission concluded that "the two objectives of harm reduction and violence prevention could most likely occur if prostitution was conducted indoors."[46] The policy implication is clear: "reassign police priorities to those types of prostitution that inflict the greatest costs," namely, street prostitution.[47]

Track Two: Controlling Street Prostitution

A major advantage of the two-track model is that resources previously devoted to the control of indoor prostitution can be transferred to where they are most needed: the street-level sex trade. Under this model, the central objective of the police and social service agencies would be (1) to protect prostitutes from violence and (2) to assist them in leaving the streets. This approach is far from the norm in the United States, but it has been applied to minors in some cities (e.g., Boston, San Francisco).[48] Under a 2008 New York law, persons under age 18 arrested for prostitution are channeled into services and programs (including safe houses, counseling, vocational training, health care) instead of being charged with a crime and prosecuted.[49] The youths are still arrested, which seems necessary in order to compel compliance, but they are not stigmatized by prosecution and formal punishment. This policy could be extended to adults involved in street prostitution.

Street prostitution in America is hardly a harmless vice. First, it is an *ecological problem* insofar as it adversely affects the quality of life of host communities. These harms include disorderly conduct on the part of prostitutes, customers, and pimps; public health dangers from discarded paraphernalia (used condoms, syringes); exposure of local residents, including children, to the sight of sex conducted in alleys, cars, bus stops, parks, and so forth; propositioning of male residents by prostitutes and propositioning and harassment of local women and teenage girls by clients; traffic congestion and noise from clients cruising in their cars; declining property values in the surrounding community; and collateral crimes such as drug use and sales, robbery, assault, and rape. The degree to which these problems occur varies over time and place, but as a general rule street prostitution is associated with a host of tangible environmental problems.[50]

Second, street prostitution is a multifaceted *social problem* whose harms are not reducible to its illegality. Many streetwalkers are underage, runaways, homeless, or economically distressed, selling sex out of desperation ("survival sex"); they are at high risk of drug abuse, unsafe sex practices, and victimization. The push factors that lead individuals into street prostitution (e.g., poverty, unemployment, running away from abusive parents) will not be alleviated if street-level transactions are simply decriminalized. For youths, preemptive intervention is needed, such as school programs to increase awareness of and options for reporting abuse by a family member, and warnings about the risks of running away from home. For adults, some European cities have experimented with permitting street prostitution in a designated zone governed by a set of rules and regulations (overseen by gatekeepers, service providers, and police). Over time, some of these zones encountered problems, such as an oversupply of prostitutes, making the area unmanageable. Moreover, the status of the workers did not change: they remained disproportionately poor, drug addicted, and socially marginalized.[51]

In settings where street prostitution is illegal and completely unregulated, as in the United States and Canada, it is fairly policy resistant. One analyst even concludes that "short of longer prison sentences for prostitutes . . . nothing seems to work."[52] Yet street prostitution is not completely incorrigible. If it is treated as a social problem rather than as a narrow law enforcement problem, it is possible to reduce its prevalence. The street population has special needs because of its manifold, adverse life experiences—including drug addiction, sexual trauma, social stigma, arrest records, and physical and mental health problems.[53] In most American cities, resources are scarce for sex-trading populations, with the exception of a few small nongovernmental organizations that attempt to help prostitutes leave the trade.[54] The dominant approach is overwhelmingly coercive rather than rehabilitative, yet past experience abundantly shows the failure of narrowly punitive intervention. Without assistance from service providers and meaningful alternatives to prostitution, there is little opportunity to exit. Reducing the amount of street prostitution requires holistic programs of temporary housing, job training, drug treatment, health care, counseling, education, and other needed services. Such multiagency interventions have been tried, with varying degrees of success, in Britain,[55] and a similar comprehensive approach in the United States stands the best chance of reducing street prostitution, bearing in mind that the push factors (homelessness, poverty, abusive relatives) will continue to feed the supply unless these forces are also tackled.

Precedents for the Two-Track Policy

A few blue-ribbon panels have recommended changes consistent with the two-track model. Commissions in Atlanta and San Francisco have advocated a dual approach for precisely the reasons just described.[56] And a landmark 1985 Canadian commission argued that abating street prostitution would require legislation allowing prostitutes to work somewhere else. It recommended a "cottage industry" approach—that is, permitting one or two prostitutes to work out of their own residence,[57] a proposal subsequently endorsed by another Canadian task force and by a British government agency.[58] Indoor work by one or a few providers was seen as preferable to work on the streets or in brothels since it gives the workers maximum autonomy and shields them against exploitation by pimps and other managers. The second Canadian commission also recommended giving provincial authorities the option of legalizing small, nonresidential brothels, subject to appropriate controls. A majority of Canadians support these proposals. In a 2009 survey, 60 percent approved of "allowing prostitutes to work indoors in brothels."[59] In England, it is legal for a single person to sell sex in his or her residence, and the Home Office recommended that it be legal for three people to work in the same residence.[60] The recommendation was rejected by the government.

Two states in the contemporary United States have implemented the two-track policy. Since 1971, Nevada has allowed rural counties the option of licensing and regulating brothels, while it retains the ban on escort and street prostitution. The brothels are discussed further in chapter 4. Rhode Island is the other U.S. example. Until 2009, Rhode Island took a dual approach that was broader than Nevada's, since it applied to all indoor prostitution, not just brothels in rural areas. A 1980 state law effectively allowed indoor prostitution by prohibiting only loitering for the purpose of soliciting sex. Loitering occurs outdoors. Solicitation that takes place indoors or on the Internet was not prohibited. Police sometimes busted massage parlors for employing workers lacking a massage license, but not for prostitution.[61] Rhode Island thus stood out for its formal (if unintentional) adoption of the two-track policy.

This situation changed in 2009, after an incident in the city of Warwick and a related one in Boston in which one escort was killed and another robbed, apparently by the same man. Heavy media coverage of these cases drew attention to the state's laissez-faire approach to indoor prostitution and led to a heated public debate and hearings in the state legislature. Among those who argued that criminalization was the wrong approach, 50 academics signed a letter opposing the bill—a letter that received considerable media coverage and was discussed in the legislature.[62] Not surprisingly, prohibitionists mounted a massive effort to convince legislators to criminalize prostitution. An op-ed article by well-known Rhode Island activist Donna Hughes attempted to alarm the public and shame politicians who were slow to accept the need for criminalization. Hughes declared that if the law remained unchanged,

> Rhode Island is headed for a human rights disaster and nationwide political embarrassment. . . . Rhode Island will continue to have an expanding number of spa-brothels, prostitution of minors in clubs, and no law that will enable the police to stop it. The hearing [on the criminalization bill] was a sordid circus, with pimps and prostitutes coming forward to oppose the legislation. . . . Senator Levesque seemed pleased and entertained by the cadre from the sex industry. . . . Never have I witnessed such a carnival. . . . I believe the Senate is going to let another year go by without a prostitution law. This will be a tragedy for victims caught in the sex industry, a black eye for Rhode Island's reputation, and a victory for the pimps.[63]

Other observers stated that there were no pimps at the hearing, but some massage-parlor workers did testify against the bill. It is ironic that Hughes warns of a "human rights disaster" if the legislature failed to criminalize indoor prostitution, given that the two-track policy had been in effect for 30 years without causing problems, let alone disastrous results.

Nevertheless, the legislature passed the bill in October 2009—thus putting an end to the state's two-track policy. In signing the legislation, Governor Donald Carcieri declared that prostitution "erodes the moral fiber of our state" and added, "For almost 30 years, Rhode Island has had the terrible distinction of being the only state outside certain counties in Nevada where indoor prostitution is not considered a crime." The symbolic dimension of the new law was echoed by Attorney General Patrick Lynch when he proclaimed that it will "end a blemish" on the state.[64]

The new law provides jail time (up to six months) or a fine (up to $1,000) for both prostitutes and their customers and permits judges to expunge the charges after one year for a convicted prostitute but not for the customer.[65] Landlords who allow prostitution on their premises face a mandatory minimum sentence of one year in prison (and a maximum five years) and a mandatory $2,000 fine (maximum $5,000) for their first offense, increasing for a subsequent offense. A few days after the law passed, massage parlors began to close. Michael Kiselica, a lawyer who represents parlor owners and their landlords, stated that his clients may sue the state because of the adverse economic effects of the new law. Kiselica asked, "What happens when you suddenly create a large number of unemployed people who the day before were gainfully and lawfully employed? What consideration did the state give to those people?"[66]

The Rhode Island and Nevada cases show that versions of the two-track policy *have been in effect* in contemporary America—for 30 years in Rhode Island and 40 years in Nevada. Thus, the policy cannot be dismissed as a utopian idea. Over the past decade, several criminalization bills had been considered but failed to pass the Rhode Island legislature (until 2009) because legislators were not convinced that the two-track approach should be abandoned. At the same time, the Rhode Island case also shows that established prostitution policy can change rather quickly, especially if activists dramatize the issue in the media and succeed in alarming the public and embarrassing policymakers. Some well-publicized violent attacks concentrated public attention on the "loophole" in the state's prostitution law, and activists capitalized on this in demanding an end to this "blemish" on Rhode Island's image.

As mentioned earlier, it is rare in the United States for a state legislature even to consider decriminalization. But Hawaii did so in 2007. The bill would have decriminalized the indoor track and zoned street prostitution:

A person commits the offense of prostitution if the person engages in, or agrees or offers to engage in, sexual conduct with another person for a fee in a public place that is likely to be observed by others who would be affronted or alarmed. . . . The legislature and counties shall designate areas within their jurisdiction as exempt from the penalty provisions. . . . Designated areas shall include portions of geographic areas that have a history of this offense. The designated areas may be described both by geographic boundaries and by time of day limitations.[67]

The first part of the bill essentially decriminalizes indoor prostitution, and the second part restricts street prostitution to certain areas. The latter therefore departs from the two-track policy because it allows street prostitution and does not provide resources to help workers get off the streets. The bill was supported by the ACLU, but it failed to pass in the legislature. One of the bill's sponsors, Rep. Bob Herkes, saw the bill as a strategic stepping stone: "It's one of those bills you do it for public dialogue instead of trying to get it passed," and the bill's advocates stated that they hoped to gain support for a similar bill in the future.[68]

The preceding discussion shows that, while blanket criminalization is the reigning approach in the United States, alternatives occasionally make it onto the public agenda. In other words, decriminalization and legalization are not totally foreign ideas in contemporary America. Decriminalization has recently been on the ballot in two cities (Berkeley and San Francisco), was considered by at least one state legislature (Hawaii), and was the key recommendation of a blue-ribbon commission (in San Francisco in 1996). Moreover, the two-track policy has been implemented in two states (Rhode Island and Nevada) and proposed by at least one official commission (in San Francisco in 1971). As we will see in later chapters, several other nations embrace some version of the two-track approach—decriminalizing brothels, escort agencies, or other indoor enterprises while continuing to ban street prostitution.

Expanding Criminalization: The Dominant Trend

Having described the different policy options as well as some recent changes in the United States, it is now time to expand the discussion by examining the most important macrolevel trend in the country over the past decade: a steadily expanding punitive approach to the sex industry. As I show in this section, *all* sectors of the sex industry, not just prostitution, have been targeted by prohibitionist forces and by the government during the past decade. Trends in the United States, therefore, contrast with those in some other countries discussed later in the book. The punitive trend may be viewed as part of a backlash to the increasing availability and mass marketing of sexual services and to what opponents inside and outside government regard as an alarming normalization of sexual commerce. The window of opportunity for moral reform opened wide during the Bush administration (2001–2008)—a regime whose interests converged almost seamlessly with the demands of prohibitionist social forces and resulted in legislation designed to curb commercial sex work.[69]

No discussion of the trend toward amplified criminalization would be complete without examining the role of sex trafficking as a policy driver. A newly discovered social problem, the term *human trafficking* was not in vogue as recently as two decades ago. In U.S. law, *trafficking* is defined as "the recruitment, harboring, transportation, provision, or obtaining of a person for labor or services through the use of force, fraud, or coercion," a definition that applies to work in agricultural, industrial, or commercial sex sectors.[70] Most commentators, activists, and government officials have focused exclusively on one area—sex trafficking.

Some analysts have published excellent critical evaluations of domestic and international trafficking policies, questioning many of the popular claims about trafficking (including the magnitude of the problem) and identifying serious flaws in the data used to support those claims.[71] But scholars have been less cognizant of the increasing conflation of trafficking with commercial sex, a theme explored here.[72] Over the past decade, the trafficking issue has driven policy debates and enforcement practices regarding the entire sex industry in the United States and in some other nations. What began in the mid-1990s as a campaign against trafficking has steadily expanded over time. Prohibitionists now associate sex trafficking with *all* sexual commerce—prostitution, pornography, and commercial stripping. Such "domain expansion" is common in social movements: once they achieve their original goals, many movements turn to other issues.

From Sex Trafficking to Prostitution

Organizations that seek to combat sex trafficking differ in their ultimate goal. One wing is committed to identifying and assisting victims (i.e., individuals who have been transported into the sex trade by force or deception) as well as the larger goal of disrupting sex-trafficking networks. Another wing has a much broader agenda. They seek to criminalize not just coercive sex trafficking but all migration into sex work. These latter organizations have increasingly monopolized the trafficking debate in the United States and other nations and have steadily expanded their compass to the entire sex industry. Here, I restrict my discussion to these dominant forces (which I call *prohibitionist* because they seek to outlaw all commercial sex). I show how, after winning victory after victory in shaping trafficking policy during the Bush administration, this movement broadened its mission to include other types of sex work.

Prohibitionists first succeeded in linking sex trafficking to prostitution.[73] To fight trafficking, they asserted, prostitution must be targeted in its own right, by increasing the penalties for participants or by criminalizing prostitution where it is currently legal. Activist Donna Hughes, for example, calls for "re-linking trafficking and prostitution, and combating the commercial sex trade as a whole."[74] Hughes claims that "most 'sex workers' are—or originally started out as—trafficked women and girls."[75] This claim is fictional: studies have not demonstrated that "most" prostitutes have been trafficked. Moreover, prostitution and trafficking differ substantively: prostitution is a type of labor, whereas migration and trafficking involve the process of recruitment and relocation to access a market. Both empirically and conceptually, it is inappropriate to fuse the two.

The U.S. government has fully adopted the conflation framework. The State Department's 2004 publication "The Link between Prostitution and Sex Trafficking" draws this "link" boldly, equating trafficking and prostitution. It also declares that prostitution "is inherently harmful"; that it "leaves women and children physically, mentally, emotionally, and spiritually devastated"; and that legal prostitution "creates a safe haven for criminals who traffic people into prostitution."[76] Officials in the Justice Department privately questioned this sweeping depiction of prostitution,[77] but this had no effect on the official position of the Bush administration.

The focus on prostitution has shaped not just official discourse but also legislation and enforcement. First, most of the enforcement efforts against human trafficking in the United States have centered on prostitution cases, with much less attention to labor trafficking.[78] And sex trafficking and prostitution have been fused: a recent investigation discovered that some multiagency law enforcement units "have focused exclusively on prostitution, making no distinction between prostitution and sex trafficking."[79] Second, the initial focus on traffickers has steadily expanded to include customers, who are seen as the root cause of trafficking—discussed later in this chapter. Third, government funding has been skewed. Activists successfully pressed for a policy that denies funding to organizations that are not sufficiently committed to eradicating prostitution. Since 2003, to be eligible for U.S. funding, any foreign nongovernmental organization working on the trafficking front must declare its opposition to prostitution.[80] The ban was also applied to researchers. In 2007, the Justice Department required those who apply for funding to conduct research on trafficking to certify that they do "not promote, support, or advocate the legalization or practice of prostitution."[81] Failure to do so would result in summary rejection. Similarly, the 2003 Global AIDS Act requires that any international organization working to curb AIDS must "have a policy explicitly opposing prostitution and sex trafficking" if it wishes to receive U.S. funding. This applies to American groups insofar as they work with or subcontract work to international organizations. Organizations that take no position on prostitution are thus ineligible for government funding.[82] These funding restrictions skew research and intervention in one direction, eliminating competing points of view and further privileging and institutionalizing the oppression paradigm. Because of the restriction, several nongovernmental organizations have declined to apply for government funding.[83]

Legal prostitution systems are a prime target. According to both prohibitionist activists and the U.S. government, legalization allegedly increases trafficking by removing the constraints on a formerly illegal and circumscribed enterprise.[84] One target is Nevada's legal brothel system. Prohibitionist activist Melissa Farley received State Department funding to investigate Nevada's brothels, resulting in a highly critical report. Remarkably, Farley provides no evidence of trafficking into the brothels and relies instead on a few individuals' opinions to make this connection:

> Women are trafficked from other countries into Nevada's legal brothels. . . . In Nevada, 27 percent of our 45 interviewees in the Nevada legal brothels *believed* that there were *undocumented immigrants* in the legal brothels. Another 11 percent said they were uncertain, thus as many as 38 percent of the women we interviewed *may have known* of internationally trafficked women in Nevada legal brothel prostitution.[85]

Another way of reporting this "finding" is that as many as 62 percent did *not* believe that women were trafficked into the brothels, while the remainder either did not have an opinion or believed that there were some undocumented immigrants, who are not necessarily "trafficked." Farley converts the *beliefs* of a *minority* with regard to immigrants into *evidence* of trafficking, and this minority consists of just twelve interviewees. Elsewhere, Farley writes that a few women in one brothel told her that women in another brothel had been trafficked from China. Farley presents this hearsay as factual and calls the women who told her this story "witnesses," lending their statements an aura of credibility.[86]

The report also discounts evidence contradicting Farley's conclusions. Workers who did not have a problem working in a brothel were simply dismissed as living a lie.[87] Similarly, a study that concluded that Nevada's legal brothels "offer the safest environment available for women to sell consensual sex acts for money"[88] was rejected by Farley because, she says, "safety is relative, given that all prostitution is associated with a high likelihood of violence."[89] Farley's methods and conclusions have been severely criticized by scholars who have studied Nevada's brothels for over a decade,[90] yet her report was given a stamp of authority when published as an official State Department report.

The State Department's own assessments appear to undercut the notion that legal prostitution systems are a magnet for sex trafficking. In its annual *Trafficking in Persons Report*, several nations where prostitution is legal (Australia, Germany, the Netherlands, New Zealand, etc.) have consistently been found to "fully comply with minimum standards for the elimination of trafficking."[91] In fact, legal prostitution *may* help *decrease* trafficking due to increased oversight. Criminalization, by contrast, appears to encourage trafficking: "It is the prohibition of prostitution and restrictions on travel," argues Alison Murray, "which attract organized crime and create the possibilities for large profits, as well as creating the prostitutes' need for protection and assistance."[92] And Kamala Kempadoo notes, "Traffickers take advantage of the illegality of commercial sex work and migration, and are able to exert an undue amount of power and control over [migrants]. . . . In such cases, it is the laws that prevent legal commercial sex work and immigration that form the major obstacles."[93] There is overwhelming evidence that organized crime thrives under conditions in which a particular vice is criminalized—amply demonstrated by drug and alcohol prohibition—and declines when it is legalized. Yet the Bush administration continued to assert that legal prostitution has the opposite effect, amplifying criminal activity, despite the lack of evidence to support this claim.

Targeting Clients

In the United States, prostitutes have always been arrested in much greater numbers than their customers have, despite the fact that customers greatly outnumber prostitutes. National data are lacking on the exact numbers of prostitutes and customers arrested (the figures report total arrests for "prostitution and commercialized vice," not broken down by suboffense and not including customers at all), but all indications are that the disparity remains wide today. Some cities, however, have vigorously pursued customers over the past decade and are part of a larger national trend toward greater enforcement against prostitutes' clients.

Customers have been targeted in different ways. Police decoys, who appear to be prostitutes, make arrests when they are solicited. Some residents have banded together to harass prostitutes and clients by following and videotaping them or by engaging in vigilante actions such as attacking cars. Public humiliation is another common approach, including "naming and shaming" alleged clients in local newspapers, on cable television, or on a police website listing the names, addresses, and pictures of men arrested for attempting to solicit a prostitute.[94] In New Haven, Connecticut, posters naming a "John of the Week" were stapled to trees in one prostitution stroll, and Miami has used freeway billboards to shame convicted clients.[95] Americans are evenly divided on these practices, with half of the public endorsing the idea of publicizing the names and photos of convicted clients.[96] In 2008, at least 280 American cities were shaming customers in some way.[97]

A second tactic is a novel form of rehabilitation: the "john school" for arrested customers. San Francisco launched its First Offenders Prostitution Program in 1995, and between 1995 and early 2008, more than 5,700 men had attended the program.[98] The program is a joint effort by the police, the prosecutor's office, the public health department, community leaders, and former prostitutes. The men avoid an arrest record and court appearance by paying a $500–$1,000 fine, attending the school, and not recidivating for one year after the arrest. As of 2008, john schools had been launched in 40 cities in the United States (as well as in Canada and Britain), all of which are modeled on San Francisco's program.[99] Every aspect of the program is designed to shame, educate, and deter the men from future contact with prostitutes. The audience hears former prostitutes describe their traumatic experiences, views a graphic slide show on sexually transmitted diseases, and is lectured by community residents about the ways that street prostitution destroys their neighborhoods. During my observations at the San Francisco school in 1998, the men were repeatedly asked how they would feel if their mothers, wives, or daughters became prostitutes and why they were "using" and "violating" prostitutes.

The paradigm shift toward clients is evident at the national and state levels as well, especially in the antitrafficking laws that contain special provisions targeting "the demand." For years, prohibitionists have been pressing for vigorous enforcement against customers.[100] Illinois has been in the vanguard of this trend with some unique interventions. In 2009, Illinois activists launched an End Demand Campaign to "advocate for the creation of resources and tools for law enforcement to hold perpetrators accountable, deter further exploitation, and increase options for prostituted and trafficked women and girls."[101] The campaign has roots in earlier efforts, including activists' successful lobbying of the state legislature to pass the Predator

Accountability Act in 2006, which allows prostitutes to seek civil damages against individuals and businesses that can be linked to their involvement in sex work. Clients and pimps can be sued if they "abuse" or "cause bodily harm" to a prostitute, but the most radical feature of the new law is the liability it imposes on businesses. A business is punishable if it "recruits, profits from, or maintains the victim in the sex trade," irrespective of whether the so-called victim was coerced. Strip clubs, massage parlors, and escort agencies that knowingly publish ads intended to recruit individuals into prostitution are the targets of this law.[102] The assets of such businesses make them lucrative targets for plaintiffs seeking financial settlements for damages. In October 2009, the Illinois attorney general and Cook Country sheriff filed a lawsuit against Craigslist for publishing advertisements for "erotic services" on its website. The lawsuit was dismissed by the court, but Craigslist agreed to increase the cost of such ads and to contribute the proceeds to charity. After other states began suing Craigslist, the company decided to close its erotic-services section in September 2010.

The growing targeting of customers in the United States is part of a larger, international trend. This approach is exemplified by Sweden, where a 1999 law punishes clients but not prostitutes on the grounds that men are the perpetrators and women are victims who should be rescued rather than prosecuted.[103] The new law was the result of heavy lobbying by actors inside and outside government who fully embraced the oppression paradigm. In fact, in the debate leading up to the new law, the notion that "prostitution was a degradation of women, a form of violence against women, was the most powerful argument" and totally eclipsed alternative views.[104]

Since 1999, some other nations have adopted the Swedish approach. In 2006, Finland passed a law outlawing the buying of sex from a trafficked woman, and in 2009, Norway and Iceland enacted legislation quite similar to Sweden's. In the same year, England and Wales passed a bill criminalizing those who buy sex from workers who are coerced into prostitution by a third party, irrespective of whether clients are aware of third-party involvement. In each case, advocates of the measures drew inspiration from the Swedish system, and in some cases Swedish and other foreign antiprostitution activists personally lobbied local politicians to pass the bills. The popularity of the Swedish approach is such that it frequently takes center stage whenever prostitution policy is on the political agenda today. It should be noted, however, that not all antiprostitution activists favor the Swedish approach: many continue to press for the criminalization and punishment of all parties involved in sex for sale, not just the clients.

Targeting Stripping and Pornography

Domain expansion is broader than prostitution. The key U.S. legislation on sex trafficking defines "commercial sexual activities" broadly, as "any sex act on account of which anything of value is given to, or received by, any person."[105] One purpose of the 2005 End Demand for Sex Trafficking bill was to "combat commercial sexual activities" in general because, according to the bill, "commercial sexual activities have a devastating impact on society. The sex trade has a dehumanizing effect on all involved." Part of the End Demand bill ended up in the 2005 Trafficking Victims Protection Reauthorization Act (TVPRA), which contains a section that repeatedly refers to the need to investigate and combat "trafficking in persons and demand for commercial sex acts in the United States"[106]—effectively blurring the line between trafficking and commercial sex. For those who "purchase commercial sex acts," the TVPRA authorized $25 million per year for increased prosecution and programs (e.g., john schools).[107]

Prohibitionists have sought to link trafficking to strip clubs. Australian activist Sheila Jeffreys claims that "trafficking in women by organized crime groups has become a common form of supply of dancers. All over Europe and North America women and girls are brought to the clubs by deception, by force, or, initially, by consent."[108] No evidence is offered to support this sweeping charge. Donna Hughes's report on trafficking (funded by the U.S. State Department) claims that "the introduction of lap dancing has almost eliminated the distinction between dancing and prostitution" and that women are trafficked to perform at strip clubs (Hughes found only six cases of this in the United States during 1998–2005).[109] Hughes maintains that strip clubs are "attractive to some criminals because they assume that since stripping is legal they will be less likely to be caught trafficking women into these markets."[110] Other prohibitionists have made similar claims, which may lead to increased police investigations of strip clubs in the future.[111]

Pornography is also under new scrutiny in the United States. Most of the groups involved in the antiprostitution movement are equally alarmed by pornography, which they have begun to associate with trafficking. In an article entitled "Pornography as Trafficking," Catharine MacKinnon equates the distribution of pornography with the trafficking of persons depicted in pornography, but MacKinnon goes further when she writes that "the pornography industry, in production, creates demand for prostitution, hence for trafficking, because it is itself a form of prostitution and trafficking."[112] Other activists argue, in less opaque terms, that there is a simple connection between trafficking and porn—that is, the two are inextricable.

A letter to President Bush, signed by over 50 leaders in the antiporn movement, urged him to crack down on this vice. Alarmed at the "explosive increase" in the availability of pornography, the signatories also claimed that "trafficking in women and children" is "linked to the spread of obscenity" and that pornography "corrupts children, ruins marriages, contributes to sex crimes against children and adults, and undermines the right of Americans to live in a decent society." The letter asked Bush to make fighting obscenity one of his "top priorities."[113] One of the signatories, Patrick Trueman, testified before Congress that "pornography is closely linked to an increase in prostitution, child prostitution, and human trafficking. . . . Pornography is a powerful factor in creating the demand for illicit sex."[114] (Trueman is the former chief of the Justice Department's obscenity branch and now legal counsel for the right-wing Family Research Council.) Donna Hughes's report for the State Department echoes this view, alleging that the producers of pornography "often rely on trafficked victims."[115] Once again, supporting evidence is lacking. The connection is simply an *assertion* by activists who seek to ban pornography.

Pressure from prohibitionist groups helps to explain the Bush administration's actions against pornography.[116] The Justice Department created a second obscenity branch and staffed the two units with prominent antiporn individuals.[117] One major figure is Bruce Taylor, who was appointed as the obscenity unit's senior legal counsel. He had previously been a lawyer for the nation's premier antipornography group (Citizens for Decency through Law, founded in 1956) and was president of another antiporn organization (the National Law Center for Children and Families).[118] Since Taylor has been such a major player in the campaign against porn both inside and outside government, his views on pornography are especially noteworthy:

> I still believe that pornography has a bad effect on society and on families, and it's not a good thing for guys to look at. It's like the training manual for how guys get to be chauvinist jerks. I mean, you don't treat a woman well if you treat her like she's treated in a porn movie. It's not the kind of thing you want your boy to be looking at or that the guy who comes to date your daughter is looking at. You don't want your husband looking at it. You don't want your boyfriend looking at it. You don't really want your wife looking at it.[119]

For Taylor, all depictions of penetration are by definition obscene, which means that "just about everything on the Internet and almost everything in the video stores and everything in the adult bookstores is still prosecutable [as] illegal obscenity."[120] This far-reaching definition of obscenity is much broader than what some jurisdictions would define as obscene. (Under *Miller v. California*, 1973, obscenity is determined by local community standards, which in practice means a jury's assessment of whether a particular work appeals to "prurient interests," depicts sexual conduct in a "patently offensive way," and lacks literary, artistic, political, or scientific value.)[121]

Appointment of staunch antiporn officials made a difference. Under their leadership, the Justice Department launched a new crackdown on adult pornography (the Clinton administration focused on child porn).[122] During the Bush administration, 361 individuals were charged with adult obscenity violations, about twice as many as were charged during the Clinton years.[123] In Bush's last year in office (2008), 54 defendants were charged, compared to 20 in the first year of Obama's administration (2009).[124]

These trends demonstrate an extraordinary amalgamation of interests between prohibitionist groups and government agencies during the Bush years. A final illustration of this interpenetration is the link between the Justice Department and a leading antiporn organization, Morality in Media (MIM). The Justice Department's website contains a section, "What Citizens Can Do about Obscenity," which encourages people to report "hardcore pornography." Since 2004, visitors who click on an icon are redirected to a MIM-run site, whose employees then conduct a review. MIM has received large government grants to fund its review of the complaints.[125] In the past few years, 67,000 citizen complaints have been passed from MIM to the Justice Department.[126] That the Justice Department's website provides links to MIM appears to reflect a seamless convergence of interests with a very partisan, conservative organization.

The advent of a new government in the United States is unlikely to alter the status quo, given how far-reaching the state's investment in prohibition has become. Right-wing political and religious forces have less access to the Obama administration than to its predecessor, but the now fully institutionalized legislation, agencies, and enforcement machinery will remain firmly in place for the foreseeable future. Moreover, many of the officials who were tasked with obscenity enforcement and trafficking policy during the Bush administration continue their work under the Obama administration.[127] Chapter 4 moves our policy discussion from the American context, where criminalization reigns supreme, to a detailed consideration of the alternatives of decriminalization and legalization in other nations.

Legal Prostitution

A New Frontier

The depiction of prostitution in the media and in government circles is almost always based on information from nations where it is illegal and subject to criminal penalties. This skews both popular perceptions and public policy. Most of the discourse regarding prostitution reflects its illegal status—with little or no consideration of alternative models. When legalization is debated in the United States, it is usually in the abstract, without reference to actually existing legal systems. Similarly, most academic studies have been conducted in nations where prostitution is criminalized, marginalized, and underground. This means that knowledge is heavily skewed by a nearly exclusive focus on only one mode of production—namely, criminalized sexual commerce. Much less is known about nations that have more liberal policies and thus present an alternative to blanket criminalization.

This huge gap in the research literature has implications both for our understanding of prostitution and for public policy. It seems important to think "outside the box" of American-style criminalization, to imagine something different and perhaps superior to the syndrome of illicit, stigmatized, and marginalized sexual commerce. As philosopher Christine Overall wrote, "It is imaginable that prostitution could always be practiced, as it occasionally is even now, in circumstances of relative safety, security, freedom, hygiene, and personal control."[1] This offers a contrasting picture to the conventional wisdom that prostitution is destined to remain a distasteful practice or oppressive institution under any and all circumstances.

Competing Views of Legalization

Can the laudable goals mentioned by Christine Overall be advanced under a system in which prostitution is legal and regulated by the government? Oppression theorists would answer with an unequivocal "no." Committed to a strict prohibitionist platform, they insist that legalization will only make the situation worse than under a regime of criminalization. Decriminalization and legalization do nothing, they claim, to alter the gender inequality inherent in sex work. Sheila Jeffreys even believes that male domination is the very reason why some nations have considered legalization, in her claim that these "patriarchal governments [are] acting in the interests of male citizens."[2] What's more, legalization is viewed as giving an official stamp of approval to a vile institution and creating a "prostitution culture" in which commercial sexual transactions are rendered acceptable. "When legal barriers disappear," Janice Raymond declares, "so too do the social and ethical barriers to treating women as sexual merchandise. Legalization of prostitution sends the message to new generations of men and boys that women are sexual commodities and that prostitution is harmless fun."[3]

These are *moral* objections that could easily be applied to commercial advertisements and to the entertainment industry more broadly, where sexual objectification is pervasive. But in addition to legalization's role in perpetuating a culture that devalues women, these authors identify more specific problems that they associate with legal prostitution, namely:

- Increased incidence of exploitation and involvement of organized crime.[4]
- Abuse: "Legitimizing prostitution as work has simply worked to normalize the violence and sexual abuse that [workers] experience on a daily basis. . . . Legalized prostitution is government-sanctioned abuse of women."[5]
- Proliferation: legal prostitution "encourages men to buy women for sex" because it makes paid sex more socially acceptable.[6]
- Trafficking: "wherever prostitution is legal, sex trafficking from other countries is significantly increased into both legal and illegal sex businesses in the region."[7]

For these reasons, oppression theorists argue, legalization is disastrous for sex workers and for the larger society.

This is hardly an abstract debate, as the oppression paradigm is the dominant one in the policy sphere. Prohibitionists have been extremely successful in popularizing this paradigm via the mass media and in gaining official government endorsement of it in the United States and abroad.[8] In many nations, the oppression paradigm is the accepted, conventional wisdom.

Before proceeding, it is important to consider the question of whether government policy makes any difference in the way prostitution is organized and experienced by workers, clients, and third parties. As we have just seen, oppression writers believe that government policy makes a huge difference, hence their campaign against legalization. But a few other scholars take the radical view that it matters little whether prostitution is illegal or legal and, if legal, what the regulations consist of. In other words, prostitution is seen as incorrigible, as almost entirely policy resistant. This conclusion is based on comparisons of different nations and the "finding" that diametrically opposed systems have little or no effect on commercial sex practices. Elizabeth Bernstein argues that policy changes in the late 1990s in Sweden, the Netherlands, and the United States resulted in "similar shifts on the ground," including

> the removal of economically disenfranchised and racially marginalized streetwalkers and their customers from gentrifying city centers; the *de facto* toleration of a small tier of predominantly white and relatively privileged indoor clients and workers; and the driving of illegal migrant sex workers further underground. . . . Whether sex work is decriminalized, legalized, or criminalized, the interests of real estate developers, municipal and national politicians, and business owners may overshadow the concerns of feminists and sex workers. . . . Despite some important surface-level contrasts . . . regimes which legalize the sex trade as well as those which claim to seek its elimination share several common threads which link them to larger changes in the global economy.[9]

There are several problems with Bernstein's formulation. First, it assumes that "the interests" of economic and political actors are uniform both within a nation and across nations. Such a monolithic picture disregards the possibility of conflicting interests between state and economic elites as well as within each sector. Second, the voices of sex workers themselves are absent from Bernstein's arguments, so it remains an open question how such macro patterns affect and are perceived by the actors involved. And third, the alleged trends are debatable. Street prostitution was not a significant part of the market in the Netherlands to begin with, and the "small tier" of upscale and mid-range indoor providers is a myth, as this sector constitutes a substantial share of the market in Sweden, the United States, and the Netherlands. Bernstein's broad assertion that a nation's policy (criminalization, decriminalization, legalization) is largely irrelevant is not convincingly argued or evidenced.

Laura Agustín makes the "no differences" argument even more forcefully. She notes that a segment of prostitution actors operate outside the law in all nations and then leaps to the conclusion that all legal regimes are a "failure":

"*Large numbers* of entrepreneurs and workers, wherever regulation is found, *always* ignore the rules and fail to participate. Given the failure of such regimes *everywhere* to be and do what they claim, it is not rational to continue to argue over which of them is best."[10] Agustín does not offer explanations for similar outcomes across different legal orders except to say that the authorities lack sufficient resources to control sex workers and their managers, who are incorrigible "everywhere." And she chides analysts who believe that policy regimes can make a difference: "The collusion of so many serious social actors in the pretense that the classic prostitution regimes are rational makes me wonder how much evidence that such regimes do not work is necessary before their many adherents give up on them. . . . Projects to control prostitution do not fit into any rational framework of social progress."[11] First, it is not clear what is meant by a "rational" policy. Second, we might ask what alternative Agustín favors. Judging from her claim that prostitution cannot be controlled, it appears that she prefers a totally unregulated system in which the state relinquishes its authority. Agustín does not say this, but it is the logical implication of her critique. And third, aside from the observation that "large numbers" of actors do not abide by the rules, Agustín presents *no evidence* for the blanket claim that all policy regimes are a failure—this after scolding other analysts for ignoring "the evidence" that government policies do "not work."

Jane Scoular is critical of Agustín's claim that law is irrelevant, but Scoular accepts the idea that "contrasting regulatory approaches have the same empirical effects."[12] She argues, like Bernstein, that the net effect of prostitution policies in Sweden and the Netherlands is the privileging of some sex workers at the expense of others. In Sweden, a 1999 law criminalized clients but not sex workers. This law led to a crackdown on street prostitution (where clients were more visible and vulnerable to arrest) and an expansion of the indoor market. In the Netherlands, legalization resulted in a two-tier system in which some workers are legal and enjoy rights while others are rendered illegal and marginalized. Disparities are indeed characteristic of both cases, but all three authors disregard the qualitative differences between the nations in question. There is a stark difference between a nation where prostitution is officially condemned and clients demonized and criminalized (Sweden) and one where workers and clients are legally free to engage in sexual commerce (the Netherlands). It is, therefore, absolutely *not* the case that these legal systems have "the same empirical effects," as Scoular and Bernstein claim, or have no effect, as Agustín insists. There may indeed be *some* similarities in the consequences of prostitution policies across nations (a conclusion that has yet to be fully documented, given the state of current research), but the empirical evidence does not justify the assertion that the effects are "the same" or that policy makes "no difference."

I maintain that it is farfetched to claim that state policy is wholly unrelated to the social organization of sex work and to participants' lived experiences. Even if many actors operate outside the legal system (e.g., not registering, not paying taxes, avoiding mandatory health exams), it still makes a difference to them whether they are regarded as criminals or as legal actors with rights. And there *is* evidence, from various nations, that the type of policy regime can affect—positively or negatively—what happens on the ground, as the remainder of this book shows. Criminalizing clients in Sweden has had the effect of further endangering street prostitutes, who, because of increased policing, now must conclude their negotiations under duress and with less time to screen clients.[13] Outlawing indoor sex work in Rhode Island in 2009 resulted in closure of massage parlors, throwing a substantial number of women out of relatively safe workplaces into more dangerous venues (if they continued to sell sex). And an analysis of Australian policies concluded that "even very limited reform processes can open new possibilities for protecting the safety and rights of sex workers. There are clear benefits that flow to workers from the availability of more legal prostitution, the most obvious of which is having the right to work without the fear of legal penalties."[14] Taken as a whole, the research on legal systems (past and present) suggests that prostitution *can* be organized in a way that is superior to blanket criminalization. At the same time, there is plenty of variation across legal systems in the nature of the regulations and their effects, both intended and unintended.

The remainder of this chapter outlines the central features of legal prostitution systems and then examines selected cases in order to highlight how they operate, the challenges they face, and what they tell us about prostitution when it is no longer illegal. Chapters 5 and 6 extend this analysis with an in-depth examination of three additional cases.

Two Types of Legalization

Legalization is defined here as *legislation that provides mechanisms for government regulation of paid sex transactions after prostitution has been decriminalized.* Regulation is what distinguishes legalization from simple decriminalization. Examples include the following: licensing of businesses, registration of workers, geographic restrictions (such as zoning in designated red-light districts or prohibitions near schools, churches, etc.), health requirements (e.g., mandatory condom use, periodic HIV and STD tests), age restrictions, and other rules for workers, managers, and clients. Prostitution is removed from the criminal law and regulated by civil law, yet the criminal law continues to apply to cases involving extortion, kidnapping, assault, rape, and other crimes.

States that liberalize their laws rarely decriminalize prostitution without coupling it with some kind of regulation. And those that simply decriminalize it without instituting safeguards put workers at risk. An extreme example of this is the city of Daulatoia in Bangladesh, where the authorities allow prostitutes to apply for "permission" to sell sex if they are over 18 years old but otherwise leave prostitution unregulated and the workers vulnerable to exploitation, abuse by madams, and violence from customers.[15] This case points to the need for government oversight, especially where workers are highly vulnerable to exploitation.

De Jure Legalization

De jure legalization involves both decriminalization and at least some formal government regulation. Because legalization involves regulation, it is inevitable that some practices will remain prohibited while others are permitted. Legalization can thus take quite different forms, as a practice allowed in one place may be prohibited in another. Nevertheless, a common objective across legal systems is harm reduction.[16] A number of scholars and policymakers have come to the conclusion that legal regulation is superior to criminalization in reducing harms in sexual commerce. As one analyst writes, "An interest in reducing the internal and external harms associated with prostitution would seem to favor a legal and regulated commercial sex industry."[17] Legalization may also have advantages over simple decriminalization in that the former involves greater control and thus offers both a practical and a symbolic dividend. State involvement in regulating vice can, over time, increase its legitimacy. The history of state regulation of gambling in the United States, as well as the more recent involvement of 15 states in regulating medical marijuana, arguably lends both of these practices greater credibility than when they were prohibited.

Recent polls, presented in table 4.1, show that majorities in several countries endorse legalization, either in the abstract or in the form of brothels. In France, a majority believes that legal brothels would make it easier to control prostitution and that the change would not lead to an increase in sexual commerce.[18] The majority supporting legalization in several other European nations contrasts with the United States, where the majority takes criminalization for granted, as shown in the previous chapter.

TABLE 4.1
Attitudes toward Legalization of Prostitution, Selected Nations

	Favor Legalization (%)
Britain (1998)[1]	61
Britain (2006)[2]	65
Canada (1998)[3]	71
Czech Republic (1999)[4]	70
France (1995)[5]	68
Germany (1999)[6]	68
Israel (2005)[7]	65
Netherlands (1997)[8]	73
New Zealand (2003)[9]	51
Portugal (2001)[10]	54
Taiwan (2009)[11]	52
Western Australia (2000)[12]	71
Western Australia (2006)[13]	64

Sources:

1. ITV Poll, reported in Agence France Presse, November 16, 1998, N=2,000 ("legalizing and licensing brothels").

2. IPSOS/MORI Poll, January 6-10, 2006, N=1,790 ("prostitution should be legalized").

3. Compas Poll, Sun Media Newspapers, reported in Edmonton Sun, October 31, 1998, N=1,479 ("legal and tightly regulated"= 65%, "completely legal"= 6%).

4. IVVM poll, reported by Czech News Agency, National News Wire, April 26, 1999 ("legalizing prostitution").

5. French poll reported in Boston Globe, January 22, 1995 ("legalized brothels").

6. Dimap poll, 1999, cited in German government explanation of the prostitution bill that became law in 2002, Parliamentary Paper BT-Drs. 14/5958, May 8, 2001.

7. Jerusalem Post, July 19, 2005, N=500 (legalization of prostitution and licensing of prostitutes).

8. Dutch poll cited in Brants (1998) ("legalization of brothels").

9. New Zealand Herald, May 14, 2003, N=500. "Don't Know" responses removed from total (legal brothels).

10. Marketest poll of residents of Lisbon and Oporto, reported in Financial Times and Diario de Noticias, August 14, 2001 ("legal brothels").

11. China Times poll, cited in The Straits Times, July 9, 2009. The reported results were 42% in favor of legalization and 39% opposed. Figure in table is converted to eliminate the "don't know" responses.

12. Sunday Times poll, March 26, 2000 (legalization of brothels).

13. Poll reported in The West Australian, February 15, 2006 (legalization of prostitution).

A separate issue is whether prostitution is considered acceptable behavior. A recent poll reported that 59 percent of the British public believed that "prostitution is a perfectly reasonable choice that women should be free to make."[19] (This tolerant attitude did not extend to family members, however, with 74 percent saying that it would be unacceptable for a female family member to work as a prostitute and 87 percent saying it would be unacceptable for a spouse or partner to pay a prostitute for sex.) The World Values Survey asks respondents whether they think "prostitution can always be justified, never be justified, or something in between." Table 4.2 reports "never justified" figures for a selection of nations. Here, we see that eastern Europe and nations where prostitution is criminalized (France, Italy, Sweden, United States) have larger proportions of their populations selecting the "never justified" option than do nations where prostitution is openly tolerated (Thailand) or legal (Australia, Germany, the Netherlands, New Zealand). Figures from the latter four countries range in the low to mid-20s, compared to 40 percent or more in eastern Europe, France, Italy, Sweden, and the United States. The exception here is Norway, ranking third in tolerance in 2007 but having followed Sweden in criminalizing the purchase of sex in 2009. In several other European nations, however, social tolerance and legal tolerance are in sync.

De Facto Legalization: A Gray Area

Some nations' policies are located in a twilight zone—one where prostitution (or aspects of it) is *illegal but regulated by the authorities*. In such systems, as long as participants do not disturb public order or violate other laws and as long as they abide by whatever rules are imposed on them by the authorities, they are allowed to operate freely. In Western Australia, the police "license" brothels, periodically inspect them, and maintain a roster of brothel workers and owners (listing names, addresses, phone numbers, tax ID numbers), yet brothels remain illegal, and "the licensees are conscious that they still have criminal status."[20] De facto regulation currently exists in Antwerp and Brussels, Belgium, and was the practice in Germany, the Netherlands, and New Zealand prior to formal decriminalization. A policy of de facto legalization can be applied to other vices as well. In the Netherlands, for example, possession and sale of cannabis remains illegal but tolerated. In 1985, the Public Prosecutions Department imposed five rules on cafes that sell marijuana: no advertising, no sales to minors, no other drugs on the premises, no sales exceeding a certain limit per customer (30 grams initially, reduced to 5 grams in 1995), and responsibility for maintaining order in the

TABLE 4.2

Attitudes Regarding Acceptability of Prostitution, Selected Nations

	Prostitution never justified (%)
Switzerland	18
Netherlands	20
Norway	21
Spain	23
Germany	24
Australia	25
New Zealand	25
Thailand	29
Britain	30
Canada	39
Sweden	40
France	41
United States	43
Bulgaria	46
Ukraine	57
Italy	58
Poland	58
Moldova	62
Russia	66
Romania	69

Source: The question asks "whether you think prostitution can always be justified, never be justified, or something in between," and respondents record their view on a 10-point continuum. World Values Survey, conducted in 2005-2006 in all listed nations except New Zealand (2004) and Norway, Spain, Switzerland, and Thailand (2007). <http://www.wvsevsdb.com/wvs/WVSAnalizeQuestion.jsp>

vicinity of their premises. Failure to comply can result in closure of the business. Subsequently, cannabis cafes were required to be licensed as well, which allows local authorities to restrict their number and location.[21] Drug sales remain illegal but are permitted and formally controlled by authorities who enforce these rules.

Observers from outside these nations may have difficulty understanding how a vice can be both illegal and regulated by the government—seeing the notion of "de facto legalization" as a contradiction in terms. This is not a matter of a clash between national and local laws or policies (as is true for medical marijuana in the United States), nor is it the same as de facto decriminalization, which is simply nonenforcement of the law. Instead, de facto legalization involves *official regulation of illegal practices* and thus reflects a disjunction between the criminal law and *formal* policies and practices. Peculiar as it may seem, in those countries where de facto legalization exists, it is justified as a pragmatic alternative to both criminalization and de jure legalization.

Thorny Issues

Unlike high-consensus crimes such as murder and robbery, vice is distinguished by moral ambivalence: vice is considered deviant and pleasurable simultaneously, and even some of those who partake of the vice have mixed feelings about it.[22] This moral ambivalence also means that vice law and public policy are fraught with controversy.

But not all vices are created equal. Some are more acceptable than others to a broader range of the population. In an analysis of drug policy, Simon Lenton lists the following conditions that increase the chances of decriminalization and legalization:

1. Support from a majority of the population
2. Survivability for politicians, that is, their support will not mean electoral suicide
3. Support from law enforcement officials
4. Support from consumers, who are theoretically the beneficiaries
5. An evidence basis for legal reform, for example, that the harms are greater under criminalization than under decriminalization or legalization
6. A policy sustainable under international treaties
7. A policy subject to regular review and evaluation[23]

Criminologist Jerome Skolnick identifies a somewhat different set of variables that help to explain the degree of acceptance of a particular vice and, by extension, the potential for decriminalization. If one or more of the following is present, the chances of toleration or legitimation increase:

1. It will provide revenue to the government (e.g., gambling casinos and lotteries).
2. It is engaged in by a large number of people (e.g., two-thirds of Americans participated in some form of gambling during the past year).[24]
3. The social status of participants is high; criminalization is easier to sustain if marginal individuals are involved (e.g., homeless heroin addicts).
4. Participants have otherwise traditional lifestyles, not being part of a deviant subculture.
5. Young people can be shielded from the vice.
6. Adults who wish to avoid the vice can be shielded from it.
7. The vice can be confined to the private sphere or at least relegated to places (e.g., casinos, brothels) that do not encroach on nonparticipants.
8. The vice does not create dependency or interfere with one's ability to fulfill obligations (e.g., addictive drugs).
9. The vice is controllable by the authorities and will not proliferate to an unmanageable level.[25]

Items 5, 6, 7, and 9 suggest the corollary superiority of indoor, building-based activity over street-level activity. In other words, indoor vice is preferable to public vice inasmuch as it is invisible to the public and does not threaten public order. The 1972 National Commission on Marihuana and Drug Abuse advocated decriminalization of possession of marijuana only in indoor settings (public possession of under one ounce would be subject to summary forfeiture; public possession of more than one ounce or public use of marijuana would be punishable by a fine of $100),[26] and most of the recent marijuana-decriminalization bills in the United States make a distinction between private (tolerated) and public (prohibited) use, just as they provide stiffer punishment for users who are underage than for adults.[27]

It is not necessary that a particular vice satisfy all of Lenton's and Skolnick's conditions in order for it to gain acceptance or legitimacy, but the more the merrier. Legal abortion, for instance, does not appreciably increase government revenue, but it appears to satisfy most of the other conditions.

What about prostitution? It can be organized in a way that yields revenue to the government, net of the cost of government regulation. Special business taxes or licensing fees can be imposed on establishments. Licensing is a central part of many legal systems; not only does it generate income for the state, but it provides the basis for periodically monitoring licensed premises and punishing violations. It can also give the authorities power to squeeze certain types of businesses out of existence. An alternative to privately owned but state-regulated businesses is the state-owned brothel. In medieval Europe, for example, some brothels were owned and managed by village officials. Regulations offered some protection to the women, for example, rules against beatings, being kept against their will, and falling into debt to the brothel owner.[28] Such state-owned brothels are a thing of the past but worth considering at least on an experimental basis because of the potential reduction of exploitation by third parties and the associated empowerment of workers.

Where prostitution is illegal, most of the sellers avoid paying taxes, or the proper amount of tax, on their proceeds. Decriminalization facilitates the paying of taxes by individual providers and business owners, although doing so is not guaranteed across the board. Some of those who are accustomed to paying no taxes will continue to evade them, at least in the immediate aftermath of legalization.

For the clients, prostitution is not associated with dependency or addiction, in the way gambling or drug use are for some consumers. Most clients are gainfully employed and have social ties to conventional institutions and thus meet the test of having traditional lifestyles apart from their paid sexual transactions. The same is true for a segment of the prostitute population, though those who work in down-market arenas (streets, low-tier brothels) are often socially isolated and detached from conventional lifestyles. Legalization may have at least some normalizing effect on their everyday lives, but the potential here is unknown.

Prohibition on youth involvement is a staple of legal vice regimes, including sex work. In addition, some states attempt to shield young people from the trade by confining it to indoor settings where underage entry is prohibited or by banning certain types of advertising. Such restrictions also safeguard adults from exposure, keeping it out of public view. German cities that have window prostitution take a rather unusual approach to shielding the public, by barricading the street that contains window units and posting signs stating, "Youth under 18 and Women Prohibited."

Controllability is trickier. Prostitution is notoriously difficult for the authorities to manage. First, legalization might lead to an overall increase in the number of participants. The number of prostitutes is partly affected by demand, though it is possible that greater supply—especially under conditions of legality—might increase demand. Supply is capped by the social stigma that taints sex work: most people will continue to shun this kind of work because they disapprove of it. With regard to the demand side, it is quite likely that the number of customers will increase once criminal penalties are abolished, although there is a threshold here as well, related to the continuing stigma of buying sex. It is also conceivable that some of those who currently buy sex where it is illegal will stop doing so when it is decriminalized if this is perceived as diminishing the desired thrill or risk involved—the "forbidden fruit" effect—but I doubt that this will reduce demand appreciably. In New Zealand, nationwide legalization in 2003 has not increased the number of prostitutes in the country.[29] Documented increases in the number of sex workers and customers in other legal systems may or may not be traceable to legalization per se, since it is impossible to know if the amount of prostitution would have increased anyway, *without* legalization. In order to restrict industry expansion, some regimes impose caps on the number of sex businesses or on the number of workers, but this has the unintended effect of forcing excluded participants to operate illegally.

Second, will prostitutes comply with the regulations? This is an extremely important question. Insofar as legalization includes stipulations as to who can and cannot engage in sex work, those ineligible (e.g., persons underage, HIV-positive, or illegal immigrants) would be forced to operate illicitly in the shadows of the regulated system. In addition, every conceivable form of legalization would be rejected by at least some eligible prostitutes, who would see no benefits in abiding by the new restrictions (e.g., mandatory registration or health examinations) and would resent the infringement on their freedom. While some streetwalkers, for example, would accept a policy zoning street transactions into a locale away from residential areas provided that it is safe and unintimidating for prostitutes and customers alike (as evidenced in some European tolerance zones, mentioned in chapter 3), others would reject this arrangement for personal reasons. Street prostitution tolerance zones are shunned if they lack places of refuge and sustenance, such as restaurants, coffee shops, grocery stores, bars, parks, and cheap hotels—amenities desired by most streetwalkers.[30] Moreover, while zoning seeks to concentrate street prostitution in a particular area, it does not necessarily remedy other problems associated with street work, such as violence and drug abuse.

One of the few academic attempts to outline a set of "best practices" is criminologist Roger Matthews's proposal for a new British approach to prostitution. Matthews advocates the following:

- Reducing and then eliminating street prostitution
- Reducing youth involvement
- Decriminalizing soliciting
- Reducing demand
- Cracking down on pimps and other exploiters

- Intensifying sanctions against those who engage in violence or coercion against prostitutes
- Enhancing opportunities to exit prostitution
- Increasing the "monitoring and surveillance" of indoor prostitution[31]

Most of these goals are unobjectionable and consistent with what other analysts would endorse. But Matthews offers few concrete steps for achieving some of his goals, and the rationale for some of them is opaque. He does not explain why reducing demand—that is, customers—is a worthy goal but instead simply assumes that we should do so. Nor does he provide any concrete indication of what the monitoring and surveillance of indoor prostitution should consist of. His proposal is so vague as to be meaningless to authorities tasked with such oversight.

If Matthews's policy package is deficient in key details and justifications, some of his proposals are nevertheless meritorious and provide a useful starting point for a more comprehensive and practical program, which I offer in the book's conclusion. When considering potential benefits of legalization, much depends on exactly what is regulated. Having said that, we can sketch some expected or desirable general benefits:

- Participants are no longer illegal actors simply because they engage in paid sex transactions, thus reducing the costs to the criminal justice system.
- Providers face less risk of being exploited by unscrupulous third parties, and criminal sanctions can be redirected to those who abuse individual workers.
- Providers, who become more accessible, can be encouraged to follow safe-sex practices and have regular medical exams.
- Underage individuals can be more easily prevented from selling sex, at least in the regulated sector.
- Safety may increase, for all participants.
- Costs to consumers are likely to decline with legalization, though this may not be viewed as a benefit to providers, whose cost per unit transaction may decline.
- Legalization reduces doubts regarding the precise services or products consumers are paying for. This can reduce the risk of misunderstandings and "rip-offs." Providers can advertise openly without fear of arrest, do not need to use euphemisms to conceal specific services and their prices, and no longer need to operate behind fronts such as salons, karaoke bars, spas, and the like. (Advertisements and signage should be sensitive to what the surrounding community will tolerate, however.)

- If a legal establishment is required to display a sticker indicating that it is a legal business, clients will know that they are buying sex lawfully. This is trickier with independent providers, who may not want to carry a card identifying them as a sex worker. But in a system in which independent sex work is allowed, the client can have a reasonable expectation that the provider is legal, unless it appears that the provider is underage or under duress. In those systems in which providers must be registered, they can be be required to show the registration card to the client.
- Nearby merchants may experience beneficial side effects from legal sex establishments—for example, increased numbers of patrons of bars, restaurants, and other businesses in the vicinity.[32]

One implication of the preceding discussion is that law reform should take into account the interests and preferences of multiple stakeholders. Some writers who discuss policy alternatives focus exclusively on the needs and desires of sex workers. Sex workers are absolutely central to the success or failure of any policy innovation, but it is also important that reforms take into account other parties as well, including local residents, the authorities, clients, and managers and owners of sex establishments.

How States Have Addressed These Issues

This section shows how some legal regimes have addressed the generic challenges described in the preceding section and serves as a prelude to our in-depth examination of three European settings. How do these models differ? And which policies seem best?

An insightful study covering a lengthy period of legal prostitution in Argentina (1875–1934) describes a litany of municipal regulations. In Buenos Aires, prostitutes were required to be registered by city authorities, to carry identity cards, to have medical examinations twice a week, and to refrain from appearing at windows and doors. The minimum age for selling sex was 22. Brothels were prohibited from displaying signage and could not be located near churches, schools, and public buildings. Brothel owners had to pay a high license fee, forcing those who could not afford the fee to operate clandestinely in bars, cabarets, casinos, or underground brothels. The number of prostitutes allowed in a brothel changed over time (only two during 1904–1908), and prostitutes working alone from home could not live in a building where anyone else sold sex. A 1908 ordinance mandated incarceration of diseased prostitutes in hospitals until they were cured.[33] Some of these rules, as we shall see, are common in legal prostitution systems today, indicating that the contours of social control have changed little over time.

Legalization of vice can have unintended consequences. During the first third of the 20th century in Argentina, successive municipal ordinances seemed incapable of producing the desired results:

> No matter how well intended the ordinance, each new measure was as counterproductive as the one it replaced. . . . Plans that might have pleased prostitutes offended pimps. When bawdy houses opened in new neighborhoods, residents complained. If the downtown was to be cleared of bordellos, outlying neighborhoods complained. . . . Yearly changes in license fees or periodic reforms of bordello ordinances created financial and political insecurity for all but the largest and wealthiest brothels. Houses opened and closed, women entered and left with incredible rapidity. . . . Regardless of what tactics police and municipal authorities used to monitor prostitutes, most failed.[34]

Such outcomes do not mean that prostitution is inherently policy resistant, but it is clear that legalization of any vice generates a host of new challenges for state officials, whose "solutions" may, as in Argentina, follow a checkered path over time. Spain, for example, shifted from prohibition to decriminalization in 1995, when it began to allow third-party involvement, but a new law in 2003 reversed the situation, recriminalizing third-party involvement. The following year, the Public Prosecutor's Office issued a circular that interpreted the law as applying only when coercion is involved or when third parties have received direct payment from prostitutes (simply renting a room used for sexual exchanges was permitted).[35] The Argentinian and Spanish examples show how a nation can radically alter its policies over a short span of time, a mere decade in the Spanish case.

Nevada

One American state, Nevada, legalized prostitution in 1971 with a law allowing rural counties to license and regulate brothels; this served to legitimate the existing brothels that were operating illegally prior to the law reform. Street or escort prostitution remains prohibited in these rural areas, and all prostitution is outlawed in the counties in which Las Vegas and Reno are located. The number of legal brothels has remained remarkably stable over time: 33 in 1973, 36 in 1997, and 28 in 2009, scattered across ten counties. This is because county officials make it difficult to obtain a new license, in order to limit the number of brothels in their jurisdiction. None of the brothels offers male prostitutes, but it is not unusual for female clients to visit as part of a husband-wife couple. Still, the vast majority of the customers are men.

Brothel owners are thoroughly screened by county or town officials; they cannot have a previous felony conviction. Workers must be at least 21 years old. State law makes condom use mandatory and requires workers to undergo weekly testing for STDs and HIV.[36] None has tested HIV-positive since testing was mandated in 1985, and unlike some other places where workers have shunned mandatory testing, it is "widely accepted among members of Nevada's brothel culture."[37]

Local governments impose additional regulations.[38] These rules govern the location of brothels, licensing procedures, and specific restrictions on workers' behavior. One universal rule is that workers must live at the brothel for the duration of their contract, which is usually three weeks at a time. If she has a husband or children, they are not allowed to reside in the same town in which she is working. The traditional rule that prevented workers from going into town when not on duty has been relaxed in recent years. Each brothel enforces its own set of rules as well. In most cases, women split half their earnings with the house, are expected to tip staff, and pay for their own health care. Overall, the package of state, county, and brothel regulations make for a tight apparatus of control over the workers. These prostitutes "are restricted in their movement due solely to the nature of their work [and] are clearly being treated differently than other service workers."[39]

Nevada's legal brothels employ a number of safety precautions (alarm buttons, listening devices, management surveillance) designed to preempt or react to an altercation. These safeguards pay off. An in-depth study by sociologists Barbara Brents and Kathryn Hausbeck concluded, "Safety was one of the most important advantages that women stressed in their choice to work in the brothels. They felt, and our research backs this up, that Nevada's legal brothels offer the safest environment available for women to sell consensual sex."[40] None of the women interviewed had ever felt the need to press an alarm button; and the police are rarely called to deal with problem customers.[41] The researchers found that Nevada's legal brothels clashed with the image presented in the oppression paradigm: these brothels were free of drug use, violence, minors, disease, and trafficking.[42] Another analyst points out that the "insulated nature of the brothels offers prostitutes near foolproof protection from theft, fraud, or crime."[43] In addition to this positive assessment of the safety record, Nevada's system advances the larger "objectives of health, safety, welfare, and morals."[44] The workers themselves are generally satisfied with the work. Alexa Albert, who conducted observations and interviews in the brothels, describes the workers as "self-aware professionals there of their own free will. . . . The women had found a genuine sense of purpose and meaning in their work."[45] Similarly, none of the workers interviewed by Brents and Hausbeck had been coerced into brothel work or were there against their will:

> All the women we interviewed stressed that they made their own choices to enter brothel work. . . . In all brothels we found that the women were strong, open, and often had close bonds with others in the house. They are in the business to make money, and some do quite well. . . . But many workers say they do it not just for the money but also because they like the work and the people they work with.[46]

These highly regulated brothels are not for everyone; many sex workers would find them too confining, and some quit after just a few days in a house. In the abstract, the restrictions may appear onerous, but the studies just cited indicate that they are not experienced negatively by those workers who are willing to abide by the norms.[47]

Counties hosting legal brothels have virtually no illegal prostitution.[48] At the same time, county officials purposely limit the number of brothels in order to restrict the size of the sex sector, with the tacit consent of existing brothel owners, who wish to limit competition.[49] This may not be wise, as one analyst argues: "A state statute should be instituted which bases the number of brothel licenses available on something less nepotistic and more objective, such as county population."[50] Nevada's decentralized approach has the advantage of giving local officials tremendous regulatory flexibility, but it also "allows unstructured and unspoken rules and even discriminatory screening of owners whose rights may be violated."[51]

Has stigma declined during the state's four decades of legal prostitution? Brothel owners aspire to being seen as respectable members of the community—in some towns sponsoring scholarships for high school students, donating to the local Rotary Club, and participating in parades and holiday festivities.[52] Polls show that a majority of Nevadans support the status quo, but it is a thin majority of 52 percent (support is higher in the counties where legal brothels exist), and only about a third favor introducing brothels to Las Vegas itself (table 3.1). Some rural counties have tried to recriminalize prostitution. In Lincoln County, prostitution was outlawed in 1978 as a result of a referendum passed by two-thirds of the county's voters. In 1999, Ely's city council voted to revoke the licenses of its three brothels and ban prostitution, but the decision was vetoed by the mayor.[53] Most other efforts to rescind legal prostitution have been unsuccessful, further demonstrating tolerance for the status quo.[54] One reason for this tacit support is the economic benefit to local governments, in the form of revenue from fees and taxes.[55] At the same time, tolerance for the brothels does not necessarily mean that the providers have been destigmatized: "The small towns tend to support the brothels, but still sometimes stigmatize the women."[56] As a rule, local women do not work in their hometown's brothels.

Is Nevada's legal prostitution a model that could be replicated elsewhere? It certainly has longevity on its side, existing for four decades now, and it demonstrates that legal prostitution *can* exist in modern America and is not a wholly foreign concept. At least some of the regulations would be endorsed by many people, though other rules would be deemed excessive. The tremendous decentralization of authority over the brothels—largely the province of counties and towns—creates a checkered arrangement that some other nations would find problematic. At the same time, we must remember that these brothels are isolated and remote from major population centers; this explains why they have remained fairly uncontroversial but also makes the Nevada model unsuited to nations that wish to legalize prostitution in urban areas.

Two Mexican Cases

Readers may not be aware that prostitution is legal and regulated in 13 of Mexico's 31 states. A study by anthropologist Patty Kelly sheds light on one such system: the Galactic Zone outside Tuxtla in the state of Chiapas.[57] Given the small scale of the Zone and Tuxtla's population of half a million, there remains plenty of illegal prostitution in the area. Moreover, some of the Galactic Zone's regulations are obtrusive, such as the mandatory health card that includes the worker's name, photo, and health status and must be renewed every three months (workers are routinely tested for syphilis and HIV).

Yet the Zone's form of legal prostitution also has some benefits. First, the Zone appears to have broad popular support. In Tuxtla, "prostitution is generally accepted (and sometimes valued) as long as it is confined and invisible," which is precisely what the Galactic Zone accomplishes.[58] Second, Zone workers have a "great deal of freedom and exercise control over their work."[59] They alone decide when to work and for how long, who they will serve, and their rates; they come and go as they please; and many take extended leaves to visit family in other parts of Mexico. Almost all of the 140 women working in the Zone are independent, free of pimps. Third, while prostitution is hardly lucrative for Zone workers, on a good day the women can earn as much as ten times the daily minimum wage in Chiapas. It is not survival sex: the workers are able to buy consumer goods that they otherwise could not afford, such as nice clothing, cell phones, jewelry, and items for their children. Fourth, working in this arena helps to bolster the women's sense of control over their lives and their self-esteem. Many began working in the Zone to support their children after escaping an unhappy, abusive, or violent relationship with a husband. The Zone allowed them to break free of dependency on their husbands and, more generally, to "find in prostitution a life better than the one they might have had."[60] There are unpleasant aspects of this highly controlled type of prostitution, but the net effect of working in the Galactic Zone is positive for the women: control over working conditions, lack of coercion, economic advancement, and enhanced self-esteem.

One of the few comparative analyses of legal and illegal prostitution is anthropologist Yasmina Katsulis's study of Tijuana, Mexico. Katsulis interviewed and observed workers in both spheres: those registered with the authorities, subjected to compulsory health exams, and holding a work card and those who had not registered. (Bars employing sex workers must be licensed and are subject to fines if their workers are not registered, but this does not apply to massage parlors, private brothels, dance halls, or escort services.) Individuals and sexually oriented establishments in Tijuana are visited periodically by government inspectors. About a thousand prostitutes are working legally at any given time, along with a larger number of illegals.

Although the registration and mandatory health checks may seem burdensome, Katsulis documents positive outcomes for those who work legally, and these benefits are quite significant. A major finding is that legal status, in itself, has diffuse effects on the workers: providing social capital, empowerment, and a sense of professionalism. The legal workers have

> better working conditions and job satisfaction, less fear about the nature of their work, and a higher degree of sophistication and confidence. . . . Registration and monthly checkups appear to encourage behaviors that are protective of health as well as provide a barrier against police harass-

ment. Registration increases the sense of legitimacy and community and is correlated with much lower levels of depression and mental stress.[61]

Moreover, the "social stigma attached to these [legal] work settings is also lessened."[62] And legal work is safer than illegal work, partly because of an improved relationship with the police, who are now more prepared to intervene in disputes between customers and workers: "for legal workers, the policing of customers offers protection against customer violence."[63]

Illegal workers, by contrast, experience police harassment, violence, fines, and incarceration; they have less stable social support networks; and they are about twice as likely as the legal workers to have been assaulted, robbed, or kidnapped. Illegal prostitution thus remains problematic in Tijuana, and Katsulis's study serves as a reminder that legalization may bypass many sex workers. The one unanswered question is *why* many Tijuana workers opt out of the legal system, but we know from research elsewhere that the reasons include fear of being formally labeled a prostitute and the increased risk of being discovered by friends and family members.

Three Australian States

In a 2005 survey, only 25 percent of Australians took the view that prostitution can "never be justified," fewer than in 1995 (29 percent) and 1981 (35 percent).[64] Prostitution is legal and regulated in several states, but each state does it differently.

Victoria was the first to decriminalize indoor prostitution, in 1986. The regulations on brothels include licenses and planning permits. Local councils have the right to refuse permits; although such decisions can be appealed, the time and cost involved discourages owners from going through the process and leads some of them to operate illegally. After the law's passage, the number of large brothels shrank from around 160 to 60 in a short span of time, because many owners were simply unable to comply with the costly new regulations. The remaining brothels were able to exercise more control over workers, who now had fewer options for employment elsewhere. Owners became more selective in hiring decisions, took a larger share of the proceeds, and imposed stricter working conditions (e.g., required attire, lineups instead of rotation, fines for being late or absent, summary firings).[65] In theory, the 1986 law held owners accountable for violations, but workers were averse to reporting them, as Alison Arnot's interviews revealed: "Generally, women were reluctant to report illegal or unethical practices of business owners and operators unless it involved the hiring and manipulation of women too young to work in the sex industry or physical attacks."[66] Reluctance to report was due to the women's unwillingness to publicly identify as sex workers. Most said that they would leave and work elsewhere if employer misconduct was a problem for them.

The situation in Victoria improved after a new law came into effect in 1995. The Prostitution Control Act contained measures designed to improve working conditions—including safe-sex rules, workers' rights to negotiate or refuse sexual services, alarm systems in brothel rooms, and so on.[67] Street prostitution remained illegal under the new law, and the penalties for street soliciting increased for both buyers and sellers. But the 1995 law did not rectify other problems. Local councils continue to issue few planning permits for new brothels; the application process for permits remains lengthy and expensive; and Victoria still has a sizeable illegal market parallel to the legal sector.[68] There are 95 licensed brothels in the state today, out of a population of 5.5 million inhabitants.[69]

Two types of sex work were decriminalized in Queensland in the 1990s: independent operators (in 1992) and brothels (in 1999). Street prostitution remains illegal, so the category of legal sole operator applies only to those who work indoors (it is estimated that only 2 percent of prostitution in Queensland is street based).[70] As of January 2009, there were 23 licensed brothels in the state (whose population is 4.5 million), and an unknown number of independents sell sex legally. There is a much larger illegal market involving persons who work (1) in unlicensed brothels, (2) cooperatively (two or more providers), or (3) for escort agencies, brokers, and other third parties.[71] The latter operate illegally because third-party involvement outside a licensed brothel is outlawed (and legal brothels are not permitted to provide out-call services). An assessment by a government agency concluded that "the inability of legal brothels to provide an escort or out-call service is the most crucial impediment to the success of the Act."[72] It is estimated that three-quarters of prostitution in Queensland involves in-call or out-call services, including both the legal sole operators and those illegally employed by third parties.[73] A contrasting case is Australia's Northern Territory, where *only* escorting is legal under a 2004 law that decriminalized both escort agencies and independent escorts. Agencies employing more than one provider must be licensed, but independent escorts are not licensed.[74]

Sole operators in Queensland are not required to hold a license and can provide services either in their own residence or elsewhere. However, their work premises must not cause a public nuisance, which the law defines as an "unreasonable annoyance" to another person.[75] It is also illegal for more than one provider to work at the same premises, even at different times of the day—which heightens their risk of victimization. Two or more workers at a single location constitute a "brothel" and would thus require licensing and the high fees associated with it, just like any other legal brothel (this differs from Victoria, where two workers may work together without being designated a brothel). Sole providers are prohibited from having any involvement with third parties (including procurers, financers) and may not employ anyone (a receptionist, broker, or driver), as this would render them no longer fully "independent." This provision of the law is enforced. In the 2007–2008 fiscal year, for example, 92 persons were charged with illegal third-party involvement in prostitution.[76]

The main reason for the sizeable illegal market is the exorbitant cost of operating a legal brothel. The start-up costs alone are staggering: a $5,500 application fee, a $7,165 license fee, and $2,867 for each room in the brothel; this puts the total initial fees for a standard five-room brothel at $27,000.[77] (Brothels are limited by law to a maximum of five sexual-service rooms, and no more than eight sex workers are allowed on the premises at any one time.) On top of the start-up costs, there is an annual license fee of $20,555 for a five-room brothel, and every three years the license must be renewed at an additional cost of $12,665 plus $2,867 for each room.[78] The flip side of these costs is that illegal brothel operators typically receive a $2,000 fine if they are caught, which means that they would have to be caught several times a year to bear the same costs as a legal operator.[79] The high licensing fees stem from the government's interest in limiting the number of brothels. In addition to reviewing applications for licenses as well as complaints against existing brothels, the Prostitution Licensing Authority is also required to advise the government on ways of helping "prostitutes to leave prostitution," arguably an inappropriate function for a licensing board.[80] (The board has no members from the sex industry or sex workers' organizations.) The Queensland government seems especially interested in keeping a lid on the legal sex industry, both by facilitating the exit of workers and by imposing very high fees on business owners.

If some of the regulations are questionable, Queensland's legal brothels themselves have been rated favorably. They are smoke- and alcohol-free, have a compulsory condom policy, and are required to train their workers in negotiating safe sex and in personal protection. A major government evaluation concluded, "There is no doubt that licensed brothels provide the safest working environment for sex workers in Queensland. . . . Legal brothels now operating in Queensland provide a sustainable model for a healthy, crime-free, and safe legal licensed brothel industry" and are a "state of the art model for the sex industry in Australia."[81] The report found that both legal brothels and sole operators had little adverse impact on the local community, whereas the (illegal) street workers "arouse significant community disquiet."[82] Other assessments are similarly positive regarding health, safety, crime, and community impact: "There is ample evidence to show . . . that the operation of licensed brothels does not have any negative impact on local areas and surrounding neighborhoods."[83] Moreover, according to the government, organized crime and corruption "are not of significant concern for the legal prostitution industry in Queensland"[84] and are essentially confined to the illegal brothels. Independent analysts agree: "Ten years of prostitution regulation appear to have been highly effective in reducing the nexus between Queensland's sex industry, [police] corruption, and organized crime."[85]

Research on legal providers in Queensland indicates that many of them are satisfied with their work. In one study, 70 percent of the 103 independent call girls and 102 licensed brothel workers interviewed said they would "definitely choose" this work if they had it to do over again, and half of each group felt that their work was a "major source of satisfaction" in their lives.[86] Almost all (97 percent) of the brothel workers said that an advantage of working in a legal brothel was the safety it provided. Only 3 percent of brothel workers, compared to 15 percent of the independents and 52 percent of a sample of illegal street prostitutes, reported that they had been "raped or bashed" by a client in the preceding 12 months, and the illegal street prostitutes were significantly more likely than the two groups of legal workers to have mental-health problems.[87] When a sample of prostitutes (drawn from all sectors in Queensland) was asked in another survey which venue was the "safest place to work," the top choice (of 77 percent) was a legal brothel, followed by private work in cooperation with others (31 percent), which is currently illegal. None said that the streets or bar work were the safest, and only 9 percent said that being a sole operator was the safest.[88] The high rating of legal brothels is a function of their extensive security measures and presence of co-workers.

Yet Queensland's system remains quite deficient: the cost of running a legal establishment is excessive and provides a strong incentive to operate illegally. Licensed brothels are at a substantial competitive disadvantage vis-à-vis their illegal counterparts, and many of the legal businesses go bankrupt in a fairly short period of time, causing instability in the legal sector.[89] The high licensing fees also preclude workers from creating their own small brothels. If the fees were dramatically reduced, this would probably induce some currently illegal operators to transition into the legal sector. In addition, it is not clear why the government has outlawed escort agencies or why it prohibits private work by two or more independent operators. The higher safety rating given to private work with colleagues over being a sole operator, noted earlier, suggests that the former should be decriminalized. Decriminalizing these providers would dramatically reduce the size of the illegal market, with added potential benefits for the health and safety of the newly legal providers. If the state's overriding goal is to limit the size of the legal sector, it has excelled magnificently, but at the expense of catalyzing the growth of a much larger, more lucrative, and potentially more exploitative and dangerous illegal sector.

Another Australian state, New South Wales (whose capital is Sydney), decriminalized street soliciting in 1979 and in the 1990s decriminalized brothels (large and small), escort agencies, and sole operators. This gives prostitutes a wider range of options than in Queensland. New South Wales does not license sex businesses, which frees owners of the costs associated with licensing and thus the temptation to operate underground that we see in Queensland. Instead of a license, local council approval is required for a brothel to operate in a particular location, and some councils have used this power to restrict brothels to industrial areas. The constellation of lawful venues makes it difficult to generalize about prostitution in New South Wales's legalized system. An example from the top echelon is described in a recent television documentary segment on a brothel in Sydney. The narrator stated that "the working conditions at Stiletto exceed those in many regular workplaces": the place is equipped with showers, a fancy dressing room, a pool table, and a gym that workers may use, and the top earners make $170,000 a year.[90] At the other end of the spectrum, street prostitution remains a problem in New South Wales. Because it is prohibited near residences, churches, and hospitals in central Sydney, there is almost nowhere that street soliciting is possible. Street work is allowed in the outer suburbs and at some highway rest stops, but the police often use their "move on" powers to disperse street workers from these locations and will arrest those who return after being told to leave.[91] In other words, street prostitution continues to be struggled over even where it has been decriminalized. Still, the overall situation in New South Wales can be judged superior to that in Queensland.[92]

New Zealand

Prior to decriminalization in New Zealand in 2003, operating a brothel was illegal but officially allowed. The law prohibited running a brothel and living off the earnings of prostitution—thus criminalizing brothel owners and managers—but the Massage Parlors Act (1978) effectively allowed indoor commercial sex. Parlor workers were required to register with the authorities, and the police conducted investigations of a parlor if they suspected that other crimes were being committed there, such as drug use, youth involvement, or organized crime.[93] The registration requirement pushed some workers into street or escort work, because they were less accessible to officials than in the massage parlors.

On the eve of decriminalization in 2003, the public was evenly divided, with 43 percent in favor and 42 percent opposed to decriminalizing prostitution and the remainder undecided.[94] Parliament was evenly divided as well, passing the bill by a slim one-vote margin. (A subsequent attempt to rescind the law failed, however.) Advocates of sex workers participated in a lengthy period of consultation and debate prior to the drafting of the bill. The premier organization, the New Zealand Prostitutes' Collective, was an active partner throughout the process, which helps to explain why some of the stated goals of the 2003 law focus so heavily on legitimizing sex work and advancing workers' rights. Arguments in favor of legal reform included harm reduction, the empowerment of workers, and enhanced control over the sex trade. The objectives of the new legislation were to reduce victimization and exploitation, institutionalize a set of labor rights for workers, eliminate the involvement of minors, reduce crimes associated with prostitution, decrease the number of illegal immigrants working in the sex trade, and curb sex trafficking.

Some analysts mistakenly categorize the current New Zealand system as decriminalization rather than legalization. Yet the new law went further than removing criminal penalties and coupled this with a number of new regulations that qualify the system as one of legalization. The 2003 act decriminalized voluntary adult prostitution and permits soliciting, brothels, escort agencies, and third-party involvement. Street prostitution is allowed, subject to local laws pertaining to public nuisances. The new regime provides for periodic inspections of prostitution premises by the police, social services, and the health department. Western Australia replicated many of these norms when its parliament voted to legalize brothel and escort prostitution in April 2008.[95]

Local regulations vary, with some councils passing bylaws and others doing nothing.[96] Advertising is governed by city councils, which may allow or ban signage in their jurisdiction or impose restrictions on the content, according to local standards of "offensiveness" to the public. Some local authorities have passed bylaws that ban signs altogether, while others restrict the content allowed on signs. Local governments are responsible for zoning regulations but may not prohibit prostitution outright.

Most controversial have been councils' rulings on the location of brothels. First, the legal definition of a brothel includes both large, formal brothels and erotic massage parlors and small, owner-operated services. The latter have argued that they should not be regulated in the same way as larger establishments. Second, some jurisdictions have tried to relegate both types of brothels to a very small part of the district. The city of Christchurch did so, confining brothels to 1 percent of the city (in the central business district) and thereby effectively excluding the small owner-operated brothels that already existed in residential areas. A court challenge in 2005 was resolved in favor of the brothel owners. The ruling stated that the city's zoning approach was much too restrictive geographically and amounted to a de facto prohibition on small owner-operated brothels. A similar court case in Auckland in 2006 was resolved in favor of the brothel owners as well, but a 2007 challenge to the city of Hamilton's zoning restriction was decided in favor of the city because the three zones it had established were not so restrictive as to be unlawful.[97]

Street prostitution exists only in Auckland, Christchurch, and Wellington. Wellington has few street workers (less than 50), and Christchurch has more (around 120, or a quarter of the city's prostitution), concentrated in a few streets. Only rarely have there been complaints from local residents. In the largest city, Auckland, street prostitution has been a problem only in Manukau, where shop owners complain about used condoms and syringes and claim that the number of street-based workers has grown since decriminalization in 2003.[98] In 2005, the Manukau City Council asked its local member of Parliament to present a bill prohibiting street prostitution in Manukau in response to the large number of street prostitutes in the area. The bill was defeated (73 to 46).[99] Had it passed, it would have signaled a major amendment to the 2003 law (by banning street prostitution), and its failure suggests that parliamentary support for the law has strengthened since 2003, when the original law passed with a thin one-vote margin. There have been no recent public opinion polls, so the level of current public support for the law is unknown. Yet prostitution was not an issue during the 2008 general election, and there was "a sense across the political divide that public and political support had cemented in favor of the law reform, with the only active debate being around street prostitution,"[100] which continues to be contentious in Manukau. As is the case in other settings, street prostitution in New Zealand is associated with greater harms (drug use, risky sex practices, violence) than indoor prostitution is, although violence appears to have decreased since decriminalization.[101]

Much like other businesses, prostitution is now governed by employment and health and safety standards. Workers have the right to refuse requests for sexual services, workers and customers are obliged to practice safe sex, and they (and employers) can be charged with an offense if they engage in unsafe sex, which is enforced by the Health Department. Employment disputes can be referred to the Labor Inspectorate. Since 2003, police practice has become increasingly protective of workers and managers. The previous system whereby sex workers were registered (under the 1978 Massage Parlors Act) has been replaced with certification of brothels that employ three or more workers, shifting the licensing from workers to business owners. The certification requirement has not led to a two-tiered system of legal and illegal sex venues,[102] largely because it is not as onerous or costly as licensing is in some other places. In New Zealand, interviews with brothel owners found that "certificates were not seen to be difficult to obtain, and neither were they considered expensive (at $200). In addition, compliance appeared to informants to be good."[103] Moreover, inspections of sex premises by the authorities have been welcomed, not resisted: "Brothel owners were often keen to show [investigators] around their premises and discuss management issues they were facing. It seemed that they were keen to be seen to be acting professionally, as any other business in the community."[104]

The act established a Prostitution Law Review Committee (PLRC) composed of current and former government officials, sex worker representatives, and members of various nongovernmental organizations. The PLRC conducts research and sponsors external reviews of the implementation and impact of the law.[105] A major evaluation in 2008 indicated that the number of prostitutes has remained about the same as prior to legalization and that there has been no increase in the number of underage workers. In addition, more than 90 percent of prostitutes (survey N = 772) were aware that they had legal and employment rights under the new law; two-thirds felt that the law gave them more leverage to refuse a client or his requests; and a majority (57 percent) felt that police attitudes had changed for the better since passage of the law.[106] Employment conditions remained inadequate, and workers remained somewhat distrustful of the authorities. Moreover, decriminalization seems to have done little to counter the "deeply ingrained moral and social stigma attached to working in the sex industry,"[107] through a nationwide poll in 2004 showed that only 25 percent of New Zealanders took the view that prostitution can "never be justified," somewhat fewer than the number who held this view prior to legalization (29 percent in 1998).[108] Overall, the PLRC concluded that legalization had achieved many of its objectives and that the majority of individuals involved in the sex industry were better off now than under the prior system.

Conclusion

The cases discussed in this chapter, in addition to what we know from other settings, point to some important challenges facing legal prostitution regimes and the various stakeholders involved. The following problems seem to be fairly common:

- Stigma and claims that prostitution is "immoral" do not magically disappear postlegalization. This affects the degree to which workers feel empowered to assert their rights to managers, clients, and government officials. Because they seek to maintain a low profile, workers may also be reluctant to report abuses to the police or other authorities.
- Public support for decriminalization or legalization is fickle. People may consider some sort of toleration preferable to criminalization *in the abstract* but can become disenchanted with actually existing legal systems (due, in part, to the dynamic sketched in the next bulleted item).
- In the aftermath of legal reform, it is common for there to be at least some opposition to the new order, from forces pressing for additional restrictions or seeking to recriminalize prostitution outright. Such resistance comes from politicians, pundits, religious leaders, antiprostitution groups, and others who oppose prostitution in principle or who react to sensationalized media coverage of a particular event or exposés of larger problems.
- Legalization creates parallel universes of legal and illegal sex work,[109] as there will always be some categories of workers who are not eligible under the legal system (minors, illegal immigrants, and perhaps those infected with STDs). And some of those workers and business owners who *are* eligible may prefer to operate in the shadows of the legal sector, due to concerns over taxation, licensing and registration, mandatory health requirements, and other "burdens." In other words, legalization cannot fully resolve the problem of illegal

prostitution, although it is intended to reduce it. New Zealand may be an exception: the inclusiveness of its legal order reduces the incentive to operate illegally.

- The owners of legal sex businesses often have difficulty adjusting to new legal strictures, particularly in the immediate aftermath of legalization. This is a natural consequence of the transition from illicit vice to lawful business. Business owners enjoyed great freedom when they operated outside the legal system and may put up stiff resistance to the imposition of some or many of the new requirements.

- Government officials face unique challenges in managing what was previously an illegal vice. A good example is the governance of medical marijuana in the 15 American states that now permit use of this drug for eligible persons, where state authorities have faced myriad, unanticipated problems. Similarly, a newly legal sex industry is likely to present challenges to officials tasked with implementing regulations, gathering needed information, and enforcing the rules—especially during the formative years immediately following legalization. Some officials have great difficulty adjusting to the new order, continuing to view sex workers and business owners as deviant actors and treating them disrespectfully and harshly, while other officials more readily take on a professional orientation, treating actors similarly to those involved in any other lawful business.

The degree to which each of these factors is a problem varies from place to place—serious and protracted in some, much less so in others. The remainder of the book examines these and other challenges in three European cases.

PART III

Case Studies

Three Red-Light Cities

5

Antwerp and Frankfurt

The previous chapter outlined a number of challenges facing governments that legalize vice and particularly prostitution. This chapter and the next pursue this question in much more depth through an examination of three European cities—Antwerp, Frankfurt, and Amsterdam. To provide contextual background, I examine, first, the main features of the Belgian, German, and Dutch systems. We will see that national context is important but not determinative of local-level commercial sex policies and arrangements. I then examine, in detail, how legal prostitution manifests itself on the ground in each city, drawing on my ethnographic data and other sources.

The material presented in chapters 5 and 6 draws on my field observations and interviews. I conducted countless hours of observations in the three cities: mapping the configuration of businesses in each red-light district, recording the behavior of people on the street, and sketching observed interactions between local sex workers and visitors. I conducted interviews with key players, including government officials, brothel and window owners, and sex worker advocates.[1] These data were supplemented with conversations with sex workers—most brief, others longer. The data are more extensive for Amsterdam and Frankfurt than for Antwerp, largely because Antwerp's red-light district is small, fairly isolated, and single purpose, whereas the other two are major sex-for-sale emporiums, making them more challenging study sites requiring a considerable time investment. I have studied Amsterdam at intervals stretching over a fairly long period of time (beginning in 1997), whereas Antwerp and Frankfurt were visited less frequently and more recently. My ethnographic data on these cases are by no means exhaustive and are presented in conjunction with information from other sources, including public opinion polls, newspaper reports, scholarly articles, government documents, secondary surveys, and clients' online discussion boards. I conducted a comprehensive review of hundreds of online client postings for the three cities on the World Sex Guide (operating in the mid-1990s), The Erotic Review, Ignatzmice, and Punternet.

The cases were selected because of both their similarities and important differences. They are major northern European cities, each with at least one geographically distinct red-light district (RLD) hosting visible commercial sex businesses. Each RLD has existed for decades. The three cities were *not* selected because they are "representative" of the nation as a whole; in fact, no city could be considered representative, as the sexual landscape of each differs in at least some respects from that of other cities in each nation. The national contexts themselves differ somewhat in their legal regimes—prostitution being de facto legal in parts of Belgium and de jure legal in Germany and the Netherlands. And each city's RLD differs from the others in appearance, constellation of businesses (erotic and other), the location and visibility of sex workers, and the kinds of people one normally finds on the street. The three cases also differ in the types of prostitution located elsewhere in the city, outside the red-light district. In short, although prostitution is permitted and regulated in each setting, the cities differ significantly in the social ecology of sex work. A *red-light district* is defined here as an area where sexually oriented businesses are clustered and publicly visible and does not include areas where prostitution is confined to street-level transactions. In the three cities examined here, street prostitution is almost nonexistent.

Antwerp's model is that of a *single-purpose* RLD organized around window prostitution. Its ecology differs radically from the much more *variegated* vice zones in Amsterdam and Frankfurt. In the latter settings, indoor prostitution is mixed in with conventional businesses (bars, cafes, snack shops), other erotic businesses (strip clubs, peep shows, live sex shows, shops selling porn and sex toys), or other vice (marijuana bars, head shops, gambling arcades). Both the clients and nearby residents are likely to view a multiuse entertainment zone that includes commercial sex differently than a single-use prostitution zone. The former allows the visitor to engage in "a package of activities that comprise the night-out, . . . [and] advantages are maximized by the location of prostitution close to other entertainment facilities."[2] Yet there can be advantages to a single-use zone as well, namely, public order, safety, and manageability by the authorities. Antwerp scores high on these measures and presents the greatest challenge to the traditional notion that vice districts are always run-down, disorderly, and dangerous. And Antwerp is by no means unique: several other cities host single-use, tranquil, and orderly RLDs—including a number of German and Dutch cities.

Ethnographic material is crucial for shedding light on the ways different red-light landscapes shape the perceptions and experiences of individuals who enter or reside in such zones. Scholars are just beginning to draw connections between the structure and ambience of red-light areas and the experiences of residents, visitors, workers, and clients. As Phil Hubbard recently wrote, the "affective geographies of these spaces could benefit from further scrutiny . . . [including] the way in which the ambience of particular settings contributes to the consumer experience by heightening or arousing specific desires . . . [and] the ways in which sex workers perform particular idealized identities to appeal to particular types of clientele."[3] These structural-experiential links are explored to some extent in this chapter and the next. I would add that the ecology of a particular red-light district is important not only sociologically but also for public policy. Different kinds of arrangements present distinctive challenges for law enforcement and order maintenance, are more or less likely to generate complaints from local residents and merchants, and increase or decrease the chances that a commercial sex sector will, at some point, become politicized and perhaps subjected to greater restrictions. Comparative analysis of different cases can help us assess the strengths and weaknesses of alternative models and perhaps contribute to the larger project of identifying arrangements that may be judged "best practices"—an admittedly complex undertaking addressed in the book's conclusion.

Historically, American red-light areas were the deliberate creation of city officials, motivated by the state's interest in controlling vice and insulating respectable areas from it.[4] European cities also experimented with official zoning, though many RLDs evolved more spontaneously (often in dockside areas frequented by sailors).[5] Today, some cities have tried to manage prostitution by relegating much of it to specific zones (Hamburg, Singapore, Tokyo), while other cities have no RLD whatsoever (e.g., Berlin, Vienna). In each of the three cities I studied, sexual commerce takes place both inside and outside designated red-light districts. The general pattern is one in which most if not all visible prostitution (in identifiable brothels, window units, or on the street) is geographically concentrated in particular locations, while less visible types (escorts, discreet or clandestine brothels) are dispersed throughout the city. Segregation is never watertight in practice, and zoning restrictions will always meet resistance from individuals who prefer to operate in the shadows. In fact, the amount of prostitution *outside* a designated RLD may be substantially greater than what takes place within it. Therefore, it is important to examine both the RLD and what lies beyond it.

It is worth noting that the populations of the three cities differ, with Amsterdam and Frankfurt being significantly larger than Antwerp—numbers that translate into different local client pools.[6] Amsterdam also has many more tourists than Frankfurt and Antwerp do, thereby creating a larger pool of foreign sex customers (in 2007, 3.9 million tourists visited Amsterdam, 1.5 million visited Frankfurt, and 636,000 visited Antwerp).[7] English is the lingua franca in these tourist-centered RLDs—captured in business names and signage, an obvious means of appealing to an international audience.

A useful starting point, which might be overlooked, is to recognize that the legal sex workers in the three settings do not risk arrest and punishment for prostitution: they are able to work with little fear of legal penalties. And this is true regardless of whether the system is one of de facto or de jure legalization. The sale of sex, per se, is not illegal in these three contexts, though third-party involvement (e.g., brothel ownership) has been either illegal in the past or is currently illegal yet tolerated (Antwerp). In other words, the owners and managers have been at greater risk for sanctions than have the sex workers themselves. Workers and third parties who operate underground, outside the legal system, are by definition subject to sanctions. This includes immigrants who lack work permits and persons who engage in street prostitution, which is forbidden in all three cities and constitutes a small share of the market in the three nations.[8]

Belgium

Belgium is a more conservative country than are Germany and the Netherlands. According to the World Values Survey, fewer Belgian than German and Dutch citizens approve of abortion and homosexuality, for example.[9] The most recent poll on prostitution that included all three nations dates from 1990, when 46 percent of Belgians said that prostitution is "never justified," compared to 33 percent in Germany and 20 percent in the Netherlands.[10] This partly explains why prostitution is only de facto legal in a few Belgian cities, rather than formally legal at the national level. Federal law in Belgium outlaws third-party involvement in prostitution, effectively criminalizing brothels, escort agencies, and other managed types. However, some of these are tolerated and regulated in some cities. Such extralegal regulation is somewhat precarious. As one Antwerp official told me, "We have to be careful in regulating prostitution as a whole because then we'd be contravening the law."[11] In fact, the regulation that does take place is technically in violation of federal law but permitted for pragmatic reasons, mirroring the de facto legalization that existed in the Netherlands prior to 2000.

Over the past decade, several legalization bills have been introduced in parliament, some of which were closely modeled on the Dutch or German laws. None passed, and competing proposals have been introduced as well, including bills that would criminalize clients (inspired by Sweden) or force local governments to close existing brothels and window prostitution.[12]

Window prostitution exists in Brussels and Antwerp and a few small cities (Ghent, Liège). Brussels's RLD is located away from the city center, near the city's north train station, whereas Antwerp's is closer to the city center but some distance from the main square. Other types of prostitution can be found in Brussels and Antwerp, in some bars and in brothels located in residential areas; the following analysis of Antwerp focuses on its windowed red-light district.

Antwerp's Red-Light Landscape

In the 1990s, Antwerp faced a growing problem with prostitution on the streets and in indoor locations scattered around the city. Window prostitution existed on three streets behind the central train station (about 60 windows in the 1990s) and in 17 streets around the old sailor's dockside area (the *Schipperskwartier*), where sailors stayed while in port and where prostitution has long thrived (comprising about 280 windows in the 1990s).[13] Things deteriorated as organized-crime groups moved into the area in the 1990s. Eastern European women were brought to the windows, there were occasional outbreaks of violence between competing crime groups, and conventional businesses and residents moved out. In 1998, residents signed a petition asking the city to clean up the district, and in 1999, the city council passed a plan with four goals: to confine prostitution to a specific red-light zone and remove it from other parts of the city, to eliminate organized crime, to reduce public nuisances, and to improve working conditions for prostitutes.[14] Street prostitution was considered a public nuisance, and the authorities began to crack down on it. In 2000, the city's social-democrat mayor began the process of squeezing prostitution out of certain areas and confining it to a three-block "tolerance zone" of neon-lit window rooms located in the old dockside area (about 20 minutes' walk from the central town square). Permits are required of owners who rent windows to sex workers, and the permits must be signed by the mayor, so it would be wrong to consider the rules simply informal. There is also a separate building code for window rooms, and compliance with the code is monitored by city officials.

The renovation of most of the units in recent years means that "the working conditions for prostitutes thereby improved drastically."[15] Antwerp's mayor describes the post-2000 changes in positive terms: "We have concentrated prostitution into three streets and that means we can put in place tough criteria. Most of these people are working in extremely good conditions. It was not like this five years ago. Now we have been able to create a situation where women are more independent [and] they are safe."[16] A 30-minute documentary, "Skippers' Quarter," confirms this verdict under the banner "Antwerp's prize-winning approach to urban renewal in its red-light district."[17] The film shows how the city dealt with problems in the area, and the award recognizes the city's creative approach to urban planning. According to the official in charge of the city's prostitution policy, Antwerp has largely succeeded in redistributing visible prostitution into this RLD. There is clandestine brothel and bar prostitution outside the area; however, most street prostitutes relocated to Brussels. The city has also tackled the large organized-crime groups, though pimps remain a problem. The official told me, "We got the big organized-crime groups out of the picture, but the individual pimps are more common, and it's very difficult to get rid of all the [third-party] in-betweens."[18] Police patrol the area in civilian clothes, monitoring anyone they think might be a pimp, and they do the same undercover work to combat male prostitution in parks. A city bylaw allows officers to stop, question, and search anyone in the RLD.

In the 1990s, approximately 4,000 cars drove through the Skippers' Quarter daily on their "tour d'amour," which gave the area a rather disorderly flavor: one observer recounted how "at four in the morning the place was packed with slow-moving cars, horns ablazing, the lads in the cars shouting at the girls in the windows dancing about."[19] Today, the RLD is a strictly pedestrian zone, with cars banned to minimize public nuisances (noise, traffic jams). There are no minors or illegals operating in the window area.[20] A small police station sits in the center of the RLD with a visible *Politie* sign. Officers patrol the area day and night, periodically visiting every sex worker and examining passports to confirm that they are adults and that they are citizens of Belgium or another European Union nation or possess documents allowing them to work in Belgium. Crimes in the prostitution sector, including assault and rape, have decreased substantially since the RLD was reinvented in 2000–2001,[21] and the police report that they have a generally positive relationship with the workers. A member of the prostitution squad, for example, stated, "Rather than being an enemy, the girls know we are here to help them and that helps us to gain their trust so we can prevent crime."[22] Additionally, residents' "complaints related to prostitution have stopped almost completely," according to an official report.[23] In 2002, the city installed a health clinic in the heart of the RLD, which offers prostitutes anonymous and free psychological counseling, tests and treatment for sexually transmitted diseases, and assistance for those who wish to leave the trade. The center's website states that "anonymity is guaranteed," with visitors identified only by their working names and birthdates and test results remaining confidential.[24] The health center provided 2,785 of these consultations in 2008.[25] It also sponsors a mobile outreach worker who visits prostitutes at their workplaces; she is a former prostitute trusted by the workers. If she learns of problems, she can pass the information along to the police or other authorities.[26]

The going rate for renting a window room in 2008 was €800 per week. Split between two women working different shifts, this amounts to €400 per week ($560). Sex workers are not allowed to reside within the RLD, but some of them live nearby. Building owners pay €2,500 ($3,500) per year in tax on each window unit, which is low relative to the amount of rental revenue. As of 2008, there were 283 windows, including 51 in one complex, the Villa Tinto, pictured in figure 5.1. Banks refuse to lend window owners money, forcing the 40 owners to lend within their own network. The owners have not formed an association to advocate for their interests, unlike in the Netherlands. However, city officials meet with all window owners twice a year, informing them of any new policies and asking the owners for input on improving the RLD. As an official told me, "We make sure every owner knows our policies and *why* they exist."[27] Most owners do not resist the authorities' requests for improvements in their buildings, perhaps because they realize they have no legal standing to oppose official dictates. About five times a year, an owner is fined by the city for failure to comply with regulations such as a defective shower, faulty electricity, or unclean facilities.[28]

About one-tenth of the window workers are transgender women, and the rest are female (males work elsewhere: in saunas, bars, and parks). Antwerp's single-purpose RLD is a good hike from the center of town, though still within walking distance. There are a couple of peep-show venues nearby, a disco, a snack shop, and one bar where prostitutes work—but the RLD proper consists almost entirely of window prostitution rooms. Almost everyone cruising the zone is male. I saw no minors, few couples, and no groups of tourists, as there is little reason to visit Antwerp's RLD unless one is seeking titillation or sex. Given the relative isolation of this district, the women are "on display" to a lower proportion of the general public than in a town-center RLD with far more pedestrians present or where cars troll through the area. The visual objectification of women is

Figure 5.1. Villa Tinto.

thus more restricted in a semi-isolated RLD such as Antwerp's. Its location also shields youth and the general public, one of the conditions for public tolerance of legal vice advanced in chapter 4.

Antwerp's red-light district is shown in figure 5.2. Unlike raucous RLDs in some other cities (including Amsterdam and Bangkok), Antwerp's is clean, tidy, and quiet. I barely heard a sound as I visited the area on separate occasions. I observed men (but no women or children) cruising the area silently, occasionally pausing to speak to one of the workers. The lack of vehicle traffic and the fact that this RLD is an enclave away from the city center contribute to its tranquil atmosphere. My observations are confirmed by clients who contribute to online message boards. When they compare the RLDs of Antwerp and Brussels, Brussels is viewed much more negatively: as somewhat unsafe, "seedy," "rough," "intimidating," and "shady." In Brussels's RLD, "you'll see some junkies/drunkards/beggars/pimp wannabes around"; "gangs looking for trouble sometimes"; and "a 'strong arm' element. I've seen big surly men in black BMW's dropping girls off."[29] The area is not particularly attractive, with lots of graffiti and litter as well as some abandoned buildings. The cars cruising slowly through the area give the place an eerie aura. Clients also complain about the curtains (instead of walls) separating window rooms in Brussels—allowing one to hear a couple in the next room—and about the lack of beds in some rooms that have a couch instead, not well suited to comfortable encounters.[30] Antwerp, by stark contrast, is described in glowing terms:

- "Very laid back and well policed."
- "The whole area seems modern and clean."
- "Probably the best RLD that I've visited. Like AMS [Amsterdam] without the bachelor party and tourist groups."
- "The best window-shopping environment that I've been in. It had a very relaxed environment to it—no gangs of the 'psst, Charlie' variety [i.e., drug sellers] hanging around, or any noticeable pimps, no stag-do's or groups of tourists snapping their cameras, just guys like you and me looking to get laid."
- "Antwerp is a secret, little known gem. Fantastic place. . . . Clean, safe. . . . Loads of choice and no frigging tourists."[31]

This atmosphere dates back several years. In a posting from 1997, a client described this RLD as "very safe to visit day or night. There is a visible police presence everywhere to make you feel secure. The selection of women is very good to excellent."[32]

When comparing the two Belgian sex markets to Amsterdam's, clients vary in which one they like best. Some described Antwerp as too tranquil, sanitized, and one-dimensional (lacking other attractions), whereas Amsterdam was judged superior as a "fun place to hang out."[33] They prefer the bustling ambience in Amsterdam and its multiple attractions (mari-

Figure 5.2. Antwerp's red-light district.

juana cafes, bars, restaurants, tourist shops, porn stores, live sex shows). But those who dislike Amsterdam's carnivalesque climate find Antwerp far superior—praising its cleanliness, safety, and lack of intoxicated, rowdy tourists and obtrusive tour groups.[34] Brussels's atmosphere, however, is almost universally ranked inferior to both Antwerp's and Amsterdam's: "Would you rather walk along the immensely scenic dimly-lit canals of Amsterdam or the very basic, very dull single street along the railroad line [Brussels's North train station] where you have to take care not to be pickpocketed or plainly robbed?"[35]

Of course, Antwerp's RLD shares certain features in common with other window-prostitution areas. An obvious universal is the women's conspicuous interest in attracting customers. They dress in sexy outfits—miniskirts, bikinis, lingerie—and their demeanor is designed to catch a man's attention. They pass the time by listening to music, dancing, eating, doing their makeup, or knocking on the window or calling out to men on the street, and they periodically take a break to disengage from the game. Walking through the area, the visitor will observe some who look bored and make little eye contact with passersby and others who are quite animated in their efforts to attract business. These dimensions of the window scene are a function of solicitation in public, akin to street prostitution behind a transparent facade. It is a different kind of presentation, much more performative than what occurs in a brothel, massage parlor, or other establishment where transactions are much more relaxed and genial.

Antwerp's window arrangement allows for some fraternization among workers. Some of the rooms have separate doors and windows, but many other units are clustered into blocs of three, five, or seven units. This has two important advantages: the women can socialize with each other, and they can collectively assert control over troublesome men. In other words, both camaraderie and empowerment are enhanced by this proximity to other workers. At the same time, such close quarters can create tensions, such as disputes over music choices, smoking, and the poaching of customers. For these reasons, some women prefer to work in separate units.[36] It would be easy for individuals standing next to each other to compete for a particular customer, though I did not observe this happening and there appears to be a norm against poaching that is usually honored.

Visibility is a prominent feature of this RLD. Everything is out in the open. Unlike Amsterdam, there are no narrow window-lined alleyways, there are no hidden areas where drinking or drug use might occur, and the lack of bars and cafes discourages visitors from loitering. I observed no malingerers in Antwerp's red-light area, unlike Amsterdam, where they are quite visible. Interestingly, Antwerp has not installed security cameras in its RLD, a fixture in Amsterdam.

The location, single-purpose orientation, and general lack of disorder help to explain why Antwerp's tolerated red-light district is relatively uncontroversial and is much less politicized than some others, including Amsterdam's (discussed in chapter 6). As noted earlier, nearby residents do not complain about it; clients are attracted to it because it is clean, orderly, and safe; youths and the general public are shielded by virtue of this RLD's isolated location; working conditions for window prostitutes have improved significantly over the past decade; and these sex workers appear to have fairly good relations with the authorities.

Germany

A 1999 poll reported that 68 percent of Germans favored legalizing prostitution.[37] This level of support is not unusual in Europe, as majorities in many other nations favor legalization as well (see table 4.1). Another survey asked about the acceptability of prostitution, and this poll allows us to compare attitudes before and after legalization in 2002. The proportion of Germans who felt that prostitution can "never be justified" declined from 42 percent in 1981 to 33 percent in 1999, dropping further to 24 percent in 2005—a trend toward greater tolerance that may have been catalyzed by legal reform in 2002.[38]

Prior to 2002, selling sex was not a crime in Germany, nor was operating a brothel. But court rulings considered prostitution to be immoral and antisocial, and prostitutes had virtually no rights.[39] It was a crime for third parties to be involved in "the furtherance of prostitution"—for example, pimping, promoting, and profiting from prostitution. This did not apply to brothel owners as long as they did not keep workers in a state of dependency, meaning any action that went beyond providing accommodation (although in practice these owners operated in some jeopardy of violating the "furtherance" measure). Building owners faced the least risk if they simply rented space to workers—hence the existence of Eros Centers, where women rent a room in which to work and are not employees of the house.[40] The first Eros Center opened in Hamburg in 1967, followed by one in Frankfurt in 1971; the centers were designed to reduce street prostitution without formally legalizing brothels.[41] Pimping was prohibited by a section of the penal code that outlawed three things: taking money from a worker in a way that reduced the person's standard of living, keeping the worker under visual surveillance, or specifying the minimum amount of money a worker must earn or the number of customers she or he must service.[42]

In the 1980s, the prostitutes' rights group Hydra and its sister groups began to press for measures that would protect workers from discrimination, winning support from the Green Party, which sponsored an antidiscrimination bill in parliament in 1990. After the Social Democrats and Greens formed a coalition government in 1998, the Greens got more leverage in advocating for legal reform. Four years later, a new bill was presented.

In the debate on the 2001 bill, most political parties expressed a desire to reduce discrimination against workers, which they hoped the bill would facilitate.[43] The general orientation in German political circles had evolved into one that views prostitution as both inevitable and in need of certain protections. There was also an explicit rejection of the oppression paradigm, as reflected in the following statement by a member of parliament, Petra Pau: "New criminological research has shown that . . . the image of the oppressed woman, who has been driven into this profession, can no longer be maintained. Prostitutes today resemble average businesswomen, . . . [and] the predominant number of prostitutes make a conscious decision to start and to go on with their activity."[44] Four of the five political parties voted for the bill, with only the Christian Democratic Union opposing it. The central goals of the 2002 law were the following:

- To remove the aura of immorality from prostitution
- To improve the legal status of prostitutes
- To improve working conditions
- To reduce crimes that accompany prostitution
- To facilitate exit from prostitution[45]

The statute decriminalized prostitution and granted adult sex workers rights to enter into contracts, to apply for social insurance, and to sue clients for nonpayment. Procuring, managing, and promoting prostitution are no longer crimes, provided that these actors do not curtail a worker's "personal or financial independence," in the words of the penal code. In addition, German penal law (§232[1]) contains a trafficking offense, defined as a situation in which someone "exploits another person's predicament or helplessness arising from being in a foreign country" and thereby induces the person into prostitution. This provision also criminalizes third-party enticement into prostitution of anyone (including German citizens) under the age of 21. The law provides a penalty (a sentence of six months to ten years) for anyone who "induces a person under 21 years of age to engage in or continue to engage in prostitution." Coercion is irrelevant; individuals are defined as victims of exploitation simply by virtue of their age.[46] German citizens aged 18–21 who are not induced, as well as those who are 21 and older and induced, are free to engage in prostitution.

The 2002 law gives sex workers certain contractual rights and prohibits managers from forcing a worker to accept a particular client or to engage in disliked sexual practices, but unlike some other legal systems, the law does not regulate other working conditions. Brothel owners are not required to provide specified amenities to ensure that their workplace is safe and hygienic. A 2006 proposal mandating health examinations for workers was rejected by the government in favor of promoting outreach work instead.[47] In general, the law has had little impact on working conditions, and third parties have no legal or economic incentive to improve them. A government report stated that there had been "hardly any measurable, positive impact" on working conditions as a result of the 2002 law and added that "it is not surprising that working conditions are not improved unless they also fulfill the economic interests of the operator."[48]

The period since legalization can also be faulted for some of the restrictions placed on sex workers as well as the absence of collateral normalization. Workers are not allowed to advertise (except on the Internet); prostitution is not accepted as a trade by Germany's trade association; and repressive police practices in some places violate the spirit of the 2002 law.

A survey conducted in 2004 of 305 prostitutes and 22 brothel owners asked whether they thought the 2002 law was "a good thing": 62 percent of prostitutes and 77 percent of brothel owners felt that it was beneficial. However, only 12 percent of prostitutes and 32 percent of owners thought that the law had brought about any improvements (understandable, given the recency of the law), while 46 percent of each group said that they hoped it would lead to further improvements. Two-fifths (43 percent) of the prostitutes felt that the statute had empowered them to assert their rights. Yet, since 2002, sex workers have initiated very few court cases against owners. Similarly rare are charges against clients who refuse to pay for services—largely because the standard practice is to demand payment in advance and because the court costs typically would exceed the amount of lost income that might be recovered, coupled with workers' desire to remain anonymous.[49] Suing a client or brothel owner would involve a public announcement of one's occupation and would expose nontaxpaying workers to tax liability. (When some sex workers have tried to register with the tax office, they have been charged back taxes for years of unreported income.[50] The amount of unpaid tax appears to be substantial,[51] and taxation enforcement differs from city to city. In some places, the local revenue office has a unit that investigates illegal brothels or other erotic establishments in search of tax evasion. The unit conducts raids on suspected premises along with the police.)

In addition, the right to enter into employment contracts with third parties is almost never asserted. Only 1 percent of the 305 workers interviewed in 2004 had an employment contract, which are disliked by workers and brothel operators alike. Prostitutes fear that employment contracts will jeopardize their anonymity, as well as their autonomy if the contract contains undesirable obligations. Owners dislike contracts because they would then have to pay insurance premiums for their employees, who also would be entitled to holiday pay, pregnancy leave, and social security benefits.[52] The government has shown little interest in convincing workers to enter into formal contracts, unlike in the Netherlands. As a government report stated,

> The majority of prostitutes wish to retain their independence (and self-determination) and this should be taken seriously.... In the Federal Government's opinion, further deliberation on the issues involved should include looking at how ... freelance work could guarantee prostitutes social protection and how their working conditions as freelancers could be improved.[53]

Regarding prostitution-related crimes, government statistics show a marked improvement since 2002. Recall that procuring/pimping was a crime prior to 2002 but is no longer an offense, provided that a worker's "personal or financial independence" is not curtailed; the latter type of pimping remains illegal under §181(a) of the penal code. Given that only a certain kind of procuring or pimping is now outlawed, we should expect a decrease in the number of procuring/pimping §181(a) cases after 2002, and official figures bear this out. In 2000, there were 1,104 such cases, steadily dropping to 298 in 2009. Similarly, §180(a) of the penal code was amended for employers who manage prostitutes: they are now liable for punishment only if they keep a prostitute personally and economically dependent on their business operation; the number of cases under §180(a) dropped dramatically between 2000 and 2009, from 1,365 to 62. Trafficking cases under §232 (exploiting someone's "predicament or helplessness arising from being in a foreign country") declined as well, from 1,016 in 2000 to 811 in 2009.[54] Regarding organized crime's role in the sex industry since 2002, the trend is less clear, given the lack of direct measures of organized-crime involvement (except perhaps the trafficking figures), but a government report did note a trend among certain business owners: "'Good' brothel operators dissociate themselves from the 'black sheep' in order to show how respectable their establishments are and thus to increase turnover [business]."[55]

Apart from the positive trend regarding prostitution-related crimes, the German government's overall assessment (five years after the passage of the 2002 law) was that the law had "only to a limited degree" achieved its goals.[56] This is understandable given the law's rather minimalist regulatory approach. Removing the aura of immorality from prostitution, one of the law's goals, is not advanced when so little has been done to harmonize this goal with other laws and official practices. Regarding the statute's other expressed goals, the government report called for "a more broad-based approach to regulating prostitution"—including additional mechanisms to improve working conditions, prevent crime, and "more efficiently monitor commercial enterprises providing sexual services" by licensing them.[57]

Aside from the general objectives of the 2002 law listed earlier, prostitution policies are locally determined: there is no single "German model." The law allows cities and towns with a population of less than 50,000 to ban prostitution and allows other jurisdictions to restrict it to certain places and prohibit it in others (called "negative zones"). Consequently, each jurisdiction has developed its own policies, and prostitution remains illegal in many parts of the country. In many German states, legal prostitution exists only in a small fraction of its cities and towns. Some municipalities ban all prostitution, whereas others (e.g., Berlin) impose very few restrictions. Most ban visible prostitution from the city center, relegate it to a zone elsewhere in the city (in some cases, to an industrial area), and stage police raids in areas where prostitution is forbidden, even when it is unobtrusive in apartments or hotels.[58] Street prostitution is permitted in only a few places and accounts for about 10 percent of prostitution in Germany.[59] Window prostitution exists in a few cities (including Hamburg, Bremen, Braunschweig, and Mannheim) where it is confined to a single street of 10–20 rooms and is hidden behind barricades with signs that forbid women and persons under age 18 from entering. Outside these few window streets, indoor workers in German red-light districts are shielded from view at the street level; the erotic nature of their workplace is visible in signage, but the prostitutes themselves are only visible after one enters the building.

Even in places where prostitution is permitted, it may be treated by officials as a deviant enterprise in need of suppression, despite the normalizing intent of the 2002 law. Leipzig, for example, has only a few legal, registered brothels, and the authorities' overall approach involves "repressive practices combined with a view of prostituting women as deviant."[60] This contrasts with cities where prostitution is treated as a quasi-conventional business whose interests are generally safeguarded by the authorities. Some cities take an "empowering approach that aims at social inclusion of sex workers" and views "sex workers and brothel owners as more or less 'normal' economic citizens."[61] For example, when the new law came into force in 2002, Dortmund officials held workshops with sex workers and brothel owners to explain the new rules. The authorities' approach to illegal prostitution also varies. In some cities, including Frankfurt, large groups of police and tax officials stage aggressive raids on brothels and nightclubs suspected of tax evasion or of harboring illegal migrant workers, whereas in other cities the monitoring is more tempered.[62]

As one would expect in any setting where prostitution has been recently legalized, there are local and national forces in Germany inside and outside government that remain opposed and have tried to turn back the clock. The Christian Democratic Union Party has advocated implementing the Swedish system criminalizing customers. Others have demanded more robust undercover police operations to bust those who sell sex outside designated zones. And the issue of trafficking is increasingly tied to prostitution in media stories, prompting calls for total repeal of the 2002 law, despite the fact that trafficking cases have declined over the past decade, as documented earlier. A coalition of activists from the churches and women's organizations has tried to convince the government to crack down in other ways: for example, to license workers and to mandate condom usage and medical exams. The police themselves have lobbied for the power to enter sexually oriented establishments at any time (without the need for a judge's warrant and thus nullifying the reasonable-suspicion requirement). A February 2011 bill in parliament would, if passed, free the police to engage in such raids and would mandate the licensing of all prostitution businesses, the registration of all prostitutes, and compulsory condom usage (currently neither workers nor sex businesses need special licenses to operate, and condom usage is not mandatory except in the state of Bavaria). All of the political parties support this bill.

Types of Prostitution

Let me sketch the contours of prostitution in Germany as a prelude to an exploration of Frankfurt's sexual landscape. I have already noted that *street prostitution* is not prevalent and is discouraged by the authorities. It accounts for about 10 percent of prostitution in Germany and 2.6 percent in Frankfurt.[63] A few municipalities have created special zones for street workers on the outskirts of the city, in an effort to remove them from the city center. The zones are modeled on similar areas in some Dutch cities. In 2001, Cologne created the first such zone, which contains drive-in cubicles where prostitutes have sex in clients' cars. The area is fenced, gated, and fitted with security cameras, and each cubicle has an alarm button for workers' safety. About 300 prostitutes work in the zone, which has reduced street prostitution in the city center.[64]

Agency-based or independent *escorting* is just as common as it is in other Western countries and is only noteworthy in Germany because escorts (as legal actors) can advertise sex freely without the need for euphemisms (such as "full service"). A sexually oriented advertising company, RTO, assists sex workers with Internet ads, designs websites, and arranges photo shoots. A manager at RTO told me that it is the only agency "that tries to build business for the sex industry." He added, "Some people say we are online pimps. But we are a cheap place to put an ad, so we are facilitating women working without pimps."[65]

Home-based sex work: In general, the authorities allow a maximum of three workers to work out of the same apartment or house, provided that at least one of them resides there and the place is registered in her or his name. It is forbidden for more than three people to sell sex in a residential unit, although the police tolerate this in some places.

Erotic bars are abundant. They include strip clubs, live sex shows, and bars where hostesses sit with men, encourage them to buy drinks, and provide sexual entertainment. Women are available for erotic touching and, depending on the place, other sexual services.

Traditional brothels vary in size, amenities, and class but usually have a parlor or bar where clients can fraternize with providers. There are house rules and a manager on the premises. At the high end, Kamilla la Dee in Berlin bills itself as "the erotic saloon in Berlin, the brothel of extraclass, where you may have excellent girlfriend sex in a beautiful, relaxed atmosphere with an intimate girlfriend on limited appointment. With her you may enjoy passionate girlfriend sex. Tender, soft, cuddly, or wild and frivolous."[66] Other conventional brothels range from similarly fancy to much less so.

Hotel-brothels (also called an eros center, sex inn, or laufhaus) are buildings where a landlord rents workers rooms for the day or half day. It is not a traditional brothel governed by house rules or where the daily activities are dictated by a manager. The workers are essentially independent providers renting a work space.

Sauna clubs offer a different kind of experience for the customer—one that includes recreation, "wellness," and nonsexual intimacy with women as well as erotic titillation and sex. Many of the clubs are known as FKK clubs (Frei Körper Kultur), which translates as "free body culture," harking back to their origins as nudist clubs. (I use the term *sauna club* interchangeably with *FKK club*, bearing in mind that not all such clubs are technically FKKs. Austria, Switzerland, and the Czech Republic have FKKs as well.) The clubs vary somewhat in price, amenities, and rules, but generally the client pays an entry fee (€25 to €80) that gives him access to a pool, sauna, food, and drink. Men wear towels or robes and chat with the sex workers on duty; the women are scantily clad, topless, or nude. The women pay the same entry fee and are considered freelancers. They receive no salary, social security, or other benefits but keep their entire earnings. The number of providers working at any given time varies tremendously, from cozy clubs with five to ten women to those with up to a hundred working at the larger emporiums.

Frankfurt's Sexual Landscape

Prostitution was de facto decriminalized in Frankfurt (on a minor scale) long before the 2002 national law liberalized the situation nationwide. In 1969, the city government decided to issue a permit for the first large brothel in the city in order to reduce street prostitution near residential areas. The police essentially forced street workers into the brothel.[67] Opened in 1971, this hotel-brothel, Crazy Sexy, is distinguished by the dancing mannequins on the building's facade (shown in figure 5.3; Crazy Sexy is now part of a chain of brothels, with sister locations in Bonn, Wiesbaden, Leipzig, and Mainz).[68] Other tolerated brothels followed, and over time, their owners gained some acceptance as entrepreneurs, although suspicion and tensions have lingered to the present time.[69] A diverse red-light district grew up around the initial brothels in the Bahnhofsviertel area, and street prostitution was almost entirely eliminated from the area by the mid-1980s.[70]

About 2,000 women sell sex in Frankfurt. A 2006 census revealed that 50 were working on the street, 1,155 in brothels, 630 in their own premises, 100 in sauna clubs (plus those in sauna clubs outside the city limits). In the main RLD in Bahnhofsviertel, it was estimated that 9,200 customers purchased sex in the hotel-brothels each day, based on the finding that 920 women were working each day and seeing an average of ten clients per day. This translates into 64,400 paid sex transactions each week in the hotel-brothels alone.[71]

An estimated 40 percent of prostitutes in the country are of German background,[72] and many of them are concentrated in escort services and brothels

Figure 5.3. Crazy Sexy brothel.

located outside the urban red-light districts. In Frankfurt's hotel-brothels, only 4 percent of the prostitutes are German; a few (7 percent) come from other western European countries, but most are from eastern Europe, Thailand, Colombia, or the Dominican Republic.[73] Eastern Europeans are the fastest growing group, constituting 20 percent of the total in 2006 (up from 6 percent in 2002).[74] Their numbers increased after 2004 when eight nations were admitted to the European Union (including Poland, Hungary, the Balkans, and the Czech Republic). Migrants are allowed to work as freelancers in a business in an EU member nation, but not as contract employees of that business. Another migrant wave came after 2007, when Bulgaria and Romania became EU members. Since then, Romanians and Bulgarians have flocked to Germany (and other western European nations),[75] so the current figure is probably significantly higher than the 20 percent reported in 2006. One estimate is that Romanians alone now constitute 20 percent of the total.

As indicated earlier in the book, estimating the number of migrants who enter a country voluntarily versus coercively is fraught with problems. However, a 2006 survey of migrant women working in the German sex industry concluded that the majority had entered the country voluntarily with the assistance of intermediaries.[76] To what extent this is true today for those Romanians and Bulgarians who entered the country after 2007 is unknown, but the fact that they are now permitted to work in Germany means that they no longer need to operate in a clandestine manner. One final point about these two groups: despite the willingness of many young Bulgarians and Romanians to migrate to red-light destinations, the population at home is more unreceptive toward prostitution than it is in most other European nations. In fact, Romanians score higher than any other European nationality on the opinion that prostitution can "never be justified"—69 percent of Romanians hold this view, as do 46 percent of Bulgarians (see table 4.2). Yet the severe lack of job opportunities in Romania and Bulgaria is a strong "push factor" explaining why so many Romanians and Bulgarians have migrated to western Europe.

The main RLD in Frankfurt's Bahnhofsviertel area is not the only sexually oriented district in the city. A tiny RLD is located miles away, on Breite Gasse street, where approximately 235 women work in four hotel-brothels.[77] One of these, Penthouse No. 1, has a bar on the top floor, where women are available as drinking companions.[78] When I visited the area in 2010, the atmosphere was placid and a few men were cruising the brothels. On a return visit a year later, there was very little action on a Friday night, with few men around and only one of the hotel-brothels occupied. Most of the women I tried to speak to in English looked perplexed or responded in some other language. A sign above the doorway of one of the brothels prohibits women and anyone under 18 from entering. There are no women on the street on this Saturday night. The women in the area's hotel-brothels vary considerably in age, ethnicity, and appearance. The Breite Gasse district is shown in figure 5.4.

Frankfurt's larger RLD in Bahnhofsviertel is a spectacle compared to Breite Gasse and much seedier than Antwerp's RLD. Many men on the street are young, in their 20s, but there are older men as well. In Germany, it is legal to drink alcohol in public, and I saw men in this RLD entering sex businesses with alcohol in hand. Few women are visible on the streets of this largely male domain: brothel workers walking to and from work, women who work at the dance clubs and erotic bars and stand outside trying to lure men in, and a few street prostitutes. On one corner is a sex arcade with video cabins. The manager told me that street prostitutes sometimes bring a man into the

Figure 5.4a, 5.4b. Breite Gasse red-light district.

cabins, pretending that he is her boyfriend (couples are allowed to go into a cabin together). When they leave, they go in separate directions, and plain-clothes police officers then alert the manager. This happens once or twice a month. Drunks and drug addicts occupy two streets; there, I saw people using drugs, drinking alcohol, and sleeping on the sidewalk. These individuals generally keep to themselves and do not hassle passersby.

My observations are confirmed in clients' online descriptions of this RLD. One says, "I have seen a host of seedy characters and other creeps in various stages of inebriation," and another calls it a "place for suckers and old men": "I don't know how anyone who has ever been to a FKK [sauna club] can go there."[79] One recommended that the owners of hotel-brothels charge people €5 ($7) to enter, to keep the "low-lifes" out. But others are not bothered by the RLD's atmosphere and value the tremendous variety of sexually oriented businesses there.

The downscale ambience of the area on the ground level is one of its most noticeable features. The aesthetics of the buildings, however, convey a classier impression, one that clashes with the vice scene on the street. The buildings' facades are adorned with neon lights, fancy decor, and erotic advertisements. The area is packed with sexually oriented places such as strip clubs, erotic bars, a sauna club, cabarets, and hotel-brothels, in addition to snack bars, casinos, and other shops (depicted in figure 5.5). To appeal to an international clientele, almost all of them have English names, such as America Peep Show, Foxy Ladies, Double D Girls & Drinks, Starstars Tabledance, Pure Platinum, New York City Bar, Miami Sauna Club, and Golden Gate. The signage features images of scantily clad or nude women or large red lips, but some attempt to conjure other fantasies, with images of palm trees (Miami Sauna Club), hearts (several Eros Centers), or a party atmosphere (Crazy Sexy's dancing mannequins).

The erotic bars and cabarets employ hostesses who sit and drink with a customer and offer sexual entertainment. Male and female solicitors stand outside these bars and try to entice or drag male pedestrians inside. If women attempt to lure customers, male touts are more aggressive, blocking the sidewalk and grabbing men who pass by. They wave and call out to men they see from afar and will even run across the street to try to entice a person into their place, often saying, "Come in just for a minute." My fieldnotes describe my experiences:

- On several occasions a man outside a bar blocked my path on the sidewalk, once forcing me into the bar, where a woman immediately appeared and tried to coax me into a curtained room "just for a minute." As I tried to leave the bar, a bouncer blocked my exit, and I had to push my way out of the place. Inside another bar, a man and a woman clung to my arms, trying to prevent me from leaving.
- I saw a tout from Bistro 91 standing in the middle of a traffic intersection beckoning to men on the four intersecting streets. After failing to get anyone interested after a couple of minutes in the street, he returned to the front of his bar.

Figure 5.5a. Bahnhofsviertel red-light district.

Figure 5.5b. Bahnhofsviertel red-light district.

Figure 5.5c and 5.5d. Bahnhofsviertel red-light district.

Figure 5.5e. Bahnhofsviertel red-light district.

Figure 5.5f. Bahnhofsviertel red-light district.

- When I walked by one of the erotic bars one night, a female solicitor convinced me to take a "free look inside." A dancer was working the poll, and a few men watched from their booths. Eight women were visible. The solicitor told me that the women will do lapdances, but she refuses to reveal the cost until I sit down and order a drink. When I ask if they do "anything else," she says, "Yes, but it is up to the woman," and will not reveal what services are available or the prices.
- This scenario is repeated a few doors away at a place that features a live sex show in addition to other attractions. I enter and see a man and woman having sex on a small stage in the center of the room. Six women sit at the bar, waiting for men to enter or for the live show to end and the stripping rotation to begin. The dancer who brought me inside says she will give me a lapdance but will not quote a price until I come in and buy a drink. She says that nude lapdances are performed in private rooms and hints that other sex acts are available, but "you have to come in to find out more."
- In two other bars, I was taken to a small room, with a couch and table, where erotic encounters take place. In one, the hostess tells me that "this is where you can play with a lady."
- At each of these places, alcohol drinks are €4–€5, but the man is also expected to buy a woman a drink for €20–€25. This is mandatory at every bar except one, where the solicitor told me that men could decline paying for the woman's drink.

Describing these places on an online discussion board, a man wrote,

> The "girls," most of them are over 30, offer plenty of promises. They will sit with you and play with you and then give you a very expensive bill, backed up by muscle. In some places you may get more but you will pay through the nose for it. . . . I have spoken to guys who have shelled out 200–300 Euros for less than an hour for a couple of drinks and a girl nuzzling their neck and stroking their ego. Unless you have a large expense account or plenty of money and a desire to be exploited, AVOID.[80]

The erotic bar scene differs radically from the atmosphere in Germany's hotel-brothels. Frankfurt's main RLD is home to a large number of these brothels, 21 at present. The women in the buildings are not visible from the street: all windows are closed and draped, and there are no rooms on the entry-level floor. The hotels are not required to register with the authorities as brothels, since owners simply rent rooms to independent providers (on a daily basis). A manager is present to accept rental payment from the women and to provide security, but this person exercises little supervision except to maintain order and a drug-free workplace. (Women are allowed to drink alcohol in their rooms, but being drunk or using drugs is frowned on by managers because it upsets order and may lead to police intervention; use of intoxicants has not been a major problem in the hotel-brothels.)[81] In 2010, the standard room rent was €130 ($180) for a 24-hour period and €90 ($125) for 12 hours. Workers who have immigrated from another country prefer the overnight stays because of convenience and to avoid paying rent for a separate apartment. They are not pressured by brothel owners to rent the rooms for long periods of time, but many of the women do so.[82] The workers I spoke to charged €30 ($42) for hand relief, oral sex, or vaginal sex, though a few charged €20 or €25 ($28 or $35). In the Netherlands and Belgium, the going rate for the same services is significantly higher: €50 ($70).

Hotel-brothels have their own distinctive signage and facades, giving many of them the appearance of a clean, classy establishment; some proprietors have invested considerably in decorating the exterior of their brothel. A few have sexually oriented interior decoration (e.g., statues of Greek goddesses, erotic paintings and wall murals, a mirror ball), but most have little if any decoration in the foyer, hallways, and stairwells—quite different from a posh brothel. The rooms are much larger than are the window units in Belgium and the Netherlands, and they are also homier, often decorated with the worker's personal effects. Each room has an alarm system to be used in the event of a problem customer. Some of the hotel-brothels feature a variety of amenities for the women, such as a tanning bed and a large kitchen. According to the website for Rotes Haus (Red House), each room is equipped with a telephone, bathroom, and international TV.[83] Frankfurt's brothel owners have been more willing than their counterparts in some other cities to make improvements in working conditions. In collaboration with the prostitutes' rights organization Doña Carmen, the owners developed a set of hygiene and safety standards for the brothels.[84]

Visitors are free to enter the premises to view the sex workers. There is no entry fee or gatekeeper restricting access, but there are security cameras at each place. Persons under 18 and women not working there are not allowed inside, and some of the brothels have signs at the front door prohibiting entry to women and underage persons. I visited all the Eros Centers in Frankfurt. The logistics are not particularly client friendly, as one must walk up four or five floors to view all the workers in each house. For local clients who have a favorite provider and know where to find her, this is not a problem, but for novices, this vertical cruising can be tiring. I was exhausted after stair climbing at a succession of places, and I saw other men winded and sweating in the hot, stuffy stairwells. Clients in web-based discussion boards frequently complain about the stairs and voice frustration about climbing to the top floor only to find no one there sometimes. They also complain about uncivil men who troll these places. One client stated, "Unfortunately, there are large numbers of men who delight in traipsing through the place, being rude about the girls, and knocking at the [closed] doors. This is very off-putting, particularly if you are mid-thrust."[85] At the same time, the logistics are not conducive to loitering in these brothels, on the part of clients, voyeurs, or pimps. I rarely saw a man hanging out in the stairwells or on the floors. There is nothing to see from the stairwells, and anyone who lingers on one of the floors would be questioned or hassled by the women.

Compared to window prostitution where workers are separated and where the windows and doors are usually closed, the hotel-brothels allow women to fraternize freely, visiting each other's room or congregating in the hallways. I saw several doing just that. Many of the floors are populated by women of the same nationality or ethnic background, facilitating socializing. That the workers can leave their rooms also gives them direct access to the men and much more opportunity to interact with potential clients than they can in window prostitution. Clients writing in online forums also like the fact that they can talk to the women freely in a secluded arena, unlike open-air RLDs, where clients are visible to the public. In the hotel-brothels, women stand or sit on stools in their doorways or linger outside their rooms and chat with men—exchanging greetings, bantering, negotiating a service, and sometimes arguing with or denigrating a man. Some gently coax, while others are more aggressive in trying to induce men to enter their rooms: the latter grab a man's arm and try to pull him into a room; others touch a guy's genitals, making compliments; and some operate in groups, surrounding a man and insisting that he make a selection. I observed all of this happening to other men in addition to experiencing it myself. One woman allowed a man in the hallway to kiss her breasts as his two friends looked on admiringly. In another place, a woman repeatedly yelled at one man, "I want your cock!" as nearby men scurried away. This direct, face-to-face marketing is much less evident in the window-prostitution model, in which the workers typically remain in their rooms and only briefly open their doors or windows to talk with a man.

I interviewed the owner of one of the hotel-brothels, who has run the place for 30 years.[86] Most of his workers are from the Dominican Republic, and there are currently 28 women working (the brothel has 34 rooms).

The majority rent rooms for 12 hours, but 40 percent rent for the entire day and live in the room. Many of the women have worked there for years, and the owner knows them well. They come into his office to get food and drink from the refrigerator, giving him the opportunity to chat with them. Two women did this during my interview, smiling and saying hello to us.

On the owner's desk, I see six video screens showing the entry to the brothel and each of its five floors. He monitors the screens constantly (as do two other managers during their shifts), and he intervenes quickly in the event of trouble with a client or when drunks are hanging out in the foyer. He tells me that the video monitoring is essential: "because you can prevent problems before they start." If a woman has a problem customer, she can quietly alert the manager by taking her phone off the hook (an alarm might cause panic and perhaps an unwanted police response). This happens, the owner says, "at least once a day" and especially on weekends, when there are a lot of men around. The main reason for altercations is attributed to communication barriers, and physical confrontations are rare—occurring about twice a year. Problems can arise if the parties do not speak the same language, if the man is drunk and disorderly, and if the woman reneges on agreed services or charges extra for such things as removing her top or more than one sexual position—what clients deride as "upselling." But this owner also says that most providers are very savvy and skilled in their ability to manage men. Novices have the most trouble because they have not yet learned how to preempt conflicts, while the more seasoned workers "are professionals and know the job" and are used to behaving in a way that prevents problems from arising.[87]

Customers are a mixed group. Male tourists are present at any time of day, as this red-light area is just a few blocks from Frankfurt's main train station. Business spikes at five to six p.m., when men leave their jobs. A large client pool consists of young, Turkish men. Facing traditional barriers on premarital sex with Turkish women, the men may visit sex workers instead. The brothel owner tells me that during the Ramadan period, Turks stop buying sex, and the prostitutes complain about the dramatic drop in business—demonstrating just how many of the clients come from this population.

Third parties experience stigma by virtue of their involvement in sexual commerce. The owner I interviewed entered the brothel business 30 years ago, when he was then running a dance club. His brother owned a brothel, facilitating his transition from dance club to brothel. The fact that such business involvement was "in the family" made the transition easy for him: "I never had a problem with it." But he is sensitive to how others view him. He lives in a village outside Frankfurt, and only his close friends know that he owns and manages an Eros Center. He says, "We can't tell anyone what we do. It's very difficult for us. We have to live two lives."

The owner also complains about the police, claiming that they conduct raids to inspect workers' documents without having reasonable suspicion of wrongdoing. When I asked if he ever meets with the police outside the brothel in order to forge a better relationship, he laughs:

> The police don't want to have contact with us. They see prostitution as an immoral activity. They like to keep it as it is, so they can make [negative] claims about us. Police don't want positive relations with owners. They like to tell people that they are not close to the owners and make it seem like a criminal business.

Officials at the sex workers' organization Doña Carmen concur that the police have a generally antagonistic relationship with the brothel owners in Frankfurt's main RLD. This is clearly inconsistent with a model of "best practices" in a system of legal prostitution, in which the police should strive to protect the rights of all parties concerned rather than acting in an adversarial or indiscriminate manner.

Like the hotel-brothels, the women working in FKK and other sauna clubs are freelancers, not employees who would be eligible for social security and other benefits. The women pay an entry fee just like the male customers (ranging from €25 to €80), and they receive a percentage of the alcohol drinks they sell customers as well as the entire fee for their sexual services. (Alcohol is not free because that might encourage men to get drunk and unmanageable and because selling drinks provides extra income for both the women and the clubs.) The entry fee for providers puts them at some economic risk: they must pay the fee even on days when they have no customers. Standard prices are €50 for the first half hour of sexual contact, €50 for each additional half hour, and additional charges for special services such as anal sex, two women, cunnilingus, and so on. The kind of service available depends on the provider, but generally they allow extensive foreplay (e.g., kissing, touching) and uncovered blow jobs—practices that are not usually on the menu in window prostitution and hotel-brothels. The services available at specific establishments are described by clients on online message boards.

The atmosphere in sauna clubs differs radically from that in hotel-brothels. The clubs vary in size and amenities, but they usually have a pool, a sauna, food, and drink. Clients walk around in towels or robes, the women are in various states of undress (scantily clad, topless, or nude), and the two parties engage in conversation, flirtation, touching, or other activities, which may or may not lead to sex. There are public areas where everyone is visible as well as private and semiprivate areas. Some clients engage in sex publicly, allowing other patrons to watch, but most prefer the privacy of a closed room.

Some men come to the club for relaxation only, and the women typically leave these men alone, not pressuring them to spend time talking with them or having sex. Women have the right to refuse services to any particular man. Clients do not select a provider from a catalogue or lineup as in traditional brothels; the connections are much more deliberative, with one party approaching the other, chatting, and later deciding if they want to take things to the next level. These clients like to "connect" with a woman prior to sexual activity; in online discussion boards, clients say that one of the main attractions of sauna clubs is that they can "hang out" with a woman both before and after sex.[88] And simply being *in the presence* of several beautiful, available women for an extended period of time is viewed as an advantage over other sex venues. An additional benefit is that clients can "sample" several providers socially before making a decision. As one client stated, "You can 'be amid women' for a while, focus on one, maybe decide you aren't 'clicking' with that one, move to another, go back to the first, and only later go for the 'main event' with the right one."[89] This man noted that such screening was simply not possible when hiring an escort or window worker or even at most traditional brothels, where the socializing time is more truncated than it is in FKKs.

In online discussion boards, clients typically sing the praises of the FKK saunas in generic terms, even if they have had a poor or mediocre experience with a particular provider. As Monk69 commented, "The atmosphere was extremely casual and felt very safe. What a great way to hobby! . . . I think a lot of American hobbyists' jaws would simply drop if they realized how good the German's have it."[90] Another client elaborates:

The FKK Clubs in Germany are the ticket if you like model perfect women and a high class venue. For about 50 euros I gained access to a club which reminded me of a chateau. Very upscale with open bar and excellent food, all included in the entry fee. I was there on a Tuesday and there were over 30 beautiful women to choose from. A must for anyone looking for a high-end erotic experience![91]

When novices ask what they can do with all the "down time" if they spend several hours in a FKK, the responses of regular clients throws light on club dynamics. When Makelove asked, "Do you ever get bored?" other posters responded with a unanimous "no." One wrote, "The FKKs are a pretty social environment. I have met and struck up interesting conversations with a variety of men and women. . . . Some gents . . . turned out to be right good buddies." Another customer stated, "These places are designed to be men's clubs and not merely brothels." And others informed Makelove of the sauna room, pool, masseur, TV, food and drink, wireless Internet, and beautiful women walking around. Consider this description of The Palace in Frankfurt: "So many amazing women! I very much enjoy the food, facilities, music, and atmosphere as well. More than the other clubs, The Palace just feels like home to me." Another client fondly reminisced about The Palace's rotating dancing platform, where he saw "middle-aged men with twenty-something girls in perfect harmony dancing with rhythm and grace."[92] Posters doubted that anyone could get bored in such a place. The sauna clubs also seem well suited for those who seek a "girlfriend experience," given the amount of time one can spend with a provider. One client remarked, "Hanging out with the girls is fun and one of the assets of visiting FKK sauna clubs."[93] At many of these clubs, clients can spend around a half hour of "social time" visiting with a woman before retiring to a room for sex.

Another man, Guava, was concerned about the possibility of pimps and procurers being involved in German saunas:

> This greatly alarms me, for I have always considered that FKK women were generally there voluntarily, and probably most are. My question is: does anyone know of any FKKs to avoid in this regard? . . . A big chunk of the freedom I feel in partaking of the FKK experience is that I imagine it's coercion-free, for the most part, as compared to other venues.[94]

None of those who responded identified an FKK to avoid, and their responses ranged from "you never know" whether some individuals have been coerced to "extremely few women in legal FKKs are enslaved." Guava thanked the others for validating what he already believed to be the case—that FKKs rank low on the coercion scale.

Naturally, there are men who complain about specific experiences—such as a provider who charged double when a client orgasmed twice in 30 minutes; a woman who violated house rules and charged for time spent interacting in the lounge and in the sauna (not just in the private room); and sex workers who renege on agreed-on services, are very conscious of time, and try to get the man to spend a minute over the base half-hour time so that she can charge for the second half hour.[95] It is clear that the women and the clubs vary considerably with respect to work styles—that is, how conversational, aggressive, money focused, GFE oriented, or time conscious they are. Some places are rated less favorably than others on these measures. One customer described the Palace in Frankfurt as "not for rookies": "Lots of sharks among the girls, lots of upselling . . . and don't forget to clock your sessions. Yes, I'm serious. Go, say, 2 minutes over, a lot of girls will try to work you for an extra €50."[96] Clients are advised to wear a watch and keep checking it. Similar cautionary tales are offered by men who have visited other sauna clubs, but problems appear to be more common at some clubs than others:

> The stopwatch thing is more important at Palace than Oase or World; it's a question of what the management will let the girls get away with. . . . I actually boycotted [Palace] for a couple of years because they treat the guys like marks. I don't see that bullshit happening at World or Oase, I really don't. Palace . . . could care less about the punters [clients], and why should they? Whenever the Messe [a nearby convention center] is booked for something, they're jammed solid [with customers] every night. But, there are some wonderful ladies who work Palace too.[97]

The providers have their issues with clients as well. Writing a post titled "How to Be a Good Guest at a FKK," Shiatsu and Cordelia (who worked at FKK World near Giessen) offered this code of conduct for clients:

- Money: a guest who claims not to have money with him "shows a lack of respect." And "don't try to get the girl to undercut the normal club prices or whine for extra time for free."
- Hygiene: the favorite guests are "very clean."
- "Be friendly": say hello to "all girls even if you don't want to go with them."
- "Don't grope the girls in the corridors."
- "Please don't talk about the other girls, your comments will only get back to the girl concerned. . . . The girls hear a lot more than you would ever imagine."
- "Make sure you go with girls who appear to make their guests cheerful and who don't dispose of them in five minutes."
- "Keep your head—try not to be obviously drunk or stoned—it acts like a magnet as girls will try and take advantage of you and relieve you of more money. . . . Not all girls are saints!"[98]

Clients report that the management at most clubs will side with the woman if a man makes a complaint.

There is only one sauna club inside Frankfurt's main RLD. The Miami Sauna Club (shown in figure 5.6) is much smaller and has fewer amenities than the more upscale clubs elsewhere in Frankfurt (Palace, Sudfass) and its suburbs. One night, I spoke to the doorman at Miami. The entry fee is €10 plus one drink (priced €8–€10), and the customer is under no obligation to buy drinks for a woman, but a menu on the door lists a "Lady Cocktail" for €40. The doorman tells me that €50 will buy "a half hour of massage, a blow-job without condom, and sex with condom"—quite inexpensive for all three services. He tries to coax me inside by inviting me to peer through a small window, where I see three topless women beckoning. A client writing online reported that his experience one night involved "7 Romanian girls who all played with our JTs [penises] despite the fact that we did not buy them drinks" and that the woman he selected for sex "failed to deliver the promised DFK [deep French kissing] and BBBJ [bareback blow job, without a con-

Figure 5.6. Miami Sauna Club.

Figure 5.7. Sudfass Sauna Club.

dom]." When he told her that lying about services would not yield repeat customers, she told him that customers rarely returned anyway.[99] Miami has less need to build a regular clientele because of its location in the midst of the tourist-heavy RLD, with high turnover in the client pool.

All other sauna clubs are located outside Frankfurt's two RLDs—in residential areas, suburbs, or small towns surrounding the city. Sudfass is the oldest club in Frankfurt (founded in 1981) and is unique in having both a hotel-brothel in one part of the building (called Amor Eros Center) and a sauna club in another part. The photo in figure 5.7 shows the entry to the hotel-brothel adorned by outsized woman's legs. Sudfass is located in a mixed commercial-residential area.

In another club on the outskirts of Frankfurt, I interviewed the owner and toured the premises.[100] Both the customers and the providers pay a €29 entry fee; the workers do not have contracts and are freelance operators. The women receive a percentage of the alcohol drinks they sell the men, but the owner tells me that they are not constantly soliciting drinks and will leave a man alone if he wishes. Customers come from the greater Frankfurt area and from the small town where the brothel is located. The age of most of the clients is between 40 and 70. Around 10–15 women are working at any given time. They range in age from 25 to 35, and most hail from Romania, Bulgaria, and Hungary. I ask what the owner looks for when he interviews new prospects. He asks them where they come from, what work they have done previously, if they have ever worked at a FKK club before—questions that one would expect in any job interview. He will reject someone who, by appearance, "does not take care of her body," telling me that "sanitation is important at FKK clubs." All of the women I saw in this club were tall, tanned, thin, white, and attractive.

The place is tastefully decorated throughout. I tour the club with the female manager, entering through a small "casino" with slot machines. There are private rooms upstairs for sexual activities, but one can elect to have sex in a public area as well. The owner tells me that one out of ten men have sex publicly. There are eleven women working and a dozen customers at the time, around six p.m. on a Thursday. The women are in various states of undress; most are topless. One is dancing nude on a small stage with a stripper pole, rock music blaring, as two men watch from couches nearby. As one man walks by the stage, the dancer playfully blocks his path with her outstretched leg. Another woman is sitting on a couch chatting with a man; two men are visible in the glass-enclosed sauna; three men are outside by the pool; one woman is lying on a couch by herself, half naked.[101] Most of the men that I see are in the 50–70 range; all are white. The owner tells me that some men come just for the sauna or to swim and bring a book to read. Several of the men are talking to other men, confirming the owner's point that the women do not cling to or pressure the men. In one large room, there is a porn film showing on a large TV screen while a couple is having sex on a couch. They do not appear to notice us.

Unlike the hotel-brothel owner discussed earlier, who had a negative view of the police, this FKK owner has had a different experience. Before he opened the place, he met with local police and asked them what they needed in order to allow him to operate freely. The police said they wanted to view the passports of everyone working at the club, and the owner shows me a binder with photocopies of passports. He tells me that the police visit once or twice a year and that he has had "no problem with them."

One might wonder how a sauna-brothel in a suburb of Frankfurt is regarded by the residents. The owner tells me that "everything is okay with them," that no one in the area has demanded that the club close, and that it is important to talk with the residents to show them that the brothel is a normal business and thus gain their acceptance. He mentions that his next-door neighbor sponsors weddings on his premises, implying that the sacred and profane can coexist within a stone's throw of each other. This owner entered the brothel business because a friend who owned a sauna got him interested in this kind of enterprise, and in my interview he presented himself as an ordinary businessman who has good relations with local people rather than feeling stigmatized and shunned.

A year later, I interviewed the manager at another FKK club in Frankfurt. The manager had friends in the brothel business and knew the owner before he started working in this club's bar, after which he became manager. He tells me he does not feel stigmatized by the nature of his work: "I never hide what I do. It's not just a business, it's what I live. I live my club and can't separate myself from it. In a good way! The people I meet don't condemn me; instead they are interested in what I do."

When I ask what he looks for when interviewing a prospective worker, he says that she must be at least 21 years old (i.e., above the legal minimum of 18), have legal papers to work in Germany, be "visually nice," and be "free of pressure" from any third party. Regarding the latter, he looks to see if someone is waiting for her outside after the interview and says that if he has any suspicions about her independence, he will not hire her. He says, "Ten years experience tells me that I will get much bigger problems if I hire someone who is controlled by someone else." He adds that 70–80 percent of the women have worked at his club for a long time, some for many years: "so we know them very well." Occasionally, a woman misbehaves: if she gets drunk, he sanctions her with a three-week suspension, and if she steals from anyone, she is immediately fired. What about problem clients? The manager tells me that they are rare and that only one case in the past ten years presented a real problem. Perhaps surprisingly, no security personnel work at the club. The manager accounts for the lack of problems from the men as "psychological": the men are vulnerable, walking around in towels or robes and thus stripped of their usual, clothed comfort zone: "That's why we don't have any stress."

At this sauna club, both customers and providers pay a €75 entry fee. The women work as freelancers "when they want and for as long as they want." They speak English along with other languages. On this Saturday night, 60 women are working in the midst of about 100 customers. When I tour the place, I see a lot of men hanging out with other men; others are sitting on couches with a woman, chatting or caressing each other. The men are diverse in age and race, while most of the women are white. They wear lingerie or are fully nude. The place is rather large, with a sauna room, a movie room, a big central room with dance music blaring, a couple of bars, and some peripheral quiet rooms where I see couples nestled on couches. The club also has a therapeutic massage room and a beauty parlor for guests. The place is upscale and tastefully decorated.[102]

My observations, coupled with clients' online descriptions of other clubs, indicate that these places are a rather distinctive kind of commercial sex venue, offering a variety of recreational options in addition to sex. Given the extended amount of time that a man can spend chatting with a woman, sharing intimacies, and perhaps bonding emotionally, the clubs seem tailor-made for men who seek a "girlfriend experience." This depends, of course, on the parties' ability to speak the same language. Providers vary in how fluent they are in German or English, but they would not work in an FKK club if they did not have a minimum of conversational skills. Moreover, like the workers who spend a great deal of time chatting with foreign men in sexually oriented bars and karaoke clubs elsewhere in the world (briefly described in chapter 2), extended conversations with clients (from different backgrounds) in sauna clubs give workers an opportunity to learn other languages and to expand their cultural repertoire, thus broadening their cognitive horizons.

Many sex workers throughout the world work out of their own premises, either by themselves or with a few other providers. In Frankfurt and many other German cities, it is legal for a maximum of three workers to sell sex in a residence, provided that at least one of them lives there and the place is registered in her or his name. I visited one of these worker-run "brothels" in Frankfurt.[103] Heidi, who runs the place, sells sex along with her three colleagues. Almost all clients are German, as are all the providers, and about five clients visit every day. Heidi tells me that appointments are not necessary, as she likes to cater to men who act on the spur of the moment as well as those who plan a visit ahead of time. The entry fee is €50, plus €150 for "straight sex" and €200 for S&M, a specialty of this house. The brothel advertises on a website and in a newspaper. Heidi likes the small scale of the enterprise; more women might create conflicts, she says. The women do not live in the house but sometimes stay overnight if they live outside the area. A customer arrives during the interview, so I am hustled away until the man retires to a room with his chosen provider. Two women are hanging out in the kitchen, and another, wearing only a thong, walks nonchalantly from one room to the next. I then tour the rooms with Heidi—viewing a large S&M dungeon, a room with a Greek theme, and a medically themed room complete with examining bed and medical supplies for men who fantasize about sex with nurses or doctors. Heidi says that the existence of this brothel is no secret to the neighbors, who are tolerant of it because it is discreet. Residential brothels can be found in cities throughout the world, but in Germany, they are legal and can operate quite openly as long as they are small-scale enterprises.

Conclusion

Antwerp and Frankfurt differ substantially in the way their red-light districts are organized and in the kinds of prostitution available elsewhere in each city. What accounts for the differences? First, Germany has, since 2002, a system in which prostitution is decriminalized and de jure legalized. In Belgium, all third-party involvement is illegal yet tolerated and regulated in certain places—de facto legalization, in other words. The legal order allows prostitution to proliferate in many different forms in Frankfurt, whereas it is more contained in Antwerp, which lacks, for example, sauna clubs, other legal brothels, and German-style erotic bars. Second and related to this difference, the authorities in Antwerp consciously designed the RLD in a way that would maximize tight control, after having experienced years of problems with prostitution throughout the city. The police in Frankfurt stage raids on premises periodically, but the sex sector is clearly less confined and controlled than is Antwerp's RLD. This is largely due to the different legal systems operating in each country, which are more constraining in Belgium, as well as each city's local policies on prostitution. Third, the absolute demand for commercial sex appears to be less in Antwerp. Frankfurt is about a third larger in population than Antwerp is, and Frankfurt has about three times more tourists visiting every year. Furthermore, Antwerp's RLD is small and fairly isolated, whereas Frankfurt has two RLDs, one of which is larger and much more varied than Antwerp's, as well as saunas and other brothels elsewhere in the city. This translates into significantly fewer people buying and selling sex and less third-party involvement in Antwerp, which reduces the frequency of problems that come to the attention of the media and the authorities and thus the chances that the sex industry will become politicized and catalyze a public backlash against it. In chapter 6, we turn to our third case: the Netherlands and specifically the city of Amsterdam, whose red-light landscape differs in important respects from those in Antwerp and Frankfurt.

6

Amsterdam

It doesn't even occur to me that prostitution should be illegal.
　　　　　　—Young woman, resident of Amsterdam[1]

The Netherlands has long tolerated prostitution. As far back as 1413, a bylaw of the city of Amsterdam permitted brothels, with the following justification:

> Because whores are necessary in big cities and especially in cities of commerce such as ours—indeed it is far better to have these women than not to have them—and also because the holy church tolerates whores on good grounds, for these reasons the court and sheriff of Amsterdam shall not entirely forbid the keeping of brothels.[2]

During the next 500 years, the tolerance policy was periodically suspended due to scandals, increases in crime, or concerns about prostitutes' welfare, but after some time, the approach typically reverted to some kind of tolerance.[3]

In the 19th century, Amsterdam had several brothels, including some luxurious houses with the following features:

> In the small drawing room gentlemen who did not want to be seen by other guests, were received. When the customer had made his choice, he could then retreat to one of the private rooms on the first floor. The big drawing room was richly decorated with mirrors in heavy gold-plated frames, crystal chandeliers, leather couches and red sofas, marble tables, and a buffet. . . . Here the customers could drink champagne with each other or with the girls, have a conversation, or dance. Often there was a piano and the girls sang. In the meantime, the gentlemen could choose a lady with whom they would go upstairs later that night. The customers often were older married gentlemen, habitués of the establishment. De

Fonteyn on de Nieuwmarkt offered its customers even more divertisse-ment. Besides a pub, a restaurant, and a beautiful ballroom, the brothel had a poolroom on the top floor where during the evening naked girls would play pool. The gentlemen could enjoy this while having a drink and a cigar. The mostly foreign girls [from France] led a sad life in the luxuri-ous brothels. They had no or hardly any personal freedom. . . . . Very sel-dom were they allowed to go in the streets and then only in [the] company of a governess.[4]

Small brothels dotted the alleys in the area that is now today's central red-light district. Women solicited clients on the street and brought them into these brothels. Other prostitutes worked in bars, where they received a per-centage of the drinks that they encouraged patrons to buy and made them-selves available to be taken out to a hotel after paying the bartender a fee—a precursor to the bar system operating in parts of Asia today.

Brothels and third-party involvement were outlawed in the Netherlands in 1911, and street prostitution was prohibited in most areas as well. The law was not strictly enforced, but with brothels now illegal, prostitutes transitioned to bars, massage salons, tobacco shops, and their own homes. In the area that is now the main red-light district, some women began sitting behind curtained windows, fully clothed and using mirrors to see approaching men, who were then alerted with hand signals and window tapping. Over time, the curtains were gradually opened, and soliciting became much less clandestine.[5] Photos at the National Archives show women sitting behind windows in the 1930s and 1940s—hence, the origins of today's much more visible window pros-titution. By the 1950s and 1960s, this red-light area was becoming "an excit-ing but also cozy entertainment district," offering not only sex for pay but also dance halls and other attractions that gave the area "great international fame."[6]

By the 1970s, some cities in the Netherlands had become a haven for pros-titution, and sex entrepreneurs throughout the country enjoyed considerable freedom in running their (technically illegal) businesses. In the early 1990s, some city governments began to regulate prostitution by conducting periodic visits to brothels and windows and even licensing such places—an example of de facto legalization, described in chapter 4 and the current regime in Ant-werp. In the Netherlands, de facto legalization (which also applies to mari-juana) typically originates at the local, municipal level but can also gain accep-tance from the national government when, for instance, the Ministry of Justice certifies a practice in policy documents, including directives to prosecutors regarding when to enforce the law and when not to.[7] The legal grounds for this categorical nonenforcement is the state's power to refrain from prosecution if it is in the public interest to do so. The vice remains unlawful, but enforcement is formally suspended by the government.

In Amsterdam, brothel and window owners in the 1990s were responsible for ensuring that their place did not interfere with public order, that certain amenities were present (e.g., a restroom), and that minors or illegal immigrants were not working on the premises. The police occasionally checked workers and removed those who were ineligible, and a few brothels were forced to close in the mid-1990s because illegal workers were discovered there.[8] However, this nascent monitoring system was much more limited than it is today. As Amsterdam's official adviser on prostitution policy stated in 1992, "As long as they obey the regulations and do not employ minors, the municipality will leave them alone."[9] And most of the limited oversight that did take place was directed at window prostitution in red-light districts, rather than at brothels or other venues outside those districts.[10]

This fairly minimalist approach was problematic: (1) it gave the authorities little opportunity to distinguish good from bad owners since all of them were technically operating illegally; (2) monitoring was sporadic and selective;[11] and (3) officials had no legal leverage to force owners to improve working conditions. It also created insecurity among proprietors, who feared that their tolerated venues could be closed at any time. As the director of a brothel owners' association told me in 1997, "These days you have to invest a lot of money when you have a club. It's a big investment, and you need security. And when we are illegal, tomorrow the community can come and say, 'Close this place. It's not [legally] allowed.' Finished."[12] A desire for stability and security explains why the brothel owners themselves pushed for legalization at this time.

The sex industry grew from the 1970s through the 1990s, becoming "so complex that its regulation badly needed more precise instruments, but existing laws had very little to offer."[13] This period also witnessed growing involvement of organized crime in Amsterdam's main red-light district, which took the form of illegal drug operations, protection rackets, and control over who could own real estate (cafes, hotels, gambling arcades) in the area.[14] A government investigation of organized crime in 1996 led to efforts to clean up the RLD, which, in turn, generated proposals for formally regulating prostitution.

A public opinion poll in 1997 reported that 73 percent of Dutch citizens favored the legalization of prostitution, and 74 percent regarded prostitution as an acceptable job.[15] Two years later, 78 percent of the population agreed with the idea that "prostitution is a job like any other, as long as there is no coercion involved."[16] The World Values Survey shows that the Netherlands is more tolerant of prostitution than are other European nations (except Switzerland) and that this tolerant attitude has not changed in recent years: in the 1990 and 2005 surveys, only 20 percent of Dutch citizens felt that prostitution can "never be justified"; by contrast, more than twice as many French respondents hold the "never justified" opinion—46 percent in 1990 and 41 percent in 2005—and Italians and Poles are even less tolerant, with 58 percent in each country selecting "never justified" in the 2005 poll.[17] Widespread Dutch tolerance and a decade of debate on new legislation in the 1990s (during which the idea of law reform gained credibility) created a favorable climate for legalization and culminated in landmark legislation amending the penal code in 2000. All the secular parties voted in favor of the bill, while the religious parties opposed it.

Importantly, there were no influential interest groups in the Netherlands opposing legalization in the late 1990s, and the dominant discourse portrayed prostitution as work rather than domination.[18] The legislation of 2000 recognized sex workers as service providers and sought to make sex work more transparent and manageable. In defending the bill, the Minister of Justice stated, "Prostitution has existed for a long time and will continue to do so. . . . Prohibition is not the way to proceed. . . . One should allow for voluntary prostitution. The authorities can then regulate prostitution, [and] it can become healthy, safe, transparent, and cleansed from criminal side-effects."[19] The 2000 legislation removed the ban on third-party involvement (e.g., running a brothel), provided for the formal licensing of sex businesses, designated prostitution as labor (subject, in theory, to labor law and employee rights), distinguished "forced" from "voluntary" prostitution, and generally sought to empower prostitutes. Other provisions include the following:

- It is a criminal offense to engage in any type of coercion, including threats and deception, in recruitment or in work requirements. Those who force an adult into prostitution or profit from a coerced adult's prostitution face a maximum of six years in prison.
- Minors (under age 18) are ineligible. Minors who are caught are not subject to arrest and punishment but instead are assisted to leave prostitution. Anyone who induces a minor into prostitution or profits from the prostitution of a minor may receive up to six years in prison (if the minor is under 16, the sanction increases to ten years incarceration).
- Clients of prostitutes under age 18 are liable to punishment (clients of individuals under 16 were already punishable under the penal code).

In addition to these statutory provisions, the federal government has attempted to create some uniformity across the country with published guidelines that recommend a particular kind of licensing system, a code of conduct for the police and other local authorities, procedures for identifying and assisting trafficked workers, and methods for conducting background checks on owners and managers.[20]

Citizens of European Union (EU) countries are allowed to work in member nations, and this applies to sex work where it is legal. A non-EU citizen working in the Netherlands is treated as an illegal immigrant, and brothel owners risk losing their license if they employ such persons. Facing risk of deportation, illegal immigrants who wish to sell sex in the Netherlands have no recourse but to engage in illegal and riskier work in underground establishments or as independent operators.

Aside from these general norms and guidelines, the 2000 law delegated to local governments most of the responsibility for devising and enforcing regulations. A municipality cannot prohibit individuals from selling sex, nor can it outlaw prostitution businesses on moral grounds, but it can limit them for pragmatic reasons. All large municipalities (over 100,000 residents) now have licensed prostitution venues, but smaller jurisdictions differ (in 2006, 31 percent of municipalities with less that 40,000 residents had at least one licensed sex establishment, but many small towns have no such businesses).[21] To prevent the expansion of the sex industry, most cities cap the number of such establishments.[22]

Types of Prostitution

As in many other countries, street prostitution in the Netherlands was long associated with drug abuse, violence, and risky sexual practices. In order to address these problems, designated tolerance zones were created in the mid-1980s, called *Tippelzones* (strolling zones). These areas were usually located away from residential neighborhoods, and Amsterdam's was on the outskirts of the city. The *Tippelzones* were intended to serve as a safe area for those who wanted to work outdoors, and each contained a kiosk offering food and drink, condoms, medical advice, a restroom with showers, and couches for relaxation. Upstairs, police or care workers could observe activities in the zone unobtrusively.[23] In cities with a *Tippelzone*, street prostitution outside the zone was a misdemeanor offense and was subject to intensified enforcement once a *Tippelzone* had been created.[24] Without such enforcement, most *Tippelzones* would have attracted few workers due to their remoteness from the central city.

From the beginning, a large proportion of the zone prostitutes were illegal immigrants from other countries.[25] Typically younger and healthier than the local, drug-addicted women working in the zones, the foreigners were a competitive threat to the locals. Illegal workers were periodically arrested and deported to their home countries, largely Romania, Bulgaria, and Albania. Over time, the zones became overcrowded (resulting in lower prices) and increasingly populated by foreign workers; approximately 300 worked in Amsterdam's *Tippelzone*.[26] With growing media attention to these problems, *Tippelzones* were closed in Amsterdam, Rotterdam, and The Hague, though they remain in Utrecht, Eindhoven, and Arnhem. As an evaluation of the zones concluded, "The success of the *Tippelzone* appears to have been its downfall, as the number of prostitutes using the zone increased exponentially and the zone could no longer be controlled."[27] Closure of Amsterdam's zone has not increased the number of street workers elsewhere in the city, which remain few in number.

Apart from the remaining *Tippelzones*, prostitution exists primarily in window rooms, brothels, clubs, hotels, and private residences. The Netherlands does not have German-style hotel-brothels and has only a few FKK-style sauna clubs (near the border with Germany), and bar prostitution is not as blatant or abundant as in Germany. Also unlike Germany, the Netherlands has a significant window-prostitution sector. Compared to other sectors, window prostitution in the Netherlands offers the greatest safety to workers, the best working conditions, and the highest income.[28] Window prostitution accounts for approximately 20 percent of the Dutch sex trade; the remainder work in brothels (25 percent) and as escorts and at home (50 percent), with only 1 percent in street prostitution.[29] There are no reliable national figures on the number of individuals working in each sector, but a 2010 survey of Amsterdam reported the following: 686 individuals working in brothels; 1,408 escorts working either independently or for an agency; 1,680 working out of their own residence; 40–45 working on the street; and a daily minimum of 570 working in window units (the number exceeding the minimum fluctuates during the year).[30] Other prostitutes work in massage parlors, bars, or other venues. The study found that there was fairly little mobility from one sector to another, but workers did move from city to city to tap into new markets.

Window prostitution is the most visible form of sex for sale and attracts the most attention from the authorities. About a dozen Dutch cities have window prostitution, and each red-light landscape differs from the others. Amsterdam's main RLD is unique because it is large, centrally located, and multipurpose. In other Dutch cities the RLDs are outside the historic city center, relatively pristine, constitute a monoculture (not nestled among other businesses), and the adjacent streets are largely residential. Almost all of the RLDs are open access; the lack of screening or entry fees allows anyone to enter these zones. Exceptions include Haarlem and Leeuwarden, where some of the houses have a turnstile and require a small fee to enter. The Hague has the largest number of window units in the Netherlands: its two window districts are outside the city center, with few shops or cafes nearby. Alkmaar's windows line a quiet cobblestone street, whereas Eindhoven has a distinctive courtyard enclave where the windowed buildings face each other. Utrecht has one window zone and a unique district where women work on canal boats. Haarlem's small window area is right next to a church several blocks from the town's central square. None of these tranquil red-light districts comes anywhere close to the circus atmosphere of Amsterdam's large RLD. In the smaller, more conservative towns, the RLD is usually situated away from the historic city center in order to keep vice out of public view. The second-largest city, Rotterdam, has no window prostitution; community groups succeeded in closing the city's window zone three decades ago.

There are both legal and illegal *workers* in the Netherlands and legal and illegal *businesses*. Workers are legal if they are Dutch citizens or come from a nation in the EU and have both a residence permit and a work permit. Only one-third of the prostitutes working in the Netherlands are Dutch, but many others are legal because of their EU status or by virtue of marriage to a Dutch citizen. Today, most foreign workers come from eastern Europe and Latin America,[31] and most eastern Europeans are Bulgarian, Hungarian, and Romanian (work permits were first made available to citizens of Hungary in 2004 and Bulgaria and Romania in 2007, the dates these nations entered the EU).

Since 2000, the emphasis has been on regulating and controlling *businesses* to a greater extent than controlling individual workers. Businesses are legal if they have been licensed by the government, which requires that they conform to certain rules regarding security (e.g., alarm systems), fire safety, building codes, and hygiene. Background checks are conducted on business owners who apply for a license, and the authorities conduct periodic site visits to determine if minors or illegal immigrants are present. Proprietors are not always in compliance with the regulations. A 2006 assessment found that one-third of all licensed sex businesses had been accused of some kind of violation and received a sanction in the past five years, mostly for employing workers lacking a valid work permit.[32] Most of the sanctions consisted of warnings; 13 percent of the places were temporarily closed and 7 percent had their licenses revoked.[33] The conventional wisdom is that abuses are much more common in illegal businesses. The illegal sector consists of unlicensed brothels, escort operations, and other underground enterprises.

Developments since Legalization

Chapter 4 noted that the process of normalizing vice can be precarious. Decriminalization can generate a popular backlash, legislation that dilutes the original law reform, or even full recriminalization if, say, an abolition-ist political party gains power. Problems with implementation of the law may attract critical or sensationalized media attention and lead to calls for a return to the previous system. In addition, the vice participants themselves may resist at least some of the regulations in a newly legal system. Work-ers may, for instance, refuse to pay taxes or register with the authorities, and business owners may fight new fees and specific, disliked regulations. What has been the Dutch experience over a decade of legal prostitution?

National Trends

Implementation of the law has been anything but smooth. The pre-2000 system of de facto regulation included informal monitoring of brothels: municipal authorities imposed some conditions on brothel owners, even though there was no formal legal basis for this arrangement.[34] Some of the more sweeping regulations imposed since 2000 have generated opposition from actors in the prostitution sector. Policy analyst Hendrik Wagenaar refers to a "large, entrenched, well-organized, and well-capitalized prosti-tution sector" as "a powerful adversary" to government authorities seeking to impose new restrictions.[35] (The organizations include the Consortium of Window Owners and two brothel-owners' associations, the Excellent Group and the Association of Operators of Relaxation Businesses.) This sector was "accustomed to managing its own affairs" and was "unwilling to give up the prerogatives and power" that they had enjoyed for years operating in a minimally regulated system. Wagenaar describes this con-text as follows: "In implementing the legalization of sex establishments, a fragmented, rivalrous police and municipal apparatus faced a powerful and highly distrustful adversary that, after decades of operating outside the legal order, was unwilling to give up its lucrative practices."[36] The loose, informal regulatory system, coupled with the power of the sex industry prior to 2000, is an important backdrop to the current system and distinguishes the Netherlands from settings where no preexisting regulations existed prior to formal legalization. However, recent years have seen a shift in the balance of power between the state and the sex industry, with the state increasingly dictating policies and the industry forced into a more subordinate, reactive role but continuing to voice opposition to new government proposals.

The same trend, of expanding government control, can be seen in the state's relations with sex workers and their advocates. Prior to 2000, the government sponsored some supportive initiatives for workers, for example, funding the prostitutes' rights organization Rode Draad (Red Thread) and a firm that conducted both research and advocacy related to sex workers' interests, the de Graaf Foundation. In a 1997 interview, the director of Red Thread, Sietske Altink, told me that the organization enjoyed a fairly collaborative relationship with the government, working with it on a variety of issues related to prostitution. Altink quipped, "We are important for them to correct their policies!"[37] Both organizations lost government funding after 2000, and the de Graaf Foundation closed. This does not mean that the interests of sex workers have been entirely jettisoned in recent years, but it does illustrate a growing state ascendancy in policymaking. The government does subsidize a rescue-oriented group, Scharlaken Koord (Scarlet Cord), which works to help women leave the sex industry, but it no longer actively supports sex workers' organizations.

Extensive field research sponsored by the Dutch government found that the legal prostitution sector has been declining over time, but it is nevertheless "much more sizeable" than the illegal sector.[38] Moreover, illegal actors are scarce in legal venues: in windows, sex clubs, and private brothels, illegal labor has been virtually eliminated due to inspections.[39] While the aggregate number of legal *workers* is reportedly higher than that of illegals, there has been a decrease in the number of legal sex *businesses* since legalization in 2000. The number of licensed sex clubs, brothels, and escort agencies fell 17 percent from 2000 to 2006 (from about 1,325 to 1,270), declining further to approximately 1,150 in 2009.[40] The number of window prostitution units has declined as well.

The diminishing number of legal businesses can be attributed to a combination of factors: (1) the costs involved in abiding by myriad regulations, (2) the aging-out of existing owners, who are not being replaced because younger individuals lack the capital to buy a place or balk at the lengthy review process in some cities, and (3) policies in some municipalities designed to reduce the number of venues by buying out some owners and forcing some others out after doing an integrity investigation.[41] I explore these dynamics later in the chapter.

Part of the impetus for legislative changes at the national level comes from the small Christian Union Party, which was part of the coalition government from 2006 to 2010. This orthodox Protestant party stands opposed to prostitution and other signs of Dutch "permissiveness" but could not dictate changes within a coalition government. Instead, it worked to convince some of the secular parties that there was a need for intensified regulation of the sex sector. In the June 2010 election, two right-wing parties (the conservative People's Party and the far-right Party for Freedom) won a huge increase in seats in Parliament, while the moderate and previously dominant Christian Democratic Party and left-wing Labor Party lost seats. This political realignment may lead to further restrictions on the sex industry in coming years.

The 2000 law delegated much of the authority for regulating prostitution to municipalities, resulting in considerable variation across jurisdictions. This decentralized model is now recognized as a problem, in that geographical differences can lead to "disparate opportunities for supervision and enforcement, which exploitative operators and human traffickers can take advantage of," according to the government's trafficking office.[42] Recent legislation is designed to introduce some minimum standards to be followed by all municipalities that permit prostitution.

These changes include, first, a mandatory licensing requirement for every establishment where commercial sex takes place and a requirement that all legal prostitution be "location bound."[43] This is a response to mobile providers who work independently and arrange liaisons via the phone or Internet, unfettered freelance work that the government defines as a problem. A Ministry of Justice official said that independents are a "big loophole" in the current law, "a black hole where everything will fall into because people will say they work alone," even if they do not, and will be left unregulated if not tied to some business.[44] If independent escorts are deemed a problem, so are those escort agencies that are currently unlicensed:

> The escort industry is particularly difficult to get a grip on, as it is not clearly organized geographically and thus falls outside the municipal sphere of enforcement. . . . Advertising and communication using websites and mobile telephone numbers have made it easier to work outside regular businesses, where it is certainly not the case that women are always independent and can decide what to do with their bodies.[45]

The police periodically check on individual escorts by arranging a hotel date where an officer posing as a client inquires about the escort's age, residential status, and ties to third parties. However, this is not considered an efficient means of control,[46] and recent legislation requires licensing of escort services, which must also have a physical location and landline telephone number. According to the government, these tools are needed to ensure that independent workers are not being exploited, coerced, or trafficked.

Second, a 2011 bill would raise the minimum age for sex workers from 18 to 21 and would require prostitutes to be registered and to carry an identification card that clients could check before buying sex. The bill is intended to reduce forced prostitution and trafficking. Prostitutes caught without a card would face a fine up to €380, and clients who visit a prostitute who does not have a card would be liable to a maximum fine of €7,600 or six months in jail.[47] This requirement has been controversial and was derided in Parliament by several political parties. Most workers will not register due to fear of losing their anonymity and concern that it would adversely affect their future employability outside the sex industry. Moreover, the very idea of registration as a tool for fighting coerced prostitution is problematic, given how difficult it is to assess a worker's circumstances at a brief registration interview. At the time of writing, the bill had not yet passed, but the requirement of carrying registration cards had been dropped due to intense lobbying against it.

The leading brothel owners' association is skeptical of the proposal to prosecute clients who patronize illegal workers. The former head of the association told me that this "won't work" because it will not be enforceable, but he also thought that the requirement would have some symbolic benefit: "It's just a signal, a good sign to the clients that they have their own responsibility" to seek out legal workers.[48] In general, the brothel owners' association wants to see greater transparency throughout the sex industry, including licensing of all businesses,[49] but it opposes registration of the sex workers themselves. The association's leaders describe registration as "ridiculous" and unnecessary because, since 2009, workers in the legal sector have been registering their self-employment status with the Chamber of Commerce for tax purposes, just like any other entrepreneurs. There is thus "no need at all for a separate registration as prostitutes; the government can't give a *reason* for this registration but feel they have to do it simply because it is *prostitution*."[50] And the current head of the brothel association believes that the registration requirement will affect some workers more than others:

The main reason for the new law is actually the escort agencies, because brothels are running okay, have their licenses, and can be found [by the authorities]. But the escort sector is footloose. You only need a telephone and a girl, and if you don't like it in one place, you move to another. Registration will affect my company [an agency whose escorts are Dutch exclusively] more than companies that hire foreign girls, because the foreign girls are less bothered by having to register. They don't have their social circles here; their friends and family are far away. But an agency with Dutch women, who want to do other careers in the future, it's going to scare them. They are afraid to loose their privacy. My girls are very concerned; some say they are going to quit and some will work illegally on their own if they have to register.[51]

The owners' association also opposes raising the minimum age to 21, for the same reason: it will push those who are 18–20 into the illegal sector.

The brothel owners have consistently opposed creation of an employer-employee relationship in their own establishments, favoring instead "independent contractor" status for their workers, which allows the owners to avoid paying benefits to the workers. Window owners consider themselves landlords who simply rent rooms, yet they are involved in both screening and monitoring those who rent windows. When a prospective renter approaches one of the window owners I interviewed, he looks for signs that she uses drugs or is connected to some third party. He will not hire a woman who uses drugs, which has happened only a few times in his 20 years as a landlord. And, he says, "If a new girl comes [to the interview] with a guy, I don't talk to her, and if a guy calls and says he has a girl, I don't speak to him." Most of the time, it is the woman's girlfriends (who are already working in a window) who introduce her to an owner. In addition to screening applicants, he ensures that the women who rent from him comply with legal regulations. He also video-monitors the men outside his windows.[52] He has 14 women working different shifts at his six windows. Other window owners engage in the same kind of screening and monitoring.

While window owners are minimally involved with the sex workers who rent from them, brothel and escort owners *do* treat their workers as employees to some extent: they impose rules regarding attire, demeanor, working hours, and so on. This means that those who work in brothels under a manager are not fully "independent" contractors, though the owners insist to the contrary. A survey of 40 owners describes the situation:

Operators are keen to stress the contractual or servicing nature of their relationship with the prostitutes, with no superior-subordinate relationship. They present themselves as people who rent out rooms and supply facilities. Sometimes agreements are set down on paper, but often they are not, as operators assume that anything set down in writing could be used against them in official arguments about their being employers. The need to present a uniform impression to potential customers, a suitable image of the business, and for the prostitutes to conduct themselves accordingly is translated into house rules, recommended prices, recommendations on dress, etc. In practice these rules are often not as voluntary as is suggested: women who do not abide by them are excluded. Many of them accept this situation, partly because they see it as part and parcel of working in the industry, partly because it provides a certain amount of protection: the operator helps to resolve quarrels with customers, for instance, and sees to it that they are accompanied in unsafe social situations. Operators regard it as wrong and unfair that the tax authorities and the UWV [workers' insurance agency] can interpret such support as indicating that they are employers.[53]

As a prominent brothel owner told me, "The tax people say we should employ them, but the health costs are high. So we prefer they stay independent workers, and the tax people allowed this—an 'opting in' to the new system."[54] In a 2006 survey of 354 prostitutes, the majority admitted that they did not pay income taxes; but since 2009 almost all of those working in licensed brothels and escort agencies have been paying their taxes in full.[55]

A 2006 survey of 49 sex proprietors found that they "have the impression that the authorities have a negative image of the industry, are putting pressure on legal businesses (licenses, fees, arguments about regular employment), and are doing hardly anything to deal with illegal prostitution."[56] It is true that officials have focused most of their attention on the legal establishments, where access is easy, compared to the clandestine, illegal operations. When I suggested to one brothel owner that perhaps the problem is the hidden nature of the illegal establishments, he responded, "The police *can* find the illegals, if you give them more authority and power. Police don't get sufficient resources, so that's why they only check the legal ones."[57] Another explanation is that the number of illegal brothels or escort agencies is much less than what some have claimed. Statements by some government officials and brothel owners that the majority of all prostitution takes place in unlicensed brothels and other venues have not been substantiated, and some experts think these claims are greatly exaggerated.

Tensions between legal and illegal sectors have arisen in other societies as well—for example, in New South Wales, Australia, where legal owners have been in the forefront in encouraging city councils to crack down on illegal brothels[58]—but such friction is not inevitable. In New Zealand, a two-tier system of legal and illegal prostitution has not developed since decriminalization in 2003.[59]

Local Trends: Expanding Control

In Amsterdam, there has been a decline in the number of legal sex businesses in recent years, a result of a larger campaign to "clean up" the city, including reducing the number of bars, casinos, and marijuana cafes. Some elites have grown increasingly concerned that the city has become a vice mecca, as a city councilor complained: "Amsterdam has a reputation that you can do everything here. That's not the way I want people to look at Amsterdam."[60] A 2007 poll of Amsterdam residents found that two-thirds (68 percent) agreed with a policy of reducing the city's image as a place where deviant behavior is tolerated, and 78 percent felt that the city should actively fight criminal involvement in the prostitution sector (surprisingly, 22 percent opposed this).[61] In the past few years, some politicians have called for the elimination of *all* prostitution. What has happened instead is gradual curtailment.

The recent downsizing of the main red-light district has roots that go back to 1996, when a parliamentary commission released a report that concluded that Amsterdam had become a major center for organized crime.[62] The following year, the Amsterdam city council appointed a manager of the RLD to coordinate efforts against organized crime, with the help of the police and tax authorities, by closing suspected businesses, withdrawing licenses, and initiating criminal investigations (the manager's team is now called the Van Traa Project). Under a law passed in 2003 (the Public Administration Probity in Decision-Making Act, known as BIBOB), local authorities are empowered to withhold or revoke a permit for any business (e.g., bar, hotel, marijuana cafe, casino, brothel, escort agency) if the owner is suspected of criminal wrongdoing or cannot prove that his or her finances are legitimate. The burden of proof is on the owner or prospective buyer. Since BIBOB is an administrative mechanism, not criminal law, the authorities do not have to prove that unlawful activity has occurred and can act on *suspicion* alone in refusing or revoking a permit.[63]

The majority of municipalities had not made use of BIBOB as of 2007;[64] it is largely an issue in Amsterdam. Still, a total of 376 businesses nationwide lost their license between 2003 and November 2009, a number that includes both sexually oriented and other businesses.[65] Amsterdam has seen the closure in recent years of a few brothels and several window units, leaving about 400 windows today. The shuttered windows and brothels were then sold to entrepreneurs not involved in the adult sector, thus reducing the number of such places.

If the RLD is further downsized, reducing legal options, it will displace prostitution to other parts of Amsterdam, to other cities, or into the illegal sector. There appears to be another counterproductive outcome of the crackdown: a reduction in small-scale operators who own a few windows and the ascendancy of large-scale operators, who buy out the small owners. Since the implementation of BIBOB and the work of the Van Traa Project, "many small brothel-owners have sold their windows to a few large players, who now own almost all brothels in the area."[66] This trend toward monopolization constricts workers' options in relocating to a brothel or window unit with a different owner (e.g., one with a good reputation) or their ability to rent at an affordable price. In fact, over the past few years, window owners have steadily increased their rental prices.

In Amsterdam, the Labor Party dominates local politics and has been in the vanguard of a crackdown on the sex industry for the past five years. Prominent politicians have claimed that some brothel and window owners are involved in money laundering, other organized crime, or trafficking of illegal migrants, and three politicians have been in the forefront of an effort to "clean up" the city's main RLD: the mayor (Job Cohen), an alderman (Lodewijk Asscher), and a city councilor (Karina Schaapman). A former sex worker turned staunch prohibitionist, Schaapman wrote a position paper on prostitution in 2005 that was based on the oppression paradigm and treated all prostitution as forced. The paper called for tighter restrictions on businesses and for raising the minimum age for sex work from 18 to 21. Her report, lobbying, and media appearances had a major influence on the views of other city councilors and helped set the stage for a crackdown, which has also been fueled by sensationalized media coverage of isolated incidents involving pimps and organized crime.[67] Alderman Asscher has stoked the fire repeatedly—calling business owners "pimps" on television, advocating raising the minimum age to 23, closing windows between four and eight a.m., mandating psychological screening of sex workers, and claiming that trafficking is a big problem in Amsterdam. The rationale for raising the minimum age is that young workers are viewed as more vulnerable to pimps, abusive clients, and traffickers, and older workers are viewed as better able to screen clients. Regarding the closing of windows for four hours in the early morning, Asscher stated, "Only the biggest creeps and boozers are walking around at those hours. Women really dread working then."[68] (The prostitutes' rights group Red Thread opposed this idea as well as raising the minimum age to 23 because it would have the effect of driving those under 23 underground.)[69] Proposals in Parliament to raise the minimum age have been opposed by Red Thread as well as the brothel and window owners' associations.

City leaders frequently try to link prostitution, pimping, and organized crime—usually citing anecdotal evidence involving a single operation and generalizing to larger patterns. Mayor Cohen declared in 2008,

> We've realized this is no longer about small-scale entrepreneurs, but that big crime organizations are involved here in trafficking women, drugs, killings, and other criminal activities. We're not banning prostitution, but we are cutting back on the whole circuit: the gambling halls, the pimps, the money laundering.[70]

Cohen's views are based in part on Schaapman's claims that pimps are ubiquitous and that many workers have been trafficked, mistakenly equating trafficking with the number of foreign workers in the Netherlands. Mayor Cohen claims,

> In the last few years we have also seen a lot of women-trafficking and women forced to be prostitutes against their will, and therefore we want to have more control. If there is control, there is transparency. . . . It is not that we want to get rid of our red-light district. We want to reduce it. Things have become unbalanced and if we do not act we will never regain control. At the heart of this project is our desire to drive back criminality and make the city welcoming for everyone.[71]

Some window workers have indeed been forced into prostitution, with one-tenth saying they have in a recent survey of 94 workers.[72] Pimping is also a problem, though its scope is a matter of debate. In 2007, the prostitutes' rights organization Red Thread launched a campaign against pimping by affixing stickers to windows that declared "Pimpfree Zone" and "Pimping Is Forbidden in the Netherlands," in an attempt to send a message to the pimps who loiter in the red-light district. If the effort does little to deter pimps, it is hoped that it helps to empower the women. Another recent initiative is the city government's attempt to tap clients for information about possible abuses of sex workers. The city created a panel of clients from three client-centered websites, where they are occasionally surveyed and can report signs (e.g., bruises, fear) that a particular sex worker might be in a problematic situation.

The extent to which organized crime is involved in the sex sector is debatable. In the full glare of the media, a single reported case can leave the impression that organized crime is more deeply embedded than it is. For instance, the most luxurious brothel in Amsterdam, the Yab Yum Club, was closed after the authorities determined that it had been taken over by the Hell's Angels. The former owner had been extorted by the Hell's Angels to give them ownership, while his name remained on the deeds.[73] The club's license was revoked in 2008, attracting great media attention. Yet, organized crime's role in the sex trade is less than what is claimed by antiprostitution forces. According to an official at the Ministry of Justice whom I interviewed, most organized crime is small scale, such as two or three pimps working together, and rarely involves large organized syndicates.[74] Most of the large-scale organized crime in the Netherlands is in the drug trade, not prostitution.[75] The director of the Prostitution Information Center in Amsterdam thinks the government's crackdown on proprietors is misplaced: "The government are trying to get rid of criminal organizations, but they have picked on the wrong people. They really have to do something about the pimps, and a pimp is never an owner of a brothel."[76] As for organized crime's involvement in sex trafficking, a government evaluation concluded that "it is likely trafficking in human beings has become more difficult, because the enforcement of the regulations has increased" since 2000.[77] An independent report to the European Parliament concurs.[78] And the government's trafficking office adds that "curtailing the licensed sector is . . . an ineffective way of preventing human trafficking and abuses, since it could cause a shift to illegal forms of prostitution, which are more difficult to monitor and regulate through policy."[79]

The high visibility of window prostitution may explain why the authorities are so concerned with the red-light district (i.e., the "image" it gives the city). What happens in such a central, visible location is easily magnified by those who are concerned about what they see as the proliferation of vice in the area—marijuana cafes, bars, porn shops, casinos, live sex shows, prostitution. (A single-use prostitution-only RLD, such as Antwerp's, is less vulnerable to charges that vice is "out of control.") Yet window prostitution accounts for only one-fifth of prostitution in Amsterdam, and the accessibility of window workers to oversight from the authorities might be grounds for expanding the number of window units rather than reducing them.

Under BIBOB, anyone who wishes to buy a window unit is subjected to an integrity evaluation by the authorities. Suspicion that the interested party is now or *might* in the future become involved in crime is sufficient to deny the application. This is a recipe for capricious action on the part of the authorities. A government assessment cites Amsterdam business owners' widespread frustration with BIBOB and a troubling lack of transparency in officials' decision-making.[80] And an analysis of the conditions under which owners now operate concluded, "In some municipalities the brothel owners encounter so many strict and unreasonable regulations [and associated costs] that it is difficult to operate legally."[81] In separate interviews, two brothel owners complained to me about the authorities' zero-tolerance approach: "Bad things are happening in illegal brothels, but if one small thing happens in my place [a legal brothel], I am closed."[82] Some owners have taken the city to court to challenge such actions, winning almost all cases in which the authorities relied on simple "suspicion" to revoke a license.

A related problem is the refusal of banks to lend money to owners of sex agencies, because, the banks claim, it is difficult to determine if the business is financially clean. Bank officials also say that American banks will not work with them if they loan money to people in the sex industry. This forces owners to seek other sources of capital, which in turn raises questions about whether the money is "dirty." An aggrieved brothel owner informed me that, despite decriminalization, the "banks still criminalize us" owners: "They say I can't get a credit card because I'm in the adult entertainment industry. Yet I've been a bank customer for 29 years! Since it's a legal business, we should be treated with respect."[83] When the head of one of the brothel owners' associations asked the Ministry of Justice to intervene when banks refuse to conduct business with sex entrepreneurs, the ministry responded that it had no power to do so.[84] To fix this problem, one Amsterdam politician recently proposed that a special bank be established to make loans to sex operators; he discussed the idea with the Dutch Association of Banks, but this has yet to happen.[85]

Neither the brothel nor window owners' associations want to return to the pre-2000 situation of illegal-but-tolerated sex work. A 2006 survey of 49 owners reported, "The majority of operators (84%) regarded the [2000] change in the law as positive. . . . The operators consider it a good thing for the authorities to intervene in the industry, but do not agree on how."[86] The police have a better reputation among window and brothel owners than do some other government officials. An officer in the window owners' association told me in 1998, prior to legalization, that the police see owners "as criminals" and that this was the main concern of other window owners.[87] Now, there has been a sea change, according to the same owner reinterviewed a decade later: "The police are our best friend at the moment; we work together with the police. They are happy with us because we take care of things."[88] Another window owner distinguished the police from another monitoring agency, the prostitution control unit of the municipal government that visits businesses to check workers' passports and work permits. This owner has a "good" relationship with the police but is very critical of the prostitution control teams, who are "looking for trouble," give women a "hard time" when checking their passports and working papers, and "treat us like we are criminals." When he has an altercation with the prostitution control squad, this owner calls the police to intervene, which usually resolves the problem.[89] In addition to conducting their own visits to the windows, the police do routine uniformed and plainclothes patrols in the RLD to maintain order, which serves the interests of business owners and sex workers alike. Officers occasionally arrest individuals who are causing a nuisance or disturbance on the streets; this happens two or three times a night. They also question individuals who loiter in the area and are suspected of being pimps.

The operators are not opposed to BIBOB in principle, which they consider useful for eliminating criminal activities. But they are opposed to the way BIBOB has been implemented in Amsterdam, with the local authorities accused of using it capriciously to cleanse the RLD of vice. The head of a brothel owners' association told me, "The biggest problem is how the local authorities *use* the law to fit with their own ideas. Their main goal is how to get them [sex businesses] out, rather than how to regulate them properly."[90] An official in the Consortium of Window Owners feels he is "walking on eggshells," fearing loss of his business license. He stated that "it's not fun doing business here anymore."[91] And a community activist in the RLD, Wim Boef, feels that the area has been unfairly stigmatized by city authorities:

All the business people in the red light district support the BIBOB law, because it's meant to separate the good from the bad. But what's happening now? It looks like Casa Rosso [the city's famous, decades-old live sex show palace] may be shut, purely on the basis of "findings" and rumors. It's a disgrace. Everyone with a business in the 1012 postcode area [the main RLD] is now regarded as a potential criminal. It's scandalous.[92]

These views are echoed by other stakeholders. After the closure of some of the windows, some women working in the RLD complained to city officials that they were being deprived of their livelihood.[93] Some of the political parties in Amsterdam have also opposed the crackdown. The Green Party has questioned why the government is so heavily focused on the red-light districts rather than outlying areas. The party supports license revocation only if owners are guilty of criminal offenses, not for economic "renewal" or cleansing vice from the RLD, which is the goal of the most powerful city leaders. As one Green Party councilor remarked, "The government's only solution is more control, without talking to sex workers and determining whether and where abuse occurs."[94] And owners and their supporters staged a street demonstration in February 2008 protesting the city government's crackdown and erecting signs in the RLD declaring, "Hands Off the Red Light!!! Enough Is Enough." Even some officials have expressed frustration about the government's approach. Two Amsterdam officials who work on prostitution issues told me, "All of the focus is on the red-light district, but the real problems are the ones we cannot see"—that is, the illegal, underground establishments.[95] And an official at the Ministry of Justice advocated a more balanced approach as well: "The legal sector is not overregulated. We need regulations, and it goes downhill fast if you don't check frequently, several times a year. The problem is that the illegal sector is not checked at all. We are trying to get more control over this."[96]

City leaders also proposed closing all of the windows in a small red-light district in the Singel area of Amsterdam, which is not part of the main RLD (Singel is discussed further later in the chapter)—this, despite the fact that local residents were generally tolerant of it and the area is relatively problem-free.[97] In addition, many of the sex workers in the area do not want to relocate to the large, central RLD. The proposal provoked strong debate in the city council and was eventually defeated.

It stands to reason that limiting the number of licenses available or imposing steep fiscal costs on legal operations will (1) inflate prices in the existing operations and/or (2) push some owners into the illegal sector. Both are occurring in Amsterdam. The decline in the number of window units has led owners to increase rental prices for the remaining units or to force workers to rent for longer periods of time, for example, a week instead of a day. At the same time, narrowing the parameters of the legal sector is almost guaranteed to expand the illegal sector, while the remaining legal operators complain that they face unfair competition from illegal businesses due to the expense of conforming to regulations.[98] Some government agencies have warned about this, noting that squeezing the legal operators is "likely to lead to a shift of prostitution to the illegal circuit."[99] "Confronted with unfair competition," the Dutch trafficking office warns, legal operators "may feel tempted to leave the legal circuit."[100] If the government is aware of this risk, it has taken few steps to remedy the situation.

Developments in Amsterdam do not necessarily apply to other Dutch cities. Perceived problems and official remedies are not universal across the country.[101] In fact, in a government-sponsored survey, a "large majority" of municipalities reported that they had seen no negative effects of the 2000 law. Of the negative effects cited by other cities, most were related to escort agencies working without a license or to prostitutes working without valid documents.[102] At the same time, most cities have imposed a freeze on the granting of new licenses; when a sex business closes, the city refuses to license a substitute business, creating a net decline over time. And Amsterdam is not the only city where the authorities have tried to close sex establishments. For example, in Alkmaar in 2009, the authorities attempted to shut all 92 windows using the BIBOB law, accusing the owner of money laundering and claiming that some of the window units had been purchased with ill-gotten money. A court decided in favor of the owner, declaring that the city had not proven its case.[103]

What about the Workers?

One of the main objectives of the 2000 decriminalization law was to improve the "social position" of individual sex workers. Such empowerment meant enhancing workers' position vis-à-vis business owners, managers, and clients (via labor rights) and improving their safety and health. The law appears to have enhanced the safety of workers and reduced coercion in the legal sector,[104] but other improvements have fallen short, according to the government, which reports that "labor relations in the licensed sector have barely changed" and that "business owners hold a solid position of power in relation to the women doing the work."[105]

What about the new restrictions that I outlined in the preceding section? As is so often the case in struggles over prostitution policies, the voices of the workers themselves are either silent or ignored. Officials claim to be acting on behalf of workers' interests without consulting them. I noted earlier that the premier sex workers' organization Red Thread has opposed almost all the recent restrictions on sex work, but it has been marginalized by the government, unlike the routine consultative role enjoyed by comparable organizations in New Zealand. A recent survey of 94 window prostitutes in Amsterdam provides some indication of how they view recent efforts to expand control over sex workers: 93 percent disagreed with the statement that "politicians know the issues of prostitutes"; 95 percent disagreed with the idea that the city's plans for the red-light district are "good for prostitutes"; 88 percent thought the current policies toward prostitution were too repressive; but the workers were more evenly split on the plan to require all sex workers to register with the authorities, with just 53 percent opposing this idea.[106] Recall that most window workers come from other countries, which may explain why some of them are willing to accept registration, given their distance from family and friends back home.

Has the relationship between sex workers and the police changed since 2000? In addition to the prostitution control units mentioned earlier, a special police squad conducts periodic visits to windows and brothels to check workers' identities and legal status and to question them about their working conditions, their motives for selling sex, and their co-workers. Police look for any signs of trafficking or exploitation.

Sex workers are not accustomed to having a cordial or supportive relationship with the police, and developing this rapport has been a major challenge for the prostitution squad, according to its leader.[107] Officers undergo three months of training during which they are taught to humanize those who sell sex, learn how to interview sex workers properly, and are taught how to spot signs of problems (nonverbal cues, bruises).[108] When the unit conducts site visits, it is supposed to operate according to a code of conduct, part of which is reproduced in table 6.1. The code attempts to professionalize contacts between officers and sex workers and to prevent officer misconduct.

I accompanied the squad when it visited window workers in June 2008. After a long conversation with one woman, the head officer told me that the woman was providing information on her pimp and that they were building a case against him by periodically visiting her. As the officers made their rounds to various windows, they conversed with the women in a routine, casual, and friendly manner.

The police have dual roles: both monitoring and assisting individual workers and maintaining order in the RLD. Other institutions in Amsterdam also strive to assist and empower sex workers. I have already mentioned the prostitutes' rights group Red Thread, which conducts outreach with individual women, advocates for sex workers in policy debates, and conducts research on the sex industry. One recent innovation that has helped to empower prostitutes is the creation of government-funded health centers that exclusively serve sex workers. Such centers exist in Amsterdam, Rotterdam, Utrecht, and The Hague. Amsterdam's Prostitution and Health Center 292 is located

TABLE 6.1

Code of Conduct, Dutch Police

- Officers' contacts with owners and managers must remain business-like.
- Officers are sworn to secrecy where private and sensitive information is concerned.
- The registration of visits to brothels and contacts with individuals who work in the sex industry must be clear and easily accessible.
- The members of the teams or units must have received proper training.
- Site visits must be conducted by teams of officers that include female officers.
- During inspections, officers must remain in contact with their colleagues.
- Officers are strongly discouraged from taking refreshments. Drinks must always be paid for.
- Officers must not drink alcohol or accept gifts, services, or promises.
- Officers have a duty to report any corrupt behavior of their colleagues to the team management.
- Officers must be aware that feelings of affection can grow, and they should be prepared to discuss these with the team.
- Officers have a duty to report advances, rumors, or other out-of-the-ordinary developments to the team leader.
- Off-duty officers are not allowed to arrange a meeting with individuals who work in the sex industry.
- Officers are not allowed to pay private visits to a brothel in the region or district where they work.

Source: Condensed "Code of Conduct," Gedragscode, 2008

near the city's main red-light district. Prior to its creation in April 2008, city authorities had less contact with sex workers, but they now have much more contact. The center's main goals are to improve sex workers' health, to enhance their social and legal position, and to empower them to resist exploitation and coercion. Not only does it provide free health care (education, contraception, STD/HIV prevention and tests) but also additional services in order to "improve the life skills and self-sufficiency of sex workers within an emancipatory vision."[109] Staff members assist all workers regardless of immigration status, are versed in six languages, and operate both on-site services and outreach to window and brothel locations a few times per week (one of the window owners allows his place to be used for health exams once a month). Some of the peer educators are former prostitutes, and the center operates with a nonjudgmental approach to prostitution. As the director told me, "We don't judge the women, and we don't distinguish legal and illegal, young or old workers. We always say everything is anonymous, and our health records only contain the individual's mobile phone number," no names or addresses. A brochure states that information is treated with absolute confidentiality by the staff. The director states, "We listen to their stories, but we don't call the police and report anything [apparent victimization] unless we think there is urgency in doing so."[110] If a sex worker states that she is a trafficking victim, the center will contact the police on the woman's behalf. In addition to health services, the center sponsors courses in Dutch (about a dozen women attend the class), as well as classes in computers, self-defense, and bookkeeping. Staff also counsel women in life skills regarding tax issues, housing, legal matters, stress-reduction techniques, and other job opportunities. The center provides separate services to male sex workers. Each week, public health workers see approximately 70 clients, social workers see 15–20 clients, and 45 women attend classes and workshops.[111] According to city council staff who work on prostitution issues, the center serves a major function: "Empowerment is the main, central issue—either while the person is in the profession or when they want to leave it. The center supports women in the profession as long as they want to do the job."[112] What sex workers learn at the center may enhance their ability to deal with clients, business owners, the authorities, and any parasitical third parties.

A different kind of service is offered by Scharlaken Koord (Scarlet Cord), which attempts to help women leave the sex industry. Founded in 1987 as an offshoot of a Christian organization (For the Salvation of the People), Scarlet Cord initially focused on helping women in the red-light district "with practical needs, instead of treating them as outcasts." At the beginning the organization "was not taken seriously" because of its religious pedigree, but over the years it has "gained more respect, because people see that we are in there working with the girls," according to the director. And with the influx in the 1990s of women from eastern Europe who were entangled in various migration networks, the organization shifted its efforts to helping women break free of pimps or leave prostitution entirely. To exit, the women "need to be helped, because there are so many psychological issues that have gone wrong" and because of other barriers to reintegration such as a lack of other work experience. The director of the organization thinks it is "naive to think you can abolish prostitution": "We are realistic knowing that prostitution will continue. We just want to give them the choice [in a context in which] there is hardly any choice. But I feel very sorry for the girls because for the majority we cannot do much, because the cause of the problem is the countries of origin." The latter is a reference to the eastern European nations from which many of the women come, where opportunities for socioeconomic advancement are extremely limited and where third parties are actively involved in recruiting women to work in western Europe.

Volunteers working at Scarlet Cord frequently visit the windows, asking women about their needs and attempting to build a trusting relationship with them. The director told me that her outreach workers usually have no problem gaining access to the women because they have developed a "talent" for communicating with them and showing that they are genuinely interested in their welfare. The organization holds periodic group meetings with prostitutes centered around empowerment and problem solving. In 2010, 95 women left prostitution as a result of Scarlet Cord's efforts. The organization also does prevention work in schools, to deter Dutch girls from entering prostitution.[113]

Having explored the Dutch legal context and trends at both the national and city levels, I now turn to the *sexual landscape* in Amsterdam, with a focus on what sex for sale looks like on the ground and the ways in which this social geography conditions the *experiences* of those who are involved in commercial sex.

Amsterdam's Sexual Landscape

Unlike Germany's hotel-brothels, where visitors view sex workers in their rooms, Dutch brothels and sex clubs are of the more traditional kind, where women introduce themselves to clients in a parlor or bar and later retire to a room. In Amsterdam, these brothels are located outside the traditional, windowed red-light districts. They range from modest "private houses" to luxurious "sex clubs" that offer various recreational activities in their bars and lounges. The brothels described in this section are a sampling of what Amsterdam has to offer.

The Yab Yum Club was the crown jewel until it closed a few years ago. One visitor writing in the World Sex Guide in 1997 described Yab Yum as having "a nice bar where you can look the girls over in a low pressure environment": "You have to request a girl to sit with you, they don't try to hustle you. There were 21 girls in the room that night. . . . The rooms are real nice, with big Jacuzzi tubs, plenty of room for two to have some fun. Hey, what a great place to visit."[114] Another client described the women at this brothel as "totally exquisite young women in tasteful evening gowns." After having sex, he "came downstairs for coffee, cognac, and cultured post-coital conversation": "Needless to say, her face and body were perfect, as were her skills as a lover and hostess. This truly was one of the golden hours of my life."[115]

I visited one upscale brothel in 2008, at the invitation of the owner. Like other high-class establishments, Societe Anonyme has a bar, a lounge, and fancy rooms for sexual encounters and also offers strip shows and lapdances in the lounge. Anonyme's brochure describes its attractions:

> Service to our guests is something Societe Anonyme feels strongly about. At this luxurious men's club in the heart of Amsterdam, you will find a warm and charming welcome and absolute privacy. At the cosy bar and stylish reception room, guests can enjoy the company of educated, sophisticated, and above all very beautiful women. Most of the ladies are local; however they speak various languages fluently. You and your business acquaintances will be treated with the utmost respect and care. . . . The rooms have been designed to evoke special atmospheres. The Hollywood room, the Japanese room, and the Jungle room accentuate just some of the many possibilities to experience complete relaxation at Societe Anonyme.

My observations confirm the physical description of the place, but no women were present when I visited in the middle of the day (it opens at eight p.m.). A client posting an online review several years ago described Anonyme as featuring "lovely friendly girls, easy atmosphere, lots of women, someone for every taste."[116]

Societe Anonyme also runs an escort service staffed by the same women who work in the brothel. It has a small namesake sign on the building and a tasteful exterior (shown in figure 6.1). But the building itself is no match for its competitor, Club Elegance (shown in figure 6.2), with its beautiful, frescoed exterior and status as an official historical site. These two brothels are located in the same neighborhood, Anonyme on a mixed residential-commercial street and Elegance on an entirely residential block. Aside from two small red lanterns on Anonyme's facade, the two buildings show no sign of being brothels.[117]

Figure 6.1. Societe Anonyme.

The interior of one midtier club is shown in figure 6.3. Midrange brothels include Club Mayfair, now closed, which occupied a red brick building in an entirely residential neighborhood, a building indistinguishable from other residences in the area.[118] In another part of the city, the Golden Key occupies a very nice building, lacking any visible indication that it offers sex for sale, whereas, a few blocks away, Ria's Men's Club boldly advertises its sexual orientation with a sign featuring four silhouetted women dancing on polls (figures 6.4 and 6.5). Ria's website states that 50 women are available and that the brothel offers an escort service as well.[119] I spoke with the manager at Ria's one day, and he told me that an hour with a woman costs €200, which includes drinks. Most of the women are from eastern Europe, he said. Ria's and Golden Key are located on Overtoom, a major street in a commercial-residential area, surrounded by well-kept neighborhoods. The two brothels fit into the landscape of other businesses on this street, including restaurants, shops, churches, and a few marijuana cafes.

Figure 6.2. Club Elegance.

Figure 6.3. Brothel interior, bar area (photo courtesy of Andre van Dorst).

Figure 6.4. The Golden Key.

The least expensive brothel, Jan Bik (see figure 6.6), is located on a side street off Haarlemerdijk, a commercial street running through a residential neighborhood. This brothel opened in 1969 and has nine sister clubs in other cities, including Rotterdam, Utrecht, and Haarlem. Jan Bik's website states that the women who work there do so independently and work in a pleasant environment: "You can still taste the informal, homely atmosphere which

Figure 6.5. Ria's Men's Club.

Figure 6.6. Jan Bik.

Club Jan Bik is famous for and experience decent prices." Jan Bik has a bar and lounge area, a whirlpool, and eight rooms. It calls itself "a proper center of love, founded on mutual respect" but also offers "topless handjob quickies between 12:00 and 8:00 pm."[120] When I knocked on the door one day, the receptionist stated that the prices are €50 for a half hour and €75 for an hour, and this includes entry to the place, the room, and "ordinary sex" with a woman (special requests cost extra). For a one-hour visit, the madam takes €30, and the provider receives €45. At any given time, five to ten women are present. This lower-tier brothel is much less expensive than most of the other legal brothels in Amsterdam and is also cheaper than the going rate for window workers (who charge €50 for 15–20 minutes). The low prices suggest that the women find other ways of making money on top of the flat rate—such as selling drinks, additional services, or more time. A client describes the place as follows: "Prices are good, girls not so much. Place is not that nice, but not terrible."[121] A website reviewing the city's brothels states that Jan Bik is "well known as the cheapest sex club in Amsterdam" and that "past visitors usually report [that] the quality of the girls reflects the low prices."[122] Still, some clients report very positive experiences on message boards.[123]

The brothels just described are located outside the city's three windowed red-light districts. I now describe the social organization and atmosphere in the three zones, based on my field observations and other sources.

The Red-Light Districts

A 1995 survey reported that about one-fifth (22 percent) of Dutch men had bought sex from a prostitute at some time (no comparable recent data exist).[124] In addition to these Dutch clients, a substantial proportion of clients in the Netherlands are foreign tourists. In a survey of 94 window workers in Amsterdam, 12 percent stated that most of their clients were tourists, 18 percent said that most were Dutch, and the remaining 70 percent said they serviced both equally.[125] No comparable data exist for other venues, but Dutch clients are more likely to visit brothels and clubs outside the red-light districts. As I indicated in chapter 5, Amsterdam hosts far more tourists (and thus potential sex clients) every year than do Antwerp and Frankfurt—twice as many as the two other cities combined. Coupled with the sheer number of visitors is the fact that Amsterdam's main red-light district is in the heart of the city, whereas Antwerp's and Frankfurt's RLDs are some distance from the city center. This means that far more people encounter Amsterdam's sexual marketplace—visitors who range from those who find the red-light area an amusing tourist attraction to heavy partiers to seekers of titillating "eye candy" or sex. Both the sheer number of people on the streets and the fact that a significant number of them are intoxicated increases the potential for disorderly behavior, altercations with sex workers, and complaints from local residents. These problems make Amsterdam's main RLD more susceptible to adverse media attention and politicization than its red-light counterparts in the two other cities.

Amsterdam has three separate red-light districts: a large one in the city center (the Wallen, with about 300 windows), one in the Singel area (with about 70 windows), and one in Ruysdaelkade near the city's cultural gem, the Rijksmuseum (about 40 windows).[126] The number of window workers exceeds the number of windows because workers typically work for one shift and rotate with one or two others. The most recent census reported that a minimum of 570 window prostitutes were working on any given day and that the number exceeding the minimum fluctuated during the year.[127] The census also found that half the window workers in the Wallen were aged 18–26 and more than half were of eastern European background, especially Hungarian.

Singel's RLD is located in a mixed commercial-residential area, while Ruysdaelkade is largely residential. Both areas cater to local Dutch clients primarily, and most tourists are unaware of them. The downside for workers is the small customer pool compared to the central RLD, which is teeming with people. According to a Ministry of Justice official I interviewed, the two small window areas are not a source of problems.[128] These small RLDs are tranquil spaces. Moreover, their very existence in residential areas and the involvement of Dutch clients suggests that window prostitution is part of the city's local culture and not just a tourist attraction. The Singel area hosts several Dutch providers who are rare in and older (30–50 years of age) than is the norm for the main RLD in the Wallen.

It is useful to describe the three red-light landscapes in some detail, as their structure and ambience influence the views and experiences of local residents, visitors, workers, and clients. Singel's RLD is depicted in figures 6.7a and 6.7b. My fieldnotes describe it as "a well-kept area, not run-down, not seedy."[129] There is graffiti along one street (Nieuwstraat) but otherwise no signs of decay. Window rooms on Nieuwstraat are away from the shops in the area, whereas the few windows on Spuistraat are nestled among residences, snack bars, a few hotels, one marijuana cafe, and some bars. A large church, the Dominicus Kerk founded in 1893, stands just a few feet away from some of the window rooms. There are no other sexually oriented places in the area, aside from a gay sex shop/cinema. About 25 women were working during the days I visited. One afternoon, I spent two hours observing the street scene from a perch in a cafe just a few yards from a row of windows. Nothing eventful was observed, and the atmosphere was placid. People walked by the windows, occasionally stopping to chat with a worker. On a return visit ten months later, in March 2011, I conducted observations from the same location, captured in my fieldnotes:

> There is a steady flow of people walking along the street, on bikes, and some cars passing through. Men carrying briefcases walk by, and a couple with two very young boys stops right in front of one of the occupied window units, to tie the boy's shoes. About one-third of the pedestrians are women. The street scene is very similar to any other mixed commercial-residential area of Amsterdam, with the window women on Spuistraat attracting little attention. Men walk by and look at the workers, but few stop to talk to them. During my three hours of observation of two windows across the street, only one woman got any inquiries from men (four times), and only one man entered her room, emerging 30 minutes later. These two women sit on their stools almost the entire time, talking on the phone, and they make no attempt to "perform" to entice men inside.

I asked the two baristas in the cafe, "What is it like having your shop so close to window prostitution?" They replied, "No problem. We've gotten along fine for ten years, since we've been here. Here, there are many kinds of places—a church, [marijuana] coffee shop, gay cinema, prostitution—and this area is tolerant of such diversity."[130] They seemed surprised by my question, and their answer was rather nonchalant. Clients who contribute to online message boards describe Singel's atmosphere in similar terms. One compared Singel to the larger, main RLD in the city center:

> I've been visiting Singel a lot more recently. I like the relaxed attitude of the girls there. They seem to have fewer restrictions than the girls in the Wallen and time [with a client] never seems to be an issue. I'd also be very surprised if there are any rip-offs there. But it really is hit and miss [as] to who is working, a really mixed bag. Sometimes there are some young and really pretty girls and sometimes quite the opposite.[131]

Another client agrees that Singel is "much more appealing [than the Wallen] for relaxed situations and rip-off free."[132]

Figure 6.7a. Spuistraat, Singel red-light district, window rooms on the left.

Figure 6.7b. Nieuwstraat, Singel red-light district.

Ruysdaelkade's RLD is even smaller than Singel's and is fully residential, as shown in figure 6.8. A few shops border this RLD, but they are not interspersed among the windows as in part of Singel. Like Singel, in Ruysdaelkade, I observed no one loitering, no disorderly people, and none of the festive and sometimes raucous "vice scene" that characterizes some red-light districts. I observed fewer people on the street than in Singel, because of

Figure 6.8. Ruysdaelkade red-light district

Figure 6.9a. The Wallen red-light district. Oude Kerk appears in the background.

Ruysdaelkade's residential nature. There are no tour groups visiting the two small RLDs because they lack the circus atmosphere of the Wallen. If not for the red lanterns and neon lights and women sitting behind windows, these areas would be indistinguishable from any other Dutch neighborhood.

Amsterdam's main red-light district in the Wallen differs radically in social ecology and ambience from the two small RLDs just described and from those in other Dutch cities and in Antwerp and Frankfurt. Each place looks and feels quite different to the visitor. Recall that Antwerp's is a tidy, quiet, single-purpose, pedestrian-only setting, while Frankfurt's main RLD is multiuse and crisscrossed by streets with vehicles passing through. In Amsterdam, the congested Wallen area sees few cars along its single-lane canal roads and none along the windowed alleys.

Amsterdam's main RLD is in the center of town and hard to miss. It is very much a *mixed-use* site offering a cornucopia of attractions—bars, marijuana cafes, restaurants, souvenir shops, clothing stores, gambling arcades, and snack bars nestled among window-prostitution rooms, live sex shows, massage parlors, and shops selling adult videos and sex toys. This kind of RLD offers visitors the opportunity to "view other goods and services they may not have pre-

Figure 6.9b. The Wallen red-light district, window rooms on the left.

Figure 6.9c. The Wallen red-light district.

viously been aware that they wanted."[133] Many of those who discuss this RLD on client websites like to recount their participation in multiple pursuits, especially combining cannabis use and paid sex. Amsterdam does not offer "everything," however; it has only one, small strip club (La Vie En Proost) and lacks German-style erotic bars, sauna clubs, and hotel-brothels.[134]

Red lights adorn the small canal bridges, and neon marquees advertise live sex shows and shops selling X-rated videos, lingerie, and sex toys. There are several stores named Red Light Souvenirs and Sex Shop, selling T-shirts, ashtrays, postcards, and other trinkets that present prostitution as an amusing curiosity. (No such shops exist in Singel or Ruysdaelkade.) During the day and night, one sees men, women, couples (some with children), and tour groups. At night, the RLD is full of life and has a boisterous party atmosphere. The street scene is captured in figure 6.9a–c.

In the very heart of the RLD is the Oude Kerk, the oldest church in Amsterdam—a jarring juxtaposition of the sacred and the profane within a few yards of each other. The church is ringed by window-prostitution units, two bars, and two marijuana cafes including the Old Church Coffee Shop. A few feet away from the Oude Kerk is a statue of Belle, whose inscription reads, "Respect Sex Workers All Over the World" (see figure 6.10). A monument of this kind is perhaps unique to Amsterdam, and it is remarkable that Belle stands virtually on church property. Belle's statue was sponsored by the nearby Prostitution Information Center (founded in 1994), which provides information on the RLD to tourists, clients, and sex workers. All of these features point to one conclusion: Amsterdam's main RLD is thoroughly integrated into the local economy and culture, quite different from many other red-light areas that are hidden away and marginal to the cultural life of the city. The character of this red-light district was established well before legalization, as I mentioned at the beginning of the chapter. A study from the 1980s describes this RLD quite similarly to its current incarnation, although more street prostitution was observed at that time than today.[135]

The very existence of an ancient RLD in the heart of the city, surrounded by other amenities and tourist attractions, contributes to the seminormalization of the window version of prostitution. The gorgeous 16th- and 17th-century gable houses, adorned with fancy red lanterns and window decorations, and the red-lit canal bridges in the heart of this RLD cast an aesthetic "halo effect" on this type of sexual commerce, leavening some of the more seedy surroundings (litter, graffiti on some buildings, and rowdy people on the street). That this RLD is itself a major tourist attraction is also important. On every visit, I have seen numerous tour groups walking the streets, including groups of 10–20 students, elderly people, teenage girls, and foreign tourists. Tour guides provide information that may help at least some tourists see prostitution in a more legitimate light. No tours are conducted in the RLDs in Singel, Ruysdaelkade, Frankfurt, or Antwerp.

It can be argued that a multiple-use RLD is superior to a single-use area as far as the workers are concerned. The juxtaposition of sexual entertainment alongside conventional businesses offers amenities to workers that are hard to come by in areas where prostitution is the sole activity. Multiple use also expands the potential customer base, as visitors who enter the area for other reasons may find themselves buying sex opportunistically, when they happen to see a provider who they are drawn to. Mixed use also increases social con-

Figure 6.10. Statue of Belle in the Wallen. The plaque reads, "Respect Sex Workers All Over the World." Oude Kerk appears in background.

trol over disorderly or predatory persons, insofar as shopkeepers are present and willing to intervene in such situations. (I have witnessed local merchants reprimanding disorderly individuals on the street.) In isolated, single-use RLDs, social control is largely relegated to on-site security personnel, co-workers, or the police.

Street prostitution (outside the few remaining *Tippelzones*) is scarce in Dutch cities, constituting only 1 percent of the total nationwide. I have been propositioned by one street worker in the Wallen, but this is quite unusual. Street prostitutes know that they are a fish out of water in a window-prostitution market and cannot compete with women who work behind the windows.

There are a few massage parlors in the RLD but no other brothels. These parlors offer erotic massage but lack the club atmosphere of a brothel with a bar and lounge where clients and providers may socialize prior to retiring to a room for sex. Massage parlor prices are higher than in the windows, but the time allotted is somewhat longer and includes massage, so the atmosphere is more relaxed and less rushed than the window experience is. The main parlors are Thai Massage and Love Club 21. After knocking on the door at Love Club, I was presented with a printed menu of services: nonsexual massage for €60; erotic massage and hand job, €75; erotic massage and sex for half an hour, €90; and erotic massage and sex for one hour, €125. Customers choose a masseuse from a group of women sitting in the parlor, but the parties do not socialize in the parlor. Thai Massage is different. The manager who opened its door told me that they offer massage and hand jobs only, and she does not allow customers to enter the building until they pay. She told me that there is "no reason" to allow a man to view the women first "since they don't give sex."[136]

Amsterdam currently has about 400 window-prostitution rooms. Almost all of its red-lit windows are small, single rooms on the first or second floor. The rooms vary somewhat in size and amenities, but all have sinks, chairs, closets, and beds. Negotiations take place while the man stands outside the window: if he decides to partake and enters the room, the woman closes a thick red curtain over the window and door. Some rooms are shrouded with black lights, accenting the woman's fluorescent attire to pique the interest of passersby. As in Antwerp, the women vary in their attire, age, attractiveness, and behavior. Almost all dress in skimpy outfits: bikinis, lingerie, thongs, translucent mesh tops, and so on. Most of them are female, but there is a small transgender cluster in one part of the Wallen. Unlike Frankfurt's hotel-brothels, where many women live for weeks at a time, in the Netherlands it is illegal for a window worker to stay in her room all day. Instead, the workers rent rooms for an eight-hour shift.

Window prostitution has the advantage of allowing the workers to set their own rules; window owners do not dictate how they should dress or behave. Window workers also make the most money in the Netherlands because of high turnover compared to escorts and brothel workers. They charge a standard €50 for about 15 minutes of manual, oral, or vaginal sex, and extras or more time will raise the price. (Window rooms in Amsterdam currently rent for €100–€150 per eight-hour shift.) A 2006 study estimated that the average gross income for window workers was €1,460 ($2,044) per week, compared to €760 ($1,064) for brothel workers and €528 ($740) for those working in massage parlors.[137] The higher income for window workers is part of the reason why 88 percent of them report being "satisfied" (of which 36 percent are "very satisfied") with their work, according to a recent survey.[138] Their job satisfaction may also be due to the relatively limited number of hours they work: 10 percent work three to four hours per day; 56 percent, five to six hours; and 34 percent, seven to eight hours. Half of them work every day, a third work a few times per week, and a sixth work once a week or a few times a month. Almost all the window workers interviewed in the survey worked in the windows exclusively: just 3 percent supplemented window work with club work, 12 percent engaged in escort work when not at their window, and none worked on the street.[139]

Almost all of Amsterdam's window rooms are single occupancy, separating workers from each other. Some rooms are connected to a bathroom and kitchen shared by several workers, but the women spend most of their time by themselves in front of the windows. This situation contrasts sharply with brothels, where workers can enjoy a party atmosphere and regular social contact with other providers, staff, and customers.

To break the monotony, most window workers "perform" in some way—drawing on their own distinctive repertoire to beckon passersby and typically displaying the same body language day after day. The women knock on their windows, dance to music, assume suggestive poses, flash private parts, and smile, wink, throw kisses, and call out to individual men. Only a few seem totally disengaged from the outside world: they read magazines, stare into space, sit catatonically, or chat on the phone. The sexiest women tend to attract groups of gawkers, while others perform seductively to get more than a passing look. The women focus their attention on specific men near their windows but also occasionally address the men in general, such as the time I saw two women lean out of their doors and yell, "Let's get some action going!" and "I'm horny." My observations are consistent with those of another researcher, who described "plenty of women hunting for men who seemed to be disinterested in them. The men's attention had to be drawn by tapping on windows, exuberantly twisting breasts and other body parts, and shouting out phrases like, 'Hey, loverboy' or 'One minute, one minute, come inside.'"[140] At least some workers take pleasure in this game, as one stated: "There was a kind of power play in the whole transaction that I enjoyed. I lured the men in and I controlled most of what happened once they were inside."[141]

Some window workers are aggressive in their efforts to snare a customer. In one narrow alley near the Old Church, I have seen men being grabbed and pulled by working women. Some will block passage with a stick, literally "hooking" and forcing the man to speak to her and insisting that he come inside. Some get agitated if a man stands and stares for too long or walks by their window repeatedly, and these women have been observed telling a man to move on or shining a laser beam at his face. Several times, I have heard women accusing lingering voyeurs of "using" them for their "masturbation fantasies" rather than paying them for their services. This is one reason why photos and video-recording are frowned on, and anyone seen doing so is subjected to a verbal tirade and may even have the equipment confiscated. The women do not want a tangible image of them that might be used for someone's private pleasure, shared with friends, or posted on the Internet—with the risk of being seen by family members or friends who are not aware the individual is selling sex. I have witnessed several altercations after photos or videos were taken. Once, a woman came out of her room and sprayed something from a plastic bottle at a man, and another time, as a group of Japanese tourists was taking photos with their cell phones, a woman stormed out of her room and called them "perverts."

A brochure produced by the Amsterdam police in the late 1990s contains a remarkable set of rules for visitors to the red-light district:

1. Have fun, but act in a normal manner.
2. Screaming and shouting. Fine 150 Guilder [$95].
3. Urinating in public. Fine 100G [$64].
4. Alcohol on the streets. Fine 80G. [$51]
5. Beware of pickpockets/robberies.
6. Prostitution, no pictures of the women.
7. Hard drugs are strictly forbidden.
8. Soft drugs [cannabis], not under 18.

Each item is followed by an explanatory paragraph. The prostitution paragraph reads,

> If you visit one of the women, we would like to remind you, they are not always women. Don't take pictures of the women, it might get you in trouble. Outside on the streets, don't shout or use bad language towards these women. Show some respect. In case you have any problem with a girl or a pimp, don't hesitate to ask a policeman/woman.[142]

These rules are periodically broken—especially the norms against shouting, public drinking, pickpocketing, taking photos, or verbally disparaging a window woman.

Based on my observations and other accounts,[143] the vast majority of the people walking through the area are spectators rather than prospective customers. Most of the men cruise individually, others in groups of two or more. A minority cause trouble: 19 percent of window workers in Amsterdam say that they have been harassed by a client, though most of them say this has occurred rarely.[144] Most of the men are quiet and simply walk through the area looking at the sights. For the most part, the men avoid eye contact with other men and do not speak to them, unless they are friends on a group outing. The stigma attached to clients makes most men wary of drawing attention to themselves. It is largely a scene of furtive window shopping, not buying.

For those who are interested in sex, the window district may be preferred over other venues because one can comparison shop with ease, viewing and interacting with sellers before making a decision. Brothels offer much more limited options, and escorts sometimes look quite different in person than on a website. Apart from those men who seek out a certain window provider because they have visited her before, many prospective clients will cruise the entire red-light district several times before selecting someone because, as one man put it, "the joy of walking around picking your favorite is immense fun."[145] The window model is also well suited to the opportunistic client, one who has not planned a sexual encounter ahead of time, whereas a liaison with an escort or visit to a brothel requires planning and may lack the element of spontaneity that some men find thrilling.

At the same time, visibility can determine whether a man partakes on any given occasion. Some men do not seem to mind entering a window room when onlookers are present, and others enjoy doing this in the presence of others especially when their choice is confirmed by other men. For example, when one man left a window occupied by a very striking blonde, another man exclaimed, "She's beautiful. I'm getting some of that!"; the departing man wrote online that hearing this affirmation of his selection "filled me with a sense of pride." But other men are reluctant to approach a window if there are other people present and will wait until they disperse before making an approach. When a large crowd has gathered outside a window whose occupant is particularly "hot," it is rare to see anyone enter her room. One client describes the nature of this dilemma: "Too many people, none was entering. Imagine having all those people waiting outside when you are [leaving]. I wanted to go, but it has to be relaxed."[146] Another man complained about the "tour groups who are gawping [*sic*] at the men-gawping-at-the-women."[147] Tour groups bother the workers as well. When a group clusters around a particular window, inadvertently intimidating potential clients, some providers will tell the tourists to leave. Finally, the high visibility of some window rooms is a deterrent for many prospective clients. The exposed windows along the main canal in the Wallen attract fewer customers than the less conspicuous windows along the narrow alleys. As a window owner told me, the "men can sneak in and sneak out" of these more hidden windows. Moreover, some men especially dislike the second-story windows along the main canal because they have to climb up a flight of stairs to reach the room, literally elevating their exposure to onlookers. I have rarely seen a man braving the spotlight in this way.

After clients complete their business and leave a window room, anywhere in this RLD, they typically walk away as quickly as possible, to minimize being seen by others. The desire to avoid such public visibility and the stigma associated with being (seen as) a "john" is one reason why some clients prefer more clandestine liaisons with escorts or in discreet brothels or even street prostitution, where the man is relatively invisible inside his car.

If tour groups are generally disliked by clients and providers alike, some people also dislike seeing families strolling through the RLD. As one client complained, "Call me old fashioned, but why do some parents think it's a good idea to bring young kids to a RLD?"[148] Others complain about visitors who are loud, drunk, or otherwise disorderly—especially on Friday and Saturday nights. On the weekends, Amsterdam is a prime destination for "stag parties"—groups of British men who arrive on a cheap flight, drink all day, and cause commotion. This is a major concern for local merchants, police, and city officials, as well as those sex workers who are accosted by these rowdy drunks. In addition to these disorderly, roving bands, I have observed some individual men calling women names, arguing with them, pounding on their doors or windows, or staring and refusing to move away. On one occasion, a group of six male youths badgered a woman by repeatedly and loudly asking if she offered "golden showers" as she repeatedly asked them to leave (a golden shower involves urination). It is not uncommon to hear men collectively and vocally rate a woman's appearance positively or negatively. I once observed a group of visibly drunk British men, one of whose members was talking to an overweight worker. His friends pulled him away, yelling, "You'll be sorry. You're too drunk to see that she's ugly." I have also witnessed men asking for sex without a condom and haggling over price, time, or services. The women have little patience for this and will quickly shut the door in the man's face, though there is sometimes shouting or cursing as well.

On the flipside, on many occasions I have heard the parties exchanging pleasantries, flirting, or joking with each other. I have heard many men compliment a working woman, saying, "You're so beautiful!" or "Hello, gorgeous!" or "You're too hot for me!" Others stop in their tracks when they see someone that they consider a goddess, staring in stunned silence. After seeing one "bombshell," a dazzled man said to his friends, "Wow! Wouldn't you like to come home to that every night?" Some men ask a woman whom they have complimented to "perform" by dancing, touching herself, bending over, or showing a breast, and some women do this spontaneously if a desirable man lingers in front of her window. But from my observations, the performative dimension is limited in most cases to beckoning, flirtation, or limited erotic body language.

My observations are confirmed by clients' postings on online discussion boards. While some of the online discussions mirror those of clients in other nations (e.g., reviews of specific providers, tales of their escapades, etiquette), other contributions are specific to window or brothel prostitution in the Netherlands. I draw on these sites here to give a more comprehensive picture of Amsterdam's red-light districts, this time from the clients' point of view. Seasoned posters educate novices on proper etiquette when approaching a window and on the way a client should act therein or at a Dutch brothel. And they criticize those who violate the rules. When one man posted his secretly recorded video of some of the window women, this was roundly condemned on the site, and another man was taken to task when he referred to one worker as a "bitch."

As one might expect, some men seek a GFE with a particular provider, particularly if they become regular clients. In online message boards, clients describe nonsexual aspects of their experiences, and some seek advice regarding a specific woman. One poster, Farid747, asked about gifts:

I'm definitely one of Agnieszka's best fans. . . . I want to offer her a gift as a sign of gratitude for the tremendous amount of joy she brings me. Don't blame me for over-romanticizing her; of course I'm no fool, but it's stronger than me, since [for] 2 weeks I can't get her out of my mind. Have any of you ever offered a gift to a window girl? What kind of present do they like?

Responders recommended jewelry, among other things, and discussed their own gift giving:

DogsAfire: I took a baseball cap to Carla one time. She collects them. She modeled it for me (wearing nothing else) and looked really cute that way. . . . Anyway, whatever you do decide to give her, make sure that it is apparent that you put some thought into it. I dislike giving flowers simply because it shows very little consideration of the individual.

Farid747: Thank you all! . . . I guess a silk scarf Yves St. Laurent or a handbag Louis Vuitton would be nice. I could easily sacrify [sacrifice] 3 or 4 sessions just to offer her a beautiful gift. Anyway, most important is not the price, it's the gesture. I wanna let her know how much I'm grateful to her for the joy that she brought, and I wanna let her know that she is so special to me ☺.[149]

Clients complain about a litany of things. Posters on online discussion boards criticize men who are rowdy, drunk, or disrespectful toward the women and revile the British stag groups. Others criticize the window type of prostitution or individual sex workers. Some lament the perfunctory nature of their sexual experiences behind the windows. One man wrote that what "you can expect from these women is an expensive rushed event," and he characterized the window sector as a "production line": "Get the customer in, get the customer out. Quality means nothing to these women."[150] What he does not mention is that clients can and do pay for longer sessions, say, €100 for 45 minutes, allowing for a less rushed experience. And some clients are *seeking* a quickie, just like street clients. Men report that some of the hottest women provide the worst services, because they see a large number of clients and therefore are less inclined to provide any particular man with a high-quality experience. Some workers also stand accused of "upselling"—that is, adding charges for every single act, such as removing a bikini top, allowing a man to touch breasts, cunnilingus, or more than one coital position. Other providers readily remove their clothes and allow a range of contact without charging extra, and rushed or impersonal services are by no means universal behind Amsterdam's windows, as clients' message boards attest. When one poster claimed that a particular street had a "reputation" for "rip-off girls," others offered contrary opinions based on their own experiences there.[151] Another online discussion revolved around Romanian sex workers and their reputation for upselling. Some men reported a great experience with a Romanian, but others thought they were inclined to exploit clients. One stated, "Normally, we eschew bashing of national origins here [on this website] but, in this case, being 50% Romanian myself, I have to agree [that] they are by far the most dishonest girls I've ever met in Amsterdam and Alkmaar."[152] Message boards can be used to "name and shame" workers who stand accused of repeatedly engaging in bad behavior. For instance, one poster complained about a particular worker who asked him to negotiate inside the room, then closed and locked the door and demanded €50 to allow him to leave, threatening to call the police if he did not pay. As he fled the room, she reportedly called him a "motherfucka" and punched him in the back. A few other posters responded that they had the same experience with her—one of them likewise claimed that he was assaulted—while others expressed shock at her behavior. Regular posters indicated that this kind of conduct was unique to her, never having been reported on the site for anyone else. When a few men said that she should be slapped or kicked, they were warned not to resort to violence, while others suggested a "Hall of Shame" be created on the board to blacklist the worst providers.[153]

Novices are counseled by seasoned clients on how to assess a particular worker's personality and thus the odds of having a satisfying experience: "If you see a girl who's even a 'maybe,' try to talk to her! It not only gives you a chance to see better what she looks like, it also shows you what her window seat smells like (is she a smoker or perfumed?), as well as what she'll sound like if/when she's talking dirty to you. Important stuff!"[154] Another says, "Pick out a woman who exhibits some personality. A friendly smile or sexy look in your direction indicate that the girl will give you a better time than a bored looking hooker will."[155] Others tell novices to determine, before entering the room, exactly what services are available, the cost of each, and how much time will be allotted. They are told not to disclose that they are first-timers, as that increases the chance of a rip-off. One newbie was informed that "complete rip-offs are fairly rare and upsells are not the end of the world—just tell them no several times."[156] One poster, Bookguy, offered a detailed list of "signs of greater levels of enjoyability" with a window woman, cues to look for when speaking to her at the door or after entering her room:

PERSONABLE: she smiles and engages you in non-selling banter.
PATIENT: she will spend a little time getting to know you in terms of your interaction style. She makes no demands on you, never says anything implying you're less of a man for whatever reason. . . .
SOBER AND INDEPENDENT: she's not under the influence of drugs or alcohol or a guy [e.g., pimp] watching out for her movements.
EXPERIENCED: she's done this before. . . .
CLEAN: her place is orderly, she takes pride in her kamer [window room] and her work. . . . She doesn't get easily distracted from your conversation or your session. . . .[157]

But a few weeks later, Bookguy offered a word of caution:

Beware, however, that she also could be misleading about how convivial she would be during a session, because she might be a great salesperson but not so great a service provider. In short, there's not really any sure way of determining whether or not the gal will be excellent at the agreed-upon services or not, at least not strictly from a mere encounter and glance from the street.[158]

He added that the "most reliable information" could be found in the reviews of specific women on client's message boards. The Ignatzmice website features a list of all known workers, their specific window location, descriptions of their physical attributes and demeanor, and reviews of their services and performance culled from years of online postings. The objective is to assist men in making informed choices and to help them locate a preferred provider if she has relocated to another window. In addition to the list, many clients post detailed online accounts of their sessions with particular providers, ranging from disastrous to fabulous. And some men wax sentimental about their all-time-favorite provider: "Even years past [sic] since I saw her I still miss and love her so much. I think she does not work any more behind the window. So I wish her all the best and happiness. If some of you know something about my sweet Dolores, please let me know."[159]

As is true for similar websites in other countries, client postings reveal an emergent subculture among sex buyers who share their experiences and advice and participate in the creation of conduct norms, but many of the Netherlands postings are specific to Dutch window or brothel prostitution. And the postings are not limited to carnal interests or to proper etiquette. The men discuss what they have observed in various brothels, windows, and clubs as well as practical issues regarding hygiene and safe sex in these places. And they debate a wide range of policy issues, sometimes posting newspaper reports and asking for comments. My review of entries found strong criticisms of Amsterdam's decision to close some of the windows; a debate on whether workers should be registered, as the national government plans to do; questions about how the 2010 Dutch election might impact the sex industry; descriptions of the plusses and minuses of RLDs in other Dutch cities; discussions on whether some providers are forced into prostitution or trafficked from another country; advice on how to spot signs that someone is working involuntarily; and what to do if one believes that a worker has been abused. That some clients are concerned to avoid situations in which a worker is exploited or abused is significant and has also been documented in studies of clients in other societies.[160]

Many of the workers have regular clients whom they see in the windows or elsewhere. In a survey, only 5 percent of window workers said that they had no regular clients, while 47 percent estimated that 30–50 percent of their clients were regulars.[161] One worker told me that she had just spent six hours with one of her regulars at a private location, earning €1,000 ($1,400), which, she said, "pays my rent for the month." I have spoken to another provider, Jasmine, on several occasions. She has worked in Amsterdam's windows for four years, has a number of regular customers, and makes lots of money. She works about seven hours a day, takes a day or two off each week, and periodically returns to her home country in southern Europe for visits with friends and family but does not sell sex there. Jasmine told me, "I like it. If I didn't, I wouldn't do it."[162]

Jasmine also sees some of her regular clients, whom she initially met in her window, in their hotel room or apartment. She does not consider herself an "escort," does not have a website, and does not give out her email address. She told me that seeing a man first in her window, over several visits, allows her to screen him before deciding whether to see him outside. Some clients do not like coming to the red-light district, preferring to see providers under more discreet circumstances. Such private encounters are much more lucrative on a per-client basis than window work is. Like most other window workers in Amsterdam, Jasmine charges €50 at the window but €400 per two-hour minimum elsewhere, at hotels or apartments, and she tells me that the date usually lasts more than two hours. She prefers out-call work, stating, "I could do this five days a week!" Some weeks she has three or four dates, but other weeks she has none, which explains why she continues working at her window.

Jasmine describes herself as completely independent, never having had a pimp or other manager. She says she does not understand why some other women have pimps and is perplexed by women who advertise and go on blind dates with clients, putting themselves at risk. For her, "It is not only about the money but also about safety." She says that the window women are "easy to get to" by men who are looking for someone to abuse, because the windows are so accessible, like street prostitution. I asked how often she has arguments or other conflicts with men who approach her window or when inside her room, and she said, "Very rarely. I avoid conflict."[163] Over time she has learned to look for signs of potential problems and screens these men out. Jasmine has established very clear boundaries with clients—no kissing and no sex without a condom, which are reserved "only for a boyfriend." From her, a client will only get a "girlfriend experience" if he has known her for a very long time; she likes to converse with customers but jealously guards what she calls her "private life."

Jasmine's story is presented here to give the reader a sense of how some window workers experience the work, and she differs from at least some other providers along axes that determine the degree of empowerment, exploitation, or risk taking—whether they are pimp managed, know their rights, engage in condomless or other risky practices, and the like.[164] Jasmine is not unique, however. Almost all the providers in the RLD insist on condoms, and Jasmine told me that the sex workers who are her friends operate with the same safeguards as she does and fully control their working conditions. The survey of window workers discussed earlier in the chapter suggests that a significant proportion of window workers share Jasmine's work etiquette, although it is by no means universal.

Conclusion

Chapter 4 argued that legalization can be judged superior to criminalization but also that much depends on the specific regulations underpinning any given legal order. The regulations shape the extent of the state's involvement, the beneficiaries, the community impact, and the degree to which the problems associated with blanket criminalization are reduced. In the aftermath of legal reform, there is naturally a period of adjustment by interested parties and often some amendments to the regulations, designed to address unanticipated problems. Competing interests make the postlegalization period at least somewhat precarious and unpredictable, perhaps resulting in changes that were not the original intent of law reform. What is the Dutch record?

First, a gulf exists between legal and illegal workers and businesses, and key stakeholders consider the illegal sector a major problem. In the legal sector, most proprietors have adjusted to the new regulations even as they find fault with some of them. We have seen that the window owners' and brothel owners' associations feel that they are under the government's microscope and overregulated, while the illegal enterprises escape oversight precisely because they are clandestine. Other interest groups offer mixed assessments of the new regime. The premier Dutch prostitutes' rights organization Red Thread considers legalization an improvement over the previous arrangement but also wants to see fewer restrictions and more guarantees of civil and labor rights. Red Thread favors a nationwide enforcement of existing labor laws; opposes caps on the number of sex businesses allowed in a jurisdiction, leaving it to what the market will bear; wants a hotline created for workers to report abuses to the authorities and a mobile unit to investigate infringements of rights; opposes restrictive controls on independent providers; and wants the state to facilitate small enterprises owned and operated by the workers themselves.[165] Red Thread opposes registration of workers and the proposal to set the minimum age at 21 instead of 18.

Second, have labor relations changed appreciably under legalization? Prostitutes now have rights vis-à-vis owners and managers, but, as is common elsewhere, most opt not to assert them.[166] As of 2004, only 60 percent of sex workers knew about the 2000 law, and of these, less than 40 percent considered it a good thing.[167] Today, awareness of the law is more widespread, but concerns about its benefits persist. It is not surprising that sex workers would be slow to assert their rights. As a population that is stigmatized and has never had rights, it is risky for prostitutes suddenly to begin claiming them. A change in their legal situation does not necessarily translate into empowerment, even when workers are aware of their rights and the specific avenues for holding employers and customers accountable. Reluctant to take an owner to court, disgruntled workers tend to change employers instead. After a decade of decriminalization, brothel owners continue to set the rules, and their workers have little leverage over working conditions. Freelance escorts and window workers are the exception because they do not work for an employer.

Third, has legalization increased the amount of prostitution? It is difficult to answer this question. The legal sector, though diminished in recent years, is nevertheless considered "much more sizeable" than the illegal sector.[168] There is a popular impression in the Netherlands that illegal prostitution has skyrocketed since legalization, but this cannot be substantiated given the underground nature of this market both before and after 2000. A 1995 survey reported that one-fifth (22 percent) of Dutch men had bought sex from a prostitute, but we have no recent survey to determine if the number has increased in recent years.[169] In addition, many clients in the Netherlands are foreign tourists who would not be represented in a survey of Dutch men. It is quite possible that the overall number of sexual transactions has not changed much over the 20-year period before and after legalization (1990–2010), given the tolerant approach taken by the authorities in the decade prior to legalization in 2000. Still, the lack of reliable data makes it impossible to say whether, or how much, it has increased. Data on the size of the market are lacking for most other nations that have legalized prostitution, but in New Zealand, the number of sex workers has not increased since legalization in 2003.[170]

Fourth, how safe are the workers in the legal venues? A Ministry of Justice evaluation concluded that the "the vast majority" of workers in legal brothels, clubs, and windows report that they "often or always feel safe."[171] Window alarms go off rarely in the main RLD in the Wallen, about twice a month. I have heard alarms on a few occasions, and each time the police arrived within a couple of minutes. Since I began conducting observations in 1997, I have seen increasing numbers of police foot patrols in the RLD over time. In addition, both the police and the window owners have installed video cameras outside the rooms, which they monitor. In an upstairs room above a row of windows, an owner I interviewed had a computer screen showing real-time video from four angles outside his window rooms. He told me that he rarely sees anything that requires his intervention.

A recent survey of 94 window workers reported that 61 percent of them had never experienced a threatening situation at work, 81 percent had never been harassed by a client, and 93 percent had never been abused at work.[172] Almost all of those who had such an experience reported that it had happened only rarely. These findings are consistent with the Ministry of Justice's assessment of safety in legal, indoor settings. When providers leave their shifts, they are typically accompanied by another sex worker, adding to safety. I have observed groups of two and three workers leaving and arriving in the window area when the shift changes in the evening.

Fifth, to what extent is coercive or parasitical third-party involvement a problem? The "great majority" of window prostitutes associate with "a so-called boyfriend or pimp," according to the government,[173] but it is impossible to tell how many workers in the more hidden sector (escorts, underground brothels) have pimps. It has been reported that "problems with pimps occur relatively frequently among East European, African, and Asian prostitutes," and most of the pimps in Amsterdam are young Moroccan or Turkish males or older eastern European men.[174] In fact, an official at the Ministry of Justice told me that the single biggest challenge since legalization has been the difficulty in curbing pimping.[175]

Eastern European pimps monitor their women via frequent phone calls, whereas some other pimps linger near window rooms, either observing their women or trying to intimidate unattached women into forming an association. The pimp will try to convince the woman that she needs protection and may threaten her if she is not interested in his "services." In the Wallen RLD, I have observed many individuals who appear to be pimps because they simply stand by a row of windows and observe without cruising, a modus operandi confirmed by the police and documented by other researchers.[176] These men linger for a long period of time, either to intimidate a particular woman or for surveillance over someone who is already connected to them. This public monitoring does not happen outside a closed brothel. Others have been observed talking to a specific woman, as described in my fieldnotes:

> On one occasion, a man talks at length to a worker, and when she starts talking to me, he kisses her and leaves. A prospective customer probably would not have done that. Later, I see him loitering outside her window. A few days later, I saw an apparent pimp arguing with a woman at her window. She does not chase him away as she would an ordinary, disputatious man.[177]

Pimps often target immigrant women, who they see as more vulnerable due to their foreigner status.[178]

The city of Eindhoven has experimented with harassing suspected pimps. When a man is observed lingering in the city's window area where loitering is not allowed, the police invite him to the police station for a conversation.[179] It is easy for the police to identify suspected pimps in Eindhoven because the RLD is in a courtyard with few people walking around, making loiterers readily visible.

What about coercive sex trafficking? In the past five years, there has been a substantial increase in the number of eastern European women entering the country, especially from Hungary, Romania, and Bulgaria, as a result of the expansion of the EU and the migration rights associated with EU status. Most of these individuals have been assisted by others in migrating to the Netherlands. As mentioned earlier in this chapter, some politicians and activists claim that coercive sex trafficking has increased dramatically in recent years, but these claims are questionable. The director of an organization that works closely with prostitutes in the Wallen, when questioned about the women working there, stated, "There are women who don't know they will work in prostitution, but they are usually in escort work. Nowadays a lot of eastern European women know beforehand that they will be working in prostitution in the Netherlands. They've been informed by their friends, their girlfriends, who are already working here and convince them to move to Holland."[180] Other analysts confirm that one of the main "pull factors" in the migration of foreign women into the sex industry is information provided to them by girlfriends who are already selling sex in the Netherlands and elsewhere in western Europe.

Government statistics on the number of "possible victims" of trafficking show a consistent increase over time, but there are two problems: (1) these statistics aggregate all types of trafficking, labor as well as sex trafficking,[181] and (2) the figures on "possible victims" refer to persons reported to the government's trafficking office, not necessarily actual victims. It is noteworthy that the number of persons *convicted* of trafficking offenses has remained fairly stable: 79 in 2003 and 73 in 2007.[182] This does not mean that the number of persons trafficked is itself stable, but it does cast doubt on the claim that trafficking has skyrocketed since prostitution was legalized in 2000. And most of the cases involving sex trafficking have involved persons working in the illegal sector, not in the windows or licensed brothels, according to government reports.[183]

While it is always difficult to draw conclusions about the magnitude of trafficking, the Dutch authorities report that legalization has helped reduce trafficking in the legal, licensed sector due to greater government oversight. The government's Rapporteur on Trafficking makes this point eloquently:

It is often said in the media that the lifting of the general ban on brothels [in 2000] has led to more THB [trafficking in human beings]. This is not a correct conclusion. Before the lifting of the general ban on brothels, THB and other (criminal) abuses were taking place in all sectors of prostitution. Some of these sectors are now under control and can be assumed to have rid themselves of their former criminal excesses, or are doing so. . . . It is possible that THB is increasing in the illegal, non-regulated or non-controlled sectors. If this were to be the case, it still cannot be assumed that the extent of THB is now at the same or even above the "old" level it was before the ban on brothels was lifted. It is in fact likely that this is not the case.[184]

If sex trafficking is minimal in the licensed, regulated sector—as these government agencies suggest—this can be interpreted as a major advantage of legalized prostitution as implemented in the Netherlands.

Sixth, what about underage prostitution? A study of 557 street and indoor prostitutes working in Amsterdam, Rotterdam, and The Hague between 2002 and 2005 found that the median age of entry into prostitution was 25 for drug-using female workers, 27 for non-drug-using female workers, and 24 for transgender workers (the age range was 20–33).[185] This was not a random sample, but it was a fairly large and diverse sample—drawn from the streets, windows, brothels, clubs, drug relief centers, and elsewhere. In a 2010 survey of 94 window workers in Amsterdam, none was a minor (23 percent were 18–21 years old, 33 percent were 22–25, and 20 percent were 26–30).[186] Research sponsored by the Ministry of Justice concluded in 2007 that there is "hardly any prostitution by minors in the licensed sector and there are no indications of a great presence of minors within the non-licensed sector either."[187] Only 5 percent of the 354 legal prostitutes interviewed started selling sex when they were younger than 18, and 10 percent of those working as unlicensed escorts began as minors.[188] Moreover, "During inspections of licensed prostitution businesses, inspectors encounter underage prostitutes only very incidentally."[189] For the five-year period between 2001 and 2005, none of the suspected victims of trafficking (i.e., those reported to the Dutch trafficking office) was 10–14 years old, 8 percent were 15–17, 39 percent were 18–23, and the remainder were 24 and older.[190]

Seventh, does stigma still color the sex trade a decade after legal reform? Legalization of vice does not imply respectability, and the individuals involved in Dutch prostitution—workers, clients, and business owners/managers—continue to experience disrepute. Although surveys mentioned earlier in the chapter suggest greater Dutch tolerance for sex work than elsewhere in Europe, this is not tantamount to full acceptance. A perfect example of this is the Dutch university student who told me that she considered prostitution "normal but also immoral." Stigma is evident in sex workers' desire to remain anonymous, including not asserting their rights when doing so would mean public identification. Few Dutch women work in the visible window sector and instead prefer the more hidden escorting or brothel work. Similarly, clients continue to feel that the public disapproves of their conduct. A survey of clients in Rotterdam found that "despite the lifting of the brothel ban seven years ago, most men feel that visiting prostitutes still belongs to the taboo sphere and many fear the possible consequences in terms of social censure and stigmatization."[191]

The owners of sex businesses struggle with stigma as well. Klein Beekman, the director of a brothel owners' association in the 1990s, told me in 1997 that his organization encouraged its members to present themselves as normal businessmen: "Get a good organization. Start talking with the government. Pay taxes. Talk with the police. Talk with everybody. . . . In the past, everybody who was working in prostitution closed the door. Now you can go to a club, and they will talk with you."[192] Beekman also tried to break down stereotypes in his frequent media appearances and in his everyday contacts with Dutch people. On one occasion, he encountered a female mayor of a small town in a bar:

> She talked loud: "So you are the pimp!" I said, "Maybe." And then I asked her, "Have you been inside a house?" She said, "No, I never was. What do you think of me?" I said, "You tell these people how bad the place is. How can you do that when you never went inside a house? You have to have been inside a house to talk like you do, or you are telling a [fictional] story. Maybe it's better that you come inside the house. I invite you, come. . . . Come with me right now. I'll take you to a place and show you everything. You can talk with everybody, and after that you can tell what you've seen." . . . I took her to the house, and the atmosphere inside the house was real good. And after ten minutes, she was sitting at the [brothel's] bar next to a guest, and she was talking with him and to the girls. And after one hour, I said, "I'll bring you back," but she said, "Oh, I'd like to stay here." And then I brought her back [to the bar], and everyone was waiting and looking. And then she said to the owner of the pub, "You should go there. It's better than here!" . . . And I see her now and then, and she never says anything wrong about the brothel anymore. And that is what I tell my [brothel-owner] colleagues—open it, show the people, [and] do the same with the government. . . . Afterward, you can say, "Okay, you want to change some things. Now, you know what's going on. Let's talk about the changes."[193]

If individual actors remain disreputable, brothels and escort agencies have become somewhat "normalized," insofar as they are officially treated as ordinary businesses. One possible by-product of legalized prostitution is that it can create a climate in which policies can be discussed in an open, conventional manner. Furthermore, the very existence and longevity of trade associations for brothel and window owners increases their credibility. In the Netherlands they are routinely consulted by government agencies and are seen as important players in policy discussions. Over a lengthy period of time, therefore, legal prostitution may win a measure of legitimacy that is not possible when it is criminalized and marginalized. But this outcome is unlikely where organized opposition is robust—where forces within the state, domestic interest groups, or foreign critics continue to condemn sex work and demand repeal of the laws legalizing it. Such opposition is growing in the Netherlands today.

Conclusion

Myths often eclipse facts when it comes to popular images of prostitution and other kinds of sex work. These myths are promulgated in the media and by politicians and partisan interest groups. Some are rooted in centuries-old stereotypes, while others are of more recent origin, such as the conflation of prostitution with sex trafficking. The fictions are only reinforced by writers who define prostitution monolithically—reducing it to patriarchal exploitation and violence or, by contrast, highlighting empowerment and therapeutic recreation. This essentialist quest is misguided. To define prostitution in such reductionist ways is to reify constructs that are best treated as *variables*, not constants.

I offer an alternative—a perspective that recognizes the complexity of sex work across time, place, and type. Empirically grounded and theoretically nuanced, the polymorphous paradigm is superior to simplistic monolithic approaches. This paradigm requires (1) major rethinking of commonsense understandings of prostitution, (2) reexamination of the factors typically associated with prostitution (e.g., violence, disease, drug addiction, organized crime, and trafficking), and (3) careful documentation of how prostitution manifests itself in different geographical settings and in different sectors of the trade. The material presented in the book provides strong evidence contradicting some popular myths as well as the central tenets of the oppression paradigm. While certain experiences are common to prostitution (coping with stigma, managing client behavior, avoiding risks), research indicates that other work-related experiences, as well as the harms typically associated with prostitution, vary greatly.

Examination of legal prostitution systems further shatters popular stereotypes. This book, along with a few other recent studies of legal prostitution,[1] throws light on a world that differs in some important respects from the conventional images of prostitution held by most people. Although no existing system is problem free, the evidence presented in this book suggests that prostitution *can* be organized in a way that is superior to blanket criminalization and marginalization. There is nothing inherent in prostitution that prevents it from being structured like other service occupations, aside from the stigma associated with it (the stigma attached to pornography and stripping does not prevent them from operating as quasi-conventional businesses). Stigma is extremely important, however, as it interferes with the smooth functioning of any legal prostitution system. Indeed, philosopher Lars Ericsson considers moralistic public attitudes toward sexuality in general and commercial sex in particular to be the biggest obstacle to the evolution of what he calls "sound prostitution." Ericsson writes,

> Our outlook as far as sex roles, relations between the sexes, and sexuality are concerned [is archaic and has] . . . negative effects not only on prostitution and prostitutes but also on the relations between the sexes generally. . . . A sound prostitution is, first of all, prostitution that is allowed to function in a social climate freed from emotional prejudice. . . . In order to improve prostitution we must first and foremost improve our attitudes toward it.[2]

A yoke of disreputability hangs over commercial sex that, if lifted, would allow existing legal prostitution systems to operate more openly and less controversially.

If stigma casts a shadow over legal prostitution systems, these regimes also face a host of practical challenges—to be expected whenever a vice is decriminalized and legalized. The magnitude and kinds of challenges vary from place to place and are usually most acute during the early formative years postlegalization. Although some jurisdictions have faced relatively few problems from a regulatory standpoint (e.g., Nevada, New Zealand, New South Wales), most others have confronted significant challenges in the aftermath of legalization. Implementing legal reforms is often a difficult and uneven process and may ignite criticism or stiff resistance from various quarters—sex workers, business owners, residents, the media, churches, local officials tasked with new responsibilities, and antiprostitution groups. In addition to opposition from forces in civil society, a legal prostitution system is usually vulnerable to denunciation from abroad as well, by some other governments and international organizations. All of this can render the normalization process quite precarious.

Philosopher Christine Overall has argued, "It is imaginable that prostitution could always be practiced, as it occasionally is even now, in circumstances of relative safety, security, freedom, hygiene, and personal control."[3] I want to emphasize the word "imaginable" in Overall's remark. This book can be read as a first step in imagining an alternative to the conventional wisdom—one in which sex work is characterized by "relative safety, security, freedom, hygiene, and personal control." Most existing legal prostitution systems have registered a degree of success in achieving one or more of these goals for at least some categories of sex workers, although none has fully realized all of these ideals.

Legalization and Gender Relations

In every legal prostitution system that I know of, the state has focused almost exclusively on women who sell sex. The regulations are applied primarily to women, with male sex workers and their managers usually left out of the monitoring system. It can be said that male prostitutes therefore benefit from decriminalization in these nations but are left largely untouched by the regulations and controls. This gender bias mirrors larger debates about prostitution policies, which pivot on the relationship between female providers and male clients. Ignoring male sex workers, critics argue that legalization ratifies and normalizes men's sexual use of women by giving prostitution the state's stamp of approval. So, whatever the practical benefits of legalization, some people will reject it because of what it seems to symbolize—men's access to women's bodies or the very notion that men have a legal "right" to buy sex from women who otherwise would be unavailable to them.[4] The existence of prostitution in general and legal prostitution in particular, critics argue, commodifies women and reinforces the broader cultural objectification of them.

This larger context is important. We have witnessed a steadily growing sexualization of Western culture over the past two decades, manifested in increasingly permissive sexual attitudes, emergence of new eroticisms, growth of the sex-toy market, and proliferation of sexual themes in music, movies, television shows, and commercial advertisements.[5] Whatever one thinks of these trends, it is clear that they are not driven solely by men; women are actively involved as well.[6] Insofar as this ubiquitous cultural sexualization serves to reinforce the public's interest in sex, whether unpaid or paid, it can be argued that these trends do not augur well for abolishing sex work. If the latter is true, prostitution will continue to exist, whether legal or not—so the question becomes one of minimizing harms and empowering workers to the maximum extent. Criminalization satisfies neither of these goals, as many feminists recognize: America's premier women's rights organization, the National Organization for Women (NOW), passed a decriminalization resolution several decades ago. The resolution declares that NOW "opposes continued prohibitive laws regarding prostitution, believing them to be punitive" and "therefore favors removal of all laws relating to the act of prostitution."[7] I now turn to a consideration of some practical aspects of legal prostitution systems.

Best Practices

The question of whether it is possible to identify gold standards applicable to all systems of legal prostitution has rarely been raised. Ericsson's "sound prostitution" ideal has the following ingredients: it is legal, voluntary, and restricted to adults; grants sex workers the same rights as other workers; and is destigmatized and recognized as fulfilling "a socially valuable function" by "decreasing the amount of sexual misery in society."[8] These are general principles, which can be distinguished from the practical challenges involved in implementing them.

Each nation that has legalized prostitution has implemented a model that differs in at least some ways from that of other nations. There has been some cross-fertilization from one setting to another, but much of the experimentation has occurred in a national vacuum. This leaves open the questions of whether we can identify a set of generic "best practices" and what the proper criteria are for evaluating a regulatory system. Some writers who discuss prostitution policies focus exclusively on the desires of sex workers. Sex workers are absolutely central to the success or failure of any new regime, but it is also important that reforms take into account (but not be determined by) the interests and preferences of *all* relevant parties—local residents, owners of sex businesses, sex workers, and state officials responsible for public order, health, and safety.

Drawing from the vice-legalization models presented in chapter 4 as well as my analysis of existing legal systems, I offer the following set of standards. These standards may not be fully comprehensive, but they do address the central pillars: visibility, eligibility, health, safety, and rights. The starting point is that *consensual adult prostitution be officially recognized as work and that participants be accorded the rights and protections available to those involved in other occupations.*

Visibility

- Minimize public visibility and encroachment on nonparticipants. Those who favor unfettered decriminalization will argue that minimizing visibility runs counter to the larger goal of normalization, but I argue that keeping prostitution as discreet as possible is a superior goal in light of the risk of backlash if the sex sector is too obtrusive. Keeping it largely out of sight will reduce the chances that residents and others will mobilize to recriminalize it. Another advantage is that workers' exposure to public view and to demeaning comments from people is reduced. I should note that this point best applies to newly legal systems in places where there is no preexisting identifiable red-light area. It is less relevant to a setting where prostitution has long existed in a particular geographical area (prior to formal legalization), such as in Amsterdam's centrally located red-light district, where commercial sex was thoroughly entrenched in the local culture and tourist economy prior to formal legalization in 2000.
- Prohibit sexually oriented businesses from locating near schools and playgrounds.
- An alternative to highly visible window prostitution is the enclosed building containing individual rooms—such as the hotel-brothels in Germany or the interior window rooms or courtyards in some places in the Netherlands. While the buildings themselves are obvious centers of sexual commerce, the workers and clients are not visible from the street.
- Street prostitution should be discouraged, in accordance with the minimum-visibility maxim and the problems associated with street prostitution set forth in chapter 3. Most states that have decriminalized prostitution ban the street variety because of the problems associated with it. The street sector is difficult to manage in a way that reduces harms and, according to some analysts, is inherently problematic. Zoning street work into a particular area rarely remedies problems even when there are amenities and safeguards in place, as in the Dutch *Tippelzones*, most of which have now been closed. Street prostitution in New Zealand and New South Wales, Australia, is allowed subject to public-nuisance laws, but the street market continues to be contentious in both places, and the workers continue to face more risks than do their indoor counterparts.
- In line with the preference for invisibility, there should be no restriction on one or two sex workers operating out of their own residences, subject only to existing laws regarding public nuisance and a prohibition on signage on the premises. More than two providers at any private location in a residential community increases the number of clients and, hence, the chances of public

annoyance. The idea of decriminalizing sole operators has a long lineage, being one of the proposals of the landmark Wolfenden Committee in Britain 50 years ago; today, some nations allow sole providers to operate freely.

- Advertising and signage should be sensitive to what the local community will tolerate. But to reduce potential offensiveness, advertising on billboards should be prohibited, and signage on sex businesses should be discreet. In some places, existing obscenity laws may be sufficient to restrict improper marketing. Advertising on the Internet should be permitted, so long as this does not take the form of unwelcome pop-up ads and instead requires consumers to search for services.

Eligibility

- Prohibit minors from participating in the sex trade. This is a common feature of legal prostitution systems and should be a universal rule. In most places, the minimum age is set at 18.
- Exclude minors from premises where sex is sold (e.g., adolescents seeking titillation, children of brothel workers).
- Instead of punishing underage prostitutes, the government should create and fund robust programs to facilitate their exit from prostitution, enlisting a network of service providers to promote rehabilitation and reintegration. The same resources should be available to adult sex workers who wish to leave the trade.
- Sex workers should not be forced to register or be licensed. This has been problematic almost everywhere it has been tried. As NOW warned decades ago, mandatory registration "will result in ongoing persecution of women who will not register because they do not wish publicly to proclaim themselves prostitutes."[9] Additional concerns include how the personal information would be used, how secure it would be, who would have access to it, and whether the records would be expunged after one stops selling sex. In short, registration has much stigmatizing potential and will be resisted by a large number of workers, who will have no option but to operate illegally and hence more vulnerably.
- Businesses should be licensed, just as any other business is. This applies to brothels, massage parlors, and escort agencies. The license should be visibly displayed on the premises, so that clients know the business is legal.
- Conduct thorough background checks on the operators of sex establishments to determine whether they have been convicted of crimes involving drugs, finances, coercion, or violence. A conviction for such crimes should be grounds for denial of a license. Prostitution-related offenses that occurred prior to legalization should not be held against actors operating under the

new system (e.g., running an illegal brothel in the past should be irrelevant). Unlike the current practice in the Netherlands, the burden of proof should not be placed on the applicants/operators, nor should they be rejected simply on the basis of suspicion of illegal activity. The authorities must prove that an operator has committed a crime.

- Conduct periodic, unannounced site visits to sex businesses, to ensure that the business is complying with the rules. The police, public health board, and building-code agency should conduct such visits in a routine and professional manner; they should not take the form of massive paramilitary raids, as occurs in some cities in Germany.

- If a licensing board exists, its role should be limited to receiving applications, conducting background checks on applicants, and reviewing another agency's site visits to licensed premises. The criteria for granting an application should be concrete—not subject to vague references about "the reputation" of an applicant, as in Queensland, Australia.[10] The licensing authority should have no policy role, as it does in Queensland, where by law it is required to advise the Minister of Justice on various matters, including ways to reduce the number of sex workers in the state. The latter function would seem to lessen the board's inclination to grant licenses, which helps to explain why so few have been granted in Queensland.

- A two-tiered structure of legal and illegal sectors is common in legal prostitution systems, but the size of each sector is influenced by the kinds of regulations adopted. The less onerous and costly the regulations, the smaller the size of the illegal sector (the latter is virtually nonexistent in New Zealand).[11] When the regulations are extensive, expensive, stigmatizing, and perceived as arbitrary or discriminatory compared to other businesses, this amplifies the temptation to opt out and operate illegally. The costs of a license and of complying with the regulations should not be such as to force operators out of the legal market, as in Queensland. The costs should be comparable to those of other service agencies: there should be no special, added "sin tax." At the same time, an overly minimalist system can be a problem. Recall the German government's judgment that the 2002 decriminalization law had "only to a limited degree" achieved its stated goals and that "a more broad-based approach to regulating prostitution is required."[12] Although crimes related to prostitution have declined since 2002, the German law does not require owners to provide good working conditions (such as hygiene and safety) in their establishments. A laissez-faire system can result in insufficient safeguards and controls, disempowering sex workers.

Health

- Encourage safe-sex practices, including condom usage. Although difficult to enforce, safe-sex practices serve the interests of all parties involved as well as public health generally. Health officials should conduct safe-sex outreach education with sex workers, clients, and managers, as they do in many existing legal prostitution systems.
- Regular health examinations should be encouraged but not mandated and should be offered free of charge to sex workers (as is the practice today in several legal prostitution systems). Compulsory testing for sexually transmitted infections stigmatizes sex workers, tests are not always accurate, and testing clean on a certain day may give the false impression that a person is sexually healthy afterward. Still, workers (and customers) should be encouraged to be tested periodically and to routinely practice safe sex.

Rights

- Guarantee workers' rights to refuse to engage in any sex act and to refuse to service a particular person. These rights supersede those of clients and business owners. Employers should be held responsible for ensuring that their workplaces are free of coercion and harassment.
- Prohibit discrimination against sex workers and business operators. An example is the systematic refusal of banks in the Netherlands to loan money to anyone involved in the sex industry, forcing them to seek other (perhaps questionable) sources of funding.
- Sex workers and business owners should be exempt from paying any unpaid taxes accrued prior to decriminalization. Taxation should not be retroactive.
- Expunge the criminal records of individuals with prostitution-related arrests and convictions received prior to legalization, freeing them of the stigma of a criminal record.

Safety

- Intensify sanctions against those who abuse sex workers. This pertains to client violence, parasitical pimping, sexual harassment by managers, and coercive or fraudulent trafficking. Regarding pimping, laws criminalizing anyone who "lives off the earnings of a prostitute" should be repealed because they could apply to a nonabusive boyfriend, friend, or husband. Punishment should be restricted to those who are violent or coercively exploitative—for example, forcing a person to work at certain times, to earn a certain amount of money before she or he can leave work, to perform disliked sex acts, and so on.

- Facilitate the reporting of abuse by educating police and other authorities to treat prostitutes as persons with rights, whose protection is the responsibility of state officials. This means sensitivity training for all officials who have professional contact with legal sex workers and requires a paradigm shift away from viewing them as deviants and prostitution as an immoral enterprise. The process can take a fairly long time, given the long history in which prostitution has been marginalized and stigmatized. We should expect some cultural lag—that is, societal toleration and acceptance lagging well behind legal reform—but where prostitution has been legalized, it is imperative that government officials learn to treat it as a conventional enterprise.
- Create a hotline through which clients and sex workers can anonymously report to the police suspected abuse of another sex worker. Such a hotline exists in the Netherlands today.

Policy Review and Enforcement
- The government should sponsor periodic review of prostitution-related laws and policies and their implementation and should rectify any problems identified in the review.
- If evaluations are conducted by an existing agency (e.g., Ministry of Justice) representatives of the sex industry (both sex workers and business owners) should be consulted during the review process. A preferable arrangement is creation of a separate agency with special expertise on the sex industry. Such an agency must include representatives of the sex industry on its board. This helps to ensure that the interests of owners and workers are taken into account in deliberations regarding law, policy, administration, or enforcement. As a Canadian panel emphasized, "sex workers should be regarded as experts in any law or policy decisions affecting the sex industry."[13] The members of New Zealand's Prostitution Law Review Committee include government officials, operators of sex businesses, and representatives of the New Zealand Prostitutes' Collective.
- In a newly legal system, it is important that prostitutes and their employers be informed of their rights and obligations under the law, and it is the government's responsibility to ensure this.
- Regulations are one thing; enforcement is another. It is crucial that the authorities actually enforce all regulations and are given the resources to do so.

In addition to allowing sole operators to work from their own residences, governments should be open to the idea of permitting worker cooperatives, that is, a small number of individuals who work together in the same (non-residential) location without a boss or manager. The workers would make all decisions collectively, provided that they comply with general norms on health, safety, and rights. This cottage-industry model was supported by three Canadian commissions as well as several other bodies[14] and is allowed in some (but not all) current legal prostitution systems. Criminologist John Lowman asks a related question: "What if escort services or other venues were to be run by non-profit societies, with some of the revenues being used to provide services for prostitutes?"[15] A prostitutes' rights organization could play this role, for example. The government might sell property to the organization, whose members would organize and run it in a way that maximizes workers' interests. A group of Dutch scholars and the sex workers' organization Red Thread recently floated a proposal for a broader public-private partnership. "The managing collective consists of (ex-) sex workers, representatives of sex workers, residents who live near the sex facility, and, if necessary, management and financial professionals. The collective leases space from the local government for affordable prices and organizes and manages the sex facility."[16] The local government's role would consist of enforcing antipimping laws, licensing and monitoring venues to ensure safe working conditions, and providing certain services (e.g., health care) to the workers.[17] This idea was more than just wishful thinking: the group located four buildings in Amsterdam with existing window units that they wanted to buy, but they could not arrange financing.[18]

What about the United States?

Is decriminalization or legalization possible in the United States? Nevada and Rhode Island show that a liberal policy is not a completely foreign idea in modern America. Yet Nevada's system of legal, regulated brothels is restricted to remote rural areas, and Rhode Island recently criminalized prostitution after 30 years of tolerance of the indoor sector. Chapter 3 showed that prostitution policies in the United States have grown more repressive over the past decade—with new laws, stiffer punishments, increased targeting of clients, and crackdowns on indoor operators in some jurisdictions. We might wonder why American prostitution policy has become steadily less tolerant in the context of two larger trends: the growing sexualization of popular culture and the gradual if incomplete normalization of some other kinds of vice or deviance over the past 40 years (gambling, marijuana use, gay rights, pornography, etc.).[19] As two analysts point out, "On the roster of victimless crimes, only the laws against prostitution have resisted [liberalizing] change in the United States during recent decades."[20] Why?

There are several reasons: (1) victimization or harm is viewed as much more prevalent in prostitution than in some of the other areas (marijuana use, gambling, gay rights); (2) a largely silent constituency: despite the fact that many sex workers and clients favor decriminalization, they have been reluctant to mobilize for reform;[21] (3) a shakier rights justification: the "right" to control what one does sexually with one's body is frequently advanced but has not persuaded policymakers (in contrast to gay rights, abortion rights, free-speech rights underlying pornography); (4) a lack of debate in political circles and in the media regarding alternatives to criminalization; (5) limited public support for decriminalization in the United States compared to many other nations and in contrast to Americans' overwhelming support for legal gambling and medical marijuana and growing support for gay rights; (6) weak or nonexistent alliances between sex workers' rights groups and other influential interest groups, especially women's rights organizations; and (7) potent opposition: a robust and influential coalition of interest groups on the right and left committed to keeping prostitution illegal and criminalizing other types of sex work.[22]

This roster of forces operating against liberalization of prostitution policies should not be taken to mean that legal reform is impossible in the United States in the future. Liberalization is clearly beyond the pale in the vast majority of jurisdictions, but it is possible that a particular city or state, one known for its tolerance, might embrace a more lenient approach in the future. Recall that San Francisco came close to embracing de facto decriminalization in 2008, when 42 percent of city residents voted for a measure that would have prevented the police from making prostitution arrests, and a remarkable de jure decriminalization bill was presented in the Hawaii legislature in 2007.[23] It is also possible that a state court might follow Canada's lead and declare the state's prostitution law unconstitutional (in September 2010, a Canadian court ruled that the prostitution laws "are not in accord with the principles of fundamental justice" because criminalization contributes to the endangerment of prostitutes).[24] Although the general trend in the United States is in the direction of greater repression, the possibility of liberalization at the local level cannot be ruled out. The experiences of nations where prostitution is legal and regulated could provide useful guidance for any American jurisdiction that decides to move in that direction.

Notes

NOTES TO CHAPTER 1

1. Parts of this chapter draw on Ronald Weitzer, "Sociology of Sex Work," *Annual Review of Sociology* 35 (2009): 213–234; Ronald Weitzer, "Sex Work: Paradigms and Policies," in Ronald Weitzer, ed., *Sex for Sale: Prostitution, Pornography, and the Sex Industry*, 2nd ed., New York: Routledge, 2010; and Ronald Weitzer, "The Mythology of Prostitution: Advocacy Research and Public Policy," *Sexuality Research and Social Policy* 7 (2010): 15–29.

2. TopTenREVIEWS provides the following figures for 2006 in the United States alone: $3.62 billion on X-rated video sales/rentals; $2.84 billion on Internet porn; $2.19 billion on cable TV, PPV, mobile, and phone sex; $2 billion on exotic dance clubs; $1.73 billion on novelties; $0.95 billion on magazines. Jerry Ropelato, "Internet Pornography Statistics," TopTenREVIEWS, http://internet-filter-review.toptenreviews.com/internet-pornography-statistics.html.

3. Eric Schlosser, "The Business of Pornography," *U.S. News and World Report*, February 10, 1997; 2006 figure from Ropelato, "Internet Pornography Statistics."

4. Ropelato, "Internet Pornography Statistics."

5. William Sherman, "The Naked Truth about Strip Clubs," *New York Daily News*, July 8, 2007.

6. James Davis and Tom Smith, *General Social Survey: Cumulative Codebook*, Chicago: National Opinion Research Center, 2008. These figures are virtually identical to those for 2002, 2004, and 2006.

7. Ibid.

8. Chris Rissel, "Experiences of Commercial Sex in a Representative Sample of Adults," *Australian and New Zealand Journal of Public Health* 27 (2003): 191–197.

9. In some other nations, even more men say they have paid for sex. In Spain, 39 percent of men have done so during their lifetime, and in northeastern Thailand, 43 percent of single men and 50 percent of married men had visited a prostitute. Ibid.; Eleanor Maticka-Tyndale, "Context and Patterns of Men's Commercial Sexual Partnerships in Northeastern Thailand," *Social Science and Medicine* 44 (1997): 199–213.

10. Ipsos MORI poll, January 6–10, 2006, N = 1,790, ages 16–64.

11. Hillary Rhodes, "Prostitution Advances in a Wired World," Associated Press, March 11, 2008; Bruce Lambert, "As Prostitutes Turn to Craigslist, Law Takes Notice," *New York Times*, September 4, 2007.

12. Figures are from the FBI's annual crime report under the category "prostitution and commercialized vice," which includes soliciting, brothel keeping, procuring, and transportation. The number of juveniles arrested is a small fraction of the total and very similar from year to year: 1,200 in 2001 and 1,156 in 2008. Federal Bureau of Investigation, *Crime in the United States*, Washington, DC: Department of Justice, 1983, 2009.

13. Lynn Comella, "Remaking the Sex Industry: The Adult Expo as a Microcosm," in Weitzer, ed., *Sex for Sale*, 2nd ed.

14. Davis and Smith, *General Social Survey*.

15. Ellison Research poll, March 11, 2008, N = 1,007. This was the view of 42 percent of men and 57 percent of women.

16. Harris Poll #76, September 20–26, 2004, N = 2,555. This was the view of 38 percent of men and 57 percent of women.

17. UMR Research poll, reported in *PC World*, January 12, 2010, N = 1,000, http://pcworld.co.nz.

18. ICM Research, Sex and Exploitation Survey, January 2008, N = 1,023. Women (68 percent) were slightly more likely to take this view than were men (62 percent).

19. Ipsos MORI poll, Prostitution Survey, June 11–12, 2008, N = 1,012.

20. Ipsos MORI poll, Prostitution Survey, August 29–31, 2008, N = 1,010.

21. *Time* magazine poll, July 26–31, 1977, N = 1,044 registered voters.

22. The question asked "whether you think prostitution can always be justified, never be justified, or something in between" and asked respondents to rank this on a ten-point continuum. World Values Survey, http://www.wvsevsdb.com/wvs/WVSAnalizeQuestion.jsp. The meaning of "justified" is opaque in the question.

23. The most recent polls are from the 1990s. See Ronald Weitzer, "The Politics of Prostitution in America," in Ronald Weitzer, ed., *Sex for Sale: Prostitution, Pornography, and the Sex Industry*, New York: Routledge, 2000.

24. The figures were 41 percent in 1984 and 33 percent in 2008, but the 2008 figure may be exceptional rather than marking a trend, given that the figures for 2004 and 2006 were 38 percent and 39 percent, respectively (Davis and Smith, *General Social Survey*). The question asked respondents which policy is closest to their own view: "There should be laws against the distribution of pornography whatever the age. There should be laws against the distribution of pornography to persons under 18. There should be no laws against the distribution of pornography." The figures presented here are for the first option, a universal ban on distribution. Women are more likely than men to want porn outlawed: 40 percent and 24 percent, respectively, in 2008.

25. Gallup, *Gallup Poll Monthly*, 1991; 46 percent thought female strippers and 45 percent thought male strippers "should be illegal at bars or clubs."

26. Arlene Carmen and Howard Moody, *Working Women: The Subterranean World of Street Prostitution*, New York: Harper and Row, 1985; Frederique Delacoste and Priscilla Alexander, eds., *Sex Work: Writings by Women in the Sex Industry*, Pittsburgh: Cleis, 1987; Nadine Strossen, *Defending Pornography*, New York: Anchor, 1995; Wendy McElroy, *XXX: A Woman's Right to Pornography*, New York: St. Martin's, 1995; Wendy Chapkis, *Live Sex Acts: Women Performing Erotic Labor*, New York: Routledge, 1997.

27. Noah Zatz, "Sex Work/Sex Act: Law, Labor, and Desire in Constructions of Prostitution," *Signs* 22 (1997): 277–308, at p. 291.

28. Chapkis, *Live Sex Acts*, p. 30.

29. Paglia, quoted in Robert Meier and Gilbert Geis, *Victimless Crime? Prostitution, Drugs, Homosexuality, Abortion*, Los Angeles: Roxbury, 1997, p. 44.

30. Shannon Bell, *Whore Carnival*, New York: Autonomedia, 1995, p. 16.

31. Annie Sprinkle, "The Forty Reasons Why Whores Are My Heroes," *Social Alternatives* 18 (1999): 8.

32. Dolores French, *Working: My Life as a Prostitute*, New York: Dutton, 1988, pp. 176, 178.

33. Paglia, quoted in Chapkis, *Live Sex Acts*, p. 22.

34. Russell Campbell, *Marked Women: Prostitutes and Prostitution in the Cinema*, Madison: University of Wisconsin Press, 2006.

35. Patty Kelly, *Lydia's Open Door: Inside Mexico's Most Modern Brothel*, Berkeley: University of California Press, 2008, pp. 202.

36. Ibid., p. 134.

37. Cleo Odzer, *Patpong Sisters: An American Woman's View of the Bangkok Sex World*, New York: Arcade, 1994, pp. 181.

38. Ibid., p. 303.

39. Sukanya Hantrakul, "Prostitution in Thailand," paper quoted in ibid., p. 133.

40. Peter Aggleton, ed., *Men Who Sell Sex*, Philadelphia: Temple University Press, 1999; Jude Uy, Jeffrey Parsons, David Bimbi, Juline Koken, and Perry Halkitis, "Gay and Bisexual Male Escorts Who Advertise on the Internet: Understanding the Reasons for and Effects of Involvement in Commercial Sex," *International Journal of Men's Health* 3 (2007): 11–26; Akiko Takeyama, "Commodified Romance in a Tokyo Host Club," in Mark McLelland and Romit Dasgupta, eds., *Genders, Transgenders, and Sexualities in Japan*, New York: Routledge, 2005.

41. Joe Thomas, "Gay Male Pornography since Stonewall," in Weitzer, ed., *Sex for Sale*, 2nd ed., p. 84. For a similar argument regarding the liberatory potential of gay porn, see Carl Stychin, "Exploring the Limits: Feminism and the Legal Regulation of Gay Male Pornography," *Vermont Law Review* 16 (1992): 857–900.

42. Katherine Frank and Michelle Carnes, "Gender and Space in Strip Clubs," in Weitzer, ed., *Sex for Sale*, 2nd ed.

43. Don Kulick, *Travesti: Sex, Gender, and Culture among Brazilian Prostitutes*, Chicago: University Chicago Press, 1998, p. 136.

44. Lydia Sausa, JoAnne Keatley, and Don Operario, "Perceived Risks and Benefits of Sex Work among Transgender Women of Color in San Francisco," *Archives of Sexual Behavior* 36 (2007): 768–777, at p. 772. See also Cymene Howe, Susanna Zaraysky, and Lois Lorentzen, "Transgender Sex Workers and Sexual Transmigration between Guadalajara and San Francisco," *Latin American Perspectives* 35 (2008): 31–50.

45. Jill Bakehorn, "Women-Made Pornography," in Weitzer, ed., *Sex for Sale*, 2nd ed.

46. Carole Pateman, *The Sexual Contract*, Stanford: Stanford University Press, 1988, pp. 199, 208.

47. Kathleen Barry, *The Prostitution of Sexuality*, New York: NYU Press, 1995; Andrea Dworkin, *Pornography: Men Possessing Women*, New York: Putnam, 1981; Andrea Dworkin, *Life and Death: Unapologetic Writings on the Continuing War against Women*, New York: Free Press, 1997; Sheila Jeffreys, *The Idea of Prostitution*, North Melbourne, Australia: Spinifex, 1997; Catharine MacKinnon, *Feminism Unmodified*, Cambridge: Harvard University Press, 1987; Catharine MacKinnon, *Toward a Feminist Theory of the State*, Cambridge: Harvard University Press, 1989.

48. Melissa Farley, "Affidavit of Melissa Farley," in *Bedford v. Attorney General of Canada*, Case No. 07-CV-329807PD1, Superior Court of Justice, Ontario, Canada, 2008, p. 16.

49. Janice Raymond, "Prostitution Is Rape That's Paid For," *Los Angeles Times*, December 11, 1995, p. B6.

50. Melissa Farley, "Prostitution, Trafficking, and Cultural Amnesia: What We Must *Not Know* in Order to Keep the Business of Sexual Exploitation Running Smoothly," *Yale Journal of Law and Feminism* 18 (2006): 101–136, at p. 114.

51. Janice Raymond, "Prostitution on Demand: Legalizing the Buyers as Sexual Consumers," *Violence Against Women* 10 (2004): 1156–1186, at p. 1183.

52. Jeffreys, *Idea of Prostitution*, p. 330.

53. Melissa Farley, "Prostitution and Trafficking in Nine Countries," *Journal of Trauma Practice* 2 (2003): 33–74, at p. 34.

54. It could be argued that the phrase "buy women" objectifies women who work in prostitution by treating them as commodities, rather than as people supplying a sexual service.

55. Jody Raphael and Deborah Shapiro, *Sisters Speak Out: The Lives and Needs of Prostituted Women in Chicago*, Chicago: Center for Impact Research, 2002, p. 137.

56. Melissa Farley, "Bad for the Body, Bad for the Heart: Prostitution Harms Women Even If Legalized or Decriminalized," *Violence Against Women* 10 (2004): 1087–1125, at p. 1102.

57. Melissa Farley, quoted in Annie Brown, "Sex Industry in Scotland: Inside the Deluded Minds of the Punters," *Daily Record* (Scotland), April 28, 2008.

58. Jan Macleod, Melissa Farley, Lynn Anderson, and Jacqueline Golding, *Challenging Men's Demand for Prostitution in Scotland*, Glasgow, Scotland: Women's Support Project, 2008, p. 27.

59. Donna Hughes, *The Demand for Victims of Sex Trafficking*, Kingston: University of Rhode Island, 2005, p. 7.

60. Dworkin, *Life and Death*, p. 145.

61. Farley, "Bad for the Body," p. 1101.

62. Farley, "Prostitution, Trafficking, and Cultural Amnesia," p. 107.

63. Ibid., p. 122.

64. Catharine MacKinnon, "Pornography as Trafficking," *Michigan Journal of International Law* 26 (2005): 993–1012, at pp. 993, 1004.

65. Ibid., p. 999.

66. These claims are repeatedly made by oppression writers and activists, in publications and on their organizations' websites, such as that of Raymond's Coalition Against Trafficking in Women and Farley's Prostitution Research and Education.

67. Marianne Hester and Nicole Westmarland, *Tackling Street Prostitution: Towards a Holistic Approach*, Research Study 279, London: Home Office, 2004.

68. Maaike van Veen, "HIV and Sexual Risk Behavior among Commercial Sex Workers in the Netherlands, *Archives of Sexual Behavior* 39 (2010): 714–723.

69. Institute for Population and Social Research, *2007 Survey of Sexual and Reproductive Health of Sex Workers in Thailand*, Salaya, Thailand: Mahidol University, 2007, pp. 19, 35. It is possible that there was some underreporting of drug use.

70. Ine Vanwesenbeeck, Ron de Graaf, Gertjan van Zessen, Cees Straver, and Jan Visser, "Professional HIV Risk Taking, Levels of Victimization, and Well-Being in Female Prostitutes in the Netherlands," *Archives of Sexual Behavior* 24 (1995): 503–515.

71. Gayle Rubin, "Thinking Sex: Notes for a Radical Theory of the Politics of Sexuality," in Carole S. Vance, ed., *Pleasure and Danger: Exploring Female Sexuality*, Boston: Routledge and Kegan Paul, 1984, p. 301.

72. Janice Raymond, "Ten Reasons for *Not* Legalizing Prostitution and a Legal Response to the Demand for Prostitution," *Journal of Trauma Practice* 2 (2003): 315–322, at p. 325.

73. Melissa Farley, *Prostitution and Trafficking in Nevada: Making the Connections*, San Francisco: Prostitution Research and Education, 2007, p. 22.

74. Ibid.

75. Ibid., p. 31.

76. Ibid., p. 33.

77. Farley, "Prostitution and Trafficking in Nine Countries," p. 52.

78. Melissa Farley, "Prostitution Harms Women Even If Indoors: Reply to Weitzer," *Violence Against Women* 11 (2005): 950–964, at p. 954.

79. This tendency is documented in Weitzer, "Mythology of Prostitution."

80. Karl Popper, *The Logic of Scientific Discovery*, New York: Basic Books, 1959.

81. Helga Hallgrimsdottir, Rachel Phillips, and Cecilia Benoit, "Fallen Women and Rescued Girls: Social Stigma and Media Narratives of the Sex Industry in Victoria, BC from 1980–2005," *Canadian Review of Sociology and Anthropology* 43 (2006): 265–280.

82. Ronald Weitzer, "Legalizing Prostitution: Morality Politics in Western Australia," *British Journal of Criminology* 49 (2009): 88–105.

83. In addition to ruling that the prostitution laws were unconstitutional because they had the effect of further endangering prostitutes, the judge stated,

> I found the evidence of Dr. Melissa Farley to be problematic. . . . Her advocacy appears to have permeated her opinions. For example, Dr. Farley's unqualified assertion in her affidavit that prostitution is inherently violent appears to contradict her own findings that prostitutes who work from indoor locations generally experience less violence. Dr. Farley's choice of language is at times inflammatory and detracts from her conclusions. For example, comments such as, "prostitution is to the community what incest is to the family," and "just as pedophiles justify sexual assault of children . . . men who use prostitutes develop elaborate cognitive schemes to justify purchase and use of women" make her opinions less persuasive. Dr. Farley stated during cross-examination that some of her opinions on prostitution were formed prior to her research, including "that prostitution is a terrible harm to women, that prostitution is abusive in its very nature, and that prostitution amounts to men paying a woman for the right to rape her." Accordingly, for these reasons, I assign less weight to Dr. Farley's evidence. . . . Similarly, I find that Drs. Raymond and Poulin were more like advocates than experts offering independent opinions to the court. At times, they made bold, sweeping statements that were not reflected in their research.

Bedford v. Canada, 2010 ONSC 4264, Superior Court of Justice, Ontario, Canada, Justice Himel, September 28, 2010, paras. 353–357. The ruling struck down the criminal-code sections that outlawed keeping a bawdy house, living on the avails of prostitution, and communicating in a public place for the purpose of engaging in prostitution.

84. Julia O'Connell Davidson, *Power, Prostitution, and Freedom*, Ann Arbor: University of Michigan Press, 1998.

85. Campbell, *Marked Women*.

86. Ine Vanwesenbeeck, "Another Decade of Social Scientific Work on Prostitution," *Annual Review of Sex Research* 12 (2001): 242–289; Frances Shaver, "Sex Work Research: Methodological and Ethical Challenges," *Journal of Interpersonal Violence* 20 (2005): 296–319; Christine Harcourt and B. Donovan, "The Many Faces of Sex Work," *Sexually Transmitted Infections* 81 (2005): 201–206.

87. See Gail Hershatter, "The Hierarchy of Shanghai Prostitution: 1870–1949," *Modern China* 15 (1989): 463–498; Ruth Karras, *Common Women: Prostitution and Sexuality in Medieval England*, New York: Oxford University Press, 1996. Over the course of the 20th century in Shanghai, for instance, "what had been essentially a luxury market in courtesans became a market primarily geared to supplying sexual services for the growing numbers of commercial and working-class men of the city." Up-market sex work persisted throughout the century, but less refined forms multiplied as well. Gail Hershatter, *Dangerous Pleasures: Prostitution and Modernity in Twentieth-Century Shanghai*, Berkeley: University of California Press, 1999, pp. 64–65.

88. Ian Urbina, "For Runaways, Sex Buys Survival," *New York Times*, October 26, 2009.

89. Michael Scott, *Street Prostitution*, Washington, DC: Department of Justice, 2001; Neil McKeganey and Marina Barnard, *Sex Work on the Streets*, Buckingham, UK: Open University Press, 1996; Judith Porter and Louis Bonilla, "The Ecology of Street Prostitution," in Weitzer, ed., *Sex for Sale*, 2nd ed.

90. Barbara Heyl, "Prostitution: An Extreme Case of Sex Stratification," in Freda Adler and Rita Simon, eds., *The Criminology of Deviant Women*, Boston: Houghton Mifflin, 1979, p. 198.

91. A New Zealand study questioned 772 street, brothel, and independent workers operating in private premises. Eight out of ten street workers began their work on the street and remained on the street at the time of the survey; 92 percent of brothel workers began their work in brothels and remained there, and 49 percent of independent call girls began as brothel workers, whereas 39 percent began as private workers. In other words, call girls were much more mobile than were the other two groups; most street and brothel workers experienced no mobility. Prostitution Law Review Committee, *Report of the Prostitution Law Review Committee on the Operation of the Prostitution Reform Act 2003*, Wellington, New Zealand: Ministry of Justice, 2008, p. 76.

92. McKeganey and Barnard, *Sex Work on the Streets*, pp. 20–21; Barbara Heyl, "The Madam as Teacher: The Training of House Prostitutes," *Social Problems* 24 (1977): 545–555. For a list of rules governing behavior in one London brothel, see the conclusion to this autobiography: Miss S, *Confessions of a Working Girl*, Naperville, IL: Sourcebooks, 2008.

93. A comparison of a large sample of customers with a nationally representative sample of American men found few differences between the two populations. The customer sample was based on men arrested mostly for soliciting street prostitutes, so it was neither random nor reflective of clients of indoor venues. Therefore, the study cannot be regarded as definitive in its comparison of the client and general male samples. Martin Monto and Nick McRee, "A Comparison of the Male Customers of Female Street Prostitutes with National Samples of Men," *International Journal of Offender Therapy and Comparative Criminology* 49 (2005): 505–529.

94. Martin Monto, "Prostitutes' Customers: Motives and Misconceptions," in Weitzer, ed., *Sex for Sale*, 2nd ed. See also Teela Sanders, *Paying for Pleasure: Men Who Buy Sex*, Portland, OR: Willan, 2008; and John Lowman and Chris Atchison, "Men Who Buy Sex: A Survey in the Greater Vancouver Regional District," *Canadian Review of Sociology and Anthropology* 43 (2006): 281–296.

95. Monto, "Prostitutes' Customers," pp. 243, 244.

96. In a British study, only 8 percent of arrested customers had a previous conviction for a sexual or violent offense: Belinda Brooks-Gordon, *The Price of Sex: Prostitution, Policy, and Society*, Portland, OR: Willan, 2006, p. 198.

97. Bridget Anderson and Julia O'Connell Davidson, *Is Trafficking in Human Beings Demand Driven? A Multi-Country Pilot Study*, Geneva: International Organization for Migration, 2003, pp. 25, 24. See also Sanders, *Paying for Pleasure*, pp. 49–52.

98. Monto, "Prostitutes' Customers," p. 243.

99. Martha Stein, *Lovers, Friends, Slaves*, New York: Berkeley, 1974, p. 312.

100. Interview with the director of the Foundation of Men and Prostitution, The Hague, May 29, 1998.

101. Mary McIntosh, "Who Needs Prostitutes? The Ideology of Male Sexual Needs," in Carol Smart and Barry Smart, eds., *Women, Sexuality, and Social Control*, London: Routledge and Kegan Paul, 1978.

102. These diverse motives are amply documented in research studies: Stein, *Lovers, Friends, Slaves*; Monto, "Prostitutes' Customers"; Sanders, *Paying for Pleasure*; McKeganey and Barnard, *Sex Work on the Streets*; Sarah Earle and Keith Sharp, *Sex in Cyberspace: Men Who Pay for Sex*, Aldershot, UK: Ashgate, 2007; Christine Milrod, "The Internet Hobbyist: Demographics and Sexual Behaviors of Male Clients of Internet Sexual Service Providers," Ph.D. diss., Institute for Advanced Study of Human Sexuality, San Francisco, 2010.

103. Charlotte Woodward, Jane Fischer, Jake Najman, and Michael Dunne, *Selling Sex in Queensland*, Brisbane, Australia: Prostitution Licensing Authority, 2004.

104. Sanders, *Paying for Pleasure*, pp. 49–52.

NOTES TO CHAPTER 2

1. In Thailand, an estimated 0.7 percent work on the street. Thomas Steinfatt, *Working at the Bar: Sex Work and Health Communication in Thailand*, Westport, CT: Ablex, 2002, p. 19.

2. See Prabha Kotiswaran, "Born unto Brothels: Toward a Legal Ethnography of Sex Work in an Indian Red-Light Area," *Law and Social Inquiry* 33 (2008): 579–629; Patty Kelly, *Lydia's Open Door: Inside Mexico's Most Modern Brothel*, Berkeley: University of California Press, 2008; Kamala Kempadoo, *Sexing the Caribbean: Gender, Race, and Sexual Labor*, New York: Routledge, 2004; Kamala Kempadoo, ed., *Sun, Sex, and Gold: Tourism and Sex Work in the Caribbean*, Lanham, MD: Rowman and Littlefield, 1999; Denise Brennan, *What's Love Got to Do with It? Transnational Desires and Sex Tourism in the Dominican Republic*, Durham: Duke University Press, 2004.

3. Louise Brown, "Performance, Status, and Hybridity in a Pakistani Red-Light District: The Cultural Production of the Courtesan," *Sexualities* 10 (2007): 409–423, at p. 418.

4. Kimberly Hoang, "Economies of Emotion, Familiarity, Fantasy, and Desire: Emotional Labor in Ho Chi Minh City's Sex Industry," *Sexualities* 13 (2010): 255–272, at p. 266.

5. Institute for Population and Social Research, *2007 Survey of Sexual and Reproductive Health of Sex Workers in Thailand*, Salaya, Thailand: Mahidol University, 2007.

6. Cleo Odzer, *Patpong Sisters: An American Woman's View of the Bangkok Sex World*, New York: Arcade, 1994, p. 65.

7. Wendy Chapkis, "Power and Control in the Commercial Sex Trade," in Ronald Weitzer, ed., *Sex for Sale: Prostitution, Pornography, and the Sex Industry*, New York: Routledge, 2000.

8. Julia O'Connell Davidson, *Power, Prostitution, and Freedom*, Ann Arbor: University of Michigan Press, 1998, pp. 46–58; Tiggey May, Alex Harocopos, and Michael Hough, *For Love or Money: Pimps and the Management of Prostitution*, Police Research Series 134, London: Home Office, 2000; Jennifer James, "Prostitute-Pimp Relationships," *Medical Aspects of Human Sexuality* 7 (1973): 147–160.

9. See, for instance, Steinfatt, *Working at the Bar*, pp. 278, 284; Henry Trotter, *Sugar Girls and Seamen: A Journey into the World of Dockside Prostitution in South Africa*, Auckland Park, South Africa: Jacana, 2008; Tiantian Zheng, *Red Lights: The Lives of Sex Workers in Postsocialist China*, Minneapolis: University of Minnesota Press, 2009; Maria Perez-y-Perez, "Discipline, Autonomy, and Ambiguity: Organizations, Markets, and Work in the Sex Industry, Christchurch, New Zealand," Ph.D. diss., University of Canterbury, Christchurch, New Zealand, 2003.

10. In Uganda, for instance, middlemen in towns along major transnational highways function as interpreters and brokers who recommend specific women based on the drivers' preferences and protect both the clients and the workers from theft, robbery, deceit, and assault—thus acting in the interests of prostitutes and clients alike. Marjolein Gysels, R. Pool, and K. Bwanika, "Truck Drivers, Middlemen, and Commercial Sex Workers," *AIDS Care* 13 (2001): 373–385.

11. Dawn Whittaker and Graham Hart, "Managing Risks: The Social Organization of Indoor Sex Work," *Sociology of Health and Illness* 18 (1996): 399–414.

12. The British researchers interviewed 135 indoor prostitutes in Birmingham, Liverpool, and Sefton: Teela Sanders and Rosie Campbell, "Designing Out Vulnerability, Building In Respect," *British Journal of Sociology* 58 (2007): 1–19. The Belgian study surveyed 83 call girls and sex workers in bars, brothels, saunas, and windows: Europap, *Report Questionnaire 2001 in Belgium*, Europap, 2001.

13. Ine Vanwesenbeeck, Ron de Graaf, Gertjan van Zessen, Cees Straver, and Jan Visser, "Professional HIV Risk Taking, Levels of Victimization, and Well-Being in Female Prostitutes in the Netherlands," *Archives of Sexual Behavior* 24 (1995): 503–515.

14. Libby Plumridge and Gillian Abel, "A Segmented Sex Industry in New Zealand: Sexual and Personal Safety of Female Sex Workers," *Australian and New Zealand Journal of Public Health* 25 (2001): 78–83, at p. 83.

15. See the studies cited in Ronald Weitzer, "Sociology of Sex Work," *Annual Review of Sociology* 35 (2009): 213–234.

16. Janet Lever and Deanne Dolnick, "Call Girls and Street Prostitutes: Selling Sex and Intimacy," in Ronald Weitzer, ed., *Sex for Sale: Prostitution, Pornography, and the Sex Industry*, 2nd ed., New York: Routledge, 2010.

17. Roberta Perkins and Frances Lovejoy, *Call Girls: Private Sex Workers in Australia*, Crawley: University of Western Australia Press, 2007, p. 51.

18. Dolores French, *Working: My Life as a Prostitute*, New York: Dutton, 1988, pp. 152–153; see also Tracy Quan, *Diary of a Manhattan Call Girl*, New York: Three Rivers, 2003.

19. Quoted in Joanne Kimberlin, "Women for Hire: Behind Closed Doors in the Escort Industry," *Virginia-Pilot*, May 18, 2008, p. A11.

20. Anonymous, *Secret Diary of a Call Girl*, New York: Grand Central, 2008, p. 140.

21. Ine Vanwesenbeeck, *Prostitutes' Well-Being and Risk*, Amsterdam: VU University Press, 1994.

22. Sarah Romans, Kathleen Potter, Judy Martin, and Peter Herbison, "The Mental and Physical Health of Female Sex Workers," *Australian and New Zealand Journal of Psychiatry* 35 (2001): 75–80.

23. John Exner, Joyce Wylie, Antonnia Leura, and Tracey Parrill, "Some Psychological Characteristics of Prostitutes," *Journal of Personality Assessment* 41 (1977): 474–485, at p. 483.

24. Ann Lucas, "The Work of Sex Work: Elite Prostitutes' Vocational Orientations and Experiences," *Deviant Behavior* 26 (2005): 513–546, at p. 541.

25. Ibid., p. 523.

26. Charlotte Woodward, Jane Fischer, Jake Najman, and Michael Dunne, *Selling Sex in Queensland*, Brisbane, Australia: Prostitution Licensing Authority, 2004, p. 39.

27. Quoted in Mark Waite, "Prostitutes Dispute Trummell Charges," *Pahrump Valley Times* (Nevada), October 5, 2007.

28. Quoted in Alexa Albert, *Brothel: Mustang Ranch and Its Women*, New York: Ballantine, 2001, p. 100.

29. See the studies cited in Weitzer, "Sociology of Sex Work"; Ine Vanwesenbeeck, "Another Decade of Social Scientific Work on Prostitution," *Annual Review of Sex Research* 12 (2001): 242–289.

30. Diana Prince, "A Psychological Study of Prostitutes in California and Nevada," Ph.D. diss., U.S. International University, San Diego, California, 1986, p. 454.

31. John Decker, *Prostitution: Regulation and Control*, Littleton, CO: Rothman, 1979, pp. 166, 174.

32. Jude Uy, Jeffrey Parsons, David Bimbi, Juline Koken, and Perry Halkitis, "Gay and Bisexual Male Escorts Who Advertise on the Internet: Understanding the Reasons for and Effects of Involvement in Commercial Sex," *International Journal of Men's Health* 3 (2007): 11–26.

33. Odzer, *Patpong Sisters*, p. 78.

34. Heidi Hoefinger, "Professional Girlfriends: Sex Workers and the Bartering of Intimacy in Phnom Penh, Cambodia," M.A. thesis, Hunter College, City University of New York, 2005, p. 85.

35. Upscale work is featured in the CNBC television documentary "Dirty Money: The Business of High-End Prostitution," which first aired in November 2008. See also Adam Goldman, "Scandal Gives Peek inside Call-Girl Ring," Associated Press, March 12, 2008.

36. Lucas, "Work of Sex Work."

37. Elizabeth Bernstein, *Temporarily Yours: Intimacy, Authenticity, and the Commerce of Sex*, Chicago: University of Chicago Press, 2007, p. 100.

38. Martha Stein, *Lovers, Friends, Slaves*, New York: Berkeley, 1974, p. 25.

39. French, *Working*, pp. 37–38.

40. Albert, *Brothel*, p. 129.

41. Martin Weinberg, Frances Shaver, and Colin Williams, "Gendered Prostitution in the San Francisco Tenderloin," *Archives of Sexual Behavior* 28 (1999): 503–521; Yasmina Katsulis, *Sex Work and the City: The Social Geography of Health and Safety in Tijuana, Mexico*, Austin: University of Texas Press, 2008.

42. This a claim frequently made by oppression writers, for example, Melissa Farley, "Prostitution and Trafficking in Nine Countries," *Journal of Trauma Practice* 2 (2003): 33–74. She insists that "psychological violence" is pervasive in all indoor sex work settings, including strip clubs.

43. Juline Koken, David Bimbi, and Jeffrey Parsons, "Male and Female Escorts: A Comparative Analysis," in Weitzer, ed., *Sex for Sale*, 2nd ed.

44. Ibid., pp. 224, 225.

45. Martin Monto, "Prostitutes' Customers: Motives and Misconceptions," in Weitzer, ed., *Sex for Sale*, 2nd ed.

46. Katherine Frank, *G-Strings and Sympathy: Strip Club Regulars and Male Desire*, Durham: Duke University Press, 2002.

47. Stein, *Lovers, Friends, Slaves*; Bernstein *Temporarily Yours*; Teela Sanders, *Paying for Pleasure: Men Who Buy Sex*, Portland, OR: Willan, 2008; Lucas, "Work of Sex Work."

48. Neil McKeganey and Marina Barnard, *Sex Work on the Streets*, Buckingham, UK: Open University Press, 1996, pp. 86–88.

49. Lever and Dolnick, "Call Girls and Street Prostitutes"; Woodward et al., *Selling Sex in Queensland*.

50. Lever and Dolnick, "Call Girls and Street Prostitutes."

51. Stein, *Lovers, Friends, Slaves*, p. 94.

52. Charrlotte Seib, Michael Dunne, Jane Fischer, and Jackob Najman, "Commercial Sexual Practices before and after Legalization in Australia," *Archives of Sexual Behavior* 39 (2010): 979–989. Almost all of the brothel and private providers had engaged in massage with clients.

53. Sarah Earle and Keith Sharp, *Sex in Cyberspace: Men Who Pay for Sex*, Aldershot, UK: Ashgate, 2007, p. 77.

54. Stein, *Lovers, Friends, Slaves*, p. 52. See also Teela Sanders, *Sex Work*, Portland, OR: Willan, 2005.

55. Prince, "Psychological Study of Prostitutes," p. 490.

56. Lucas, "Work of Sex Work," p. 531.

57. Seib et al., "Commercial Sexual Practices."

58. Christine Milrod, "The Internet Hobbyist: Demographics and Sexual Behaviors of Male Clients of Internet Sexual Service Providers," Ph.D. diss., Institute for Advanced Study of Human Sexuality, San Francisco, 2010, p. 114.

59. See, for instance, Andrew Jacobs, "Call Girls, Updated," *New York Times*, October 12, 2004.

60. See, for instance, Voon Chin Phua, "The Love That Binds: Transnational Relationships in Sex Work," *Sexuality and Culture* 13 (2009): 91–110.

61. Koken et al., "Male and Female Escorts"; Michael Smith, Christian Grov, and David Seal, "Agency Based Male Sex Work," *Journal of Men's Studies* 16 (2008): 193–210; Mark Padilla, *Caribbean Pleasure Industry: Tourism, Sexuality, and AIDS in the Dominican Republic*, Chicago: University of Chicago Press, 2007.

62. Bernstein, *Temporarily Yours*, pp. 69, 120.

63. Gail Hershatter, *Dangerous Pleasures: Prostitution and Modernity in Twentieth-Century Shanghai*, Berkeley: University of California Press, 1999, p. 37.

64. Ibid., p. 109.

65. Stein, *Lovers, Friends, Slaves*, p. 11.

66. Tammy Castle and Jenifer Lee, "Ordering Sex in Cyberspace: A Content Analysis of Escort Websites," *International Journal of Cultural Studies* 11 (2008): 108–121.

67. Thomas Holt and Kristie Blevins, "Examining Sex Work from the Clients' Perspective," *Deviant Behavior* 28 (2007): 333–354; CNBC, "Dirty Money."

68. Earle and Sharp, *Sex in Cyberspace*.

69. Milrod, "Internet Hobbyist," p. 112.

70. Sanders, *Paying for Pleasure*, p. 93.

71. Ibid., p. 109.

72. Lucas, "Work of Sex Work," p. 531.

73. Quoted in Diane Suchetka and Jim Nichols, "Sex for Sale: The Men Who Buy It," *Cleveland Plain Dealer*, March 21, 2008.

74. *Dexter*, season 3, Showtime, 2008.

75. Johngaltnh, posting on theeroticreview.com, September 2009.

76. Earle and Sharp, *Sex in Cyberspace*.

77. Stein, *Lovers, Friends, Slaves*, p. 314.

78. Perkins and Lovejoy, *Call Girls*, p. 107.

79. Sanders, *Paying for Pleasure*, pp. 60, 98.

80. Ibid., pp. 53–55.

81. Nearly two-thirds of the customers interviewed in one study felt guilty for cheating on their regular sex partners. Perkins and Lovejoy, *Call Girls*, p. 107.

82. Earle and Sharp, *Sex in Cyberspace*; Bernstein, *Temporarily Yours*, pp. 131–133.

83. Sanders, *Paying for Pleasure*, p. 104.

84. Julia O'Connell Davidson, "The Anatomy of 'Free Choice' Prostitution," *Gender, Work, and Organization* 2 (1995): 1–10, at p. 4. See also Sanders, *Sex Work*.

85. French, *Working*, p. 29.

86. Anonymous, *Secret Diary*, p. 231.

87. Perkins and Lovejoy (*Call Girls*, p. 107) found that half of the brothel workers and two-fifths of the calls girls in their study had problems with obsessive clients.

88. *Honeymooning* is the term used by street workers in the HBO documentary "Downtown Girls: The Hookers of Honolulu," 2005.

89. Stein, *Lovers, Friends, Slaves*, p. 23.

90. Ibid.

91. Perkins and Lovejoy, *Call Girls*, p. 112.

92. Anonymous, *Secret Diary*, p. 150.

93. Quoted in Mike Celizic, "Former Call Girl Opens Up about the Industry," MSNBC.msn.com, March 12, 2008.

94. Quoted in Perkins and Lovejoy, *Call Girls*, p. 63.

95. Quoted in Perez-y-Perez, "Discipline, Autonomy, and Ambiguity," p. 204.

96. Bernstein, *Temporarily Yours*, p. 103.

97. Perkins and Lovejoy, *Call Girls*, p. 110; cf. Perez-y-Perez, "Discipline, Autonomy, and Ambiguity," p. 195.

98. Brennan, *What's Love Got to Do with It?* p. 24.

99. Steinfatt, *Working at the Bar*, pp. 177, 254–255.

100. Ibid. See also Kempadoo, ed., *Sun, Sex, and Gold*; Eric Ratliff, "Women as 'Sex Workers,' Men as 'Boyfriends': Shifting Identities in Philippine Go-Go Bars and Their Significance in STD/AIDS Control," *Anthropology and Medicine* 6 (1999): 79–101; Lin Lean Lim, *The Sex Sector: The Economic and Social Bases of Prostitution in Southeast Asia*, Geneva: International Labor Office, 1998.

101. The 1995 survey was conducted by Dieter Kleiber and Martin Wilke, cited in Martin Oppermann, "Introduction," in Martin Oppermann, ed., *Sex Tourism and Prostitution*, Elmsford, NY: Cognizant Communication, 1998.

102. Ibid., p. 14.

103. Padilla, *Caribbean Pleasure Industry*; see also Phua, "Love That Binds."

104. Erik Cohen, "Lovelorn Farangs: The Correspondence between Foreign Men and Thai Girls," *Anthropological Quarterly* 59 (1986): 115–127; Brennan, *What's Love Got to Do with It?*; Kempadoo, ed., *Sun, Sex, and Gold*.

105. Trotter, *Sugar Girls and Seamen*.

106. Ibid., p. 16.

107. Ara Wilson, *The Intimate Economies of Bangkok*, Berkeley: University of California Press, 2004, pp. 89, 90.

108. Hoefinger, "Professional Girlfriends"; Saundra Sturdevant and Brenda Stoltzfus, *Let the Good Times Roll: Prostitution and the U.S. Military in Asia*, New York: New Press, 1993; Katherine Moon, *Sex among Allies: Military Prostitution in U.S.-Korea Relations*, New York: Columbia University Press, 1997.

109. Steinfatt, *Working at the Bar*, pp. 251, 309.

110. Wilson, *Intimate Economies of Bangkok*, p. 95.

111. Hoefinger, "Professional Girlfriends," pp. 43, 46.

112. Deborah Pruitt and Suzanne LaFont, "For Love and Money: Romance Tourism in Jamaica," *Annals of Tourism Research* 22 (1995): 422–440, at p. 427.

113. Jacqueline Sanchez Taylor, "Female Sex Tourism: A Contradiction in Terms?" *Feminist Review* 83 (2006): 43–59, at pp. 49–50.

114. Edward Herold, Rafael Garcia, and Tony DeMoya, "Female Tourists and Beach Boys: Romance or Sex Tourism?" *Annals of Tourism Research* 28 (2001): 978–997, at p. 982.

115. Phua, "Love That Binds"; Padilla, *Caribbean Pleasure Industry*; Cohen, "Lovelorn Farangs."

116. Susan Frohlick, "'I'm More Sexy Here': Erotic Subjectivities of Female Tourists in the 'Sexual Paradise' of the Costa Rican Caribbean," in Tanu Priya Uteng and Tim Cresswell, eds., *Gendered Mobilities*, Aldershot, UK: Ashgate, 2008.

117. Jacqueline Sanchez Taylor, "Dollars Are a Girl's Best Friend: Female Tourists' Sexual Behavior in the Caribbean," *Sociology* 34 (2001): 749–764, at p. 755.

118. Pruitt and LaFont, "For Love and Money."

119. Taylor, "Dollars Are a Girl's Best Friend."

120. Joan Phillips, "Tourist-Oriented Prostitution in Barbados: The Case of the Beach Boy and the White Female Tourist," in Kempadoo, ed., *Sun, Sex, and Gold*, p. 191.

121. Frohlick, "I'm More Sexy Here."

122. Akiko Takeyama, "Commodified Romance in a Tokyo Host Club," in Mark McLelland and Romit Dasgupta, eds., *Genders, Transgenders, and Sexualities in Japan*, New York: Routledge, 2005, pp. 203–204.

123. Ibid., p. 204.

124. *The Great Happiness Space*, DVD, Jake Clennell Productions, 2006.

125. Such research could further investigate the circumstances under which women become clients, power relations between female clients and male providers, objectification of male sex workers, and the balance between romance and prostitution.

1. John Dombrink and Daniel Hillyard, *Sin No More*, New York: NYU Press, 2007, chap. 1.

2. In a 2010 poll, 81 percent agreed that doctors "should be allowed to prescribe marijuana for medical purposes to treat their patients." The vast majority of both Democrats (85 percent) and Republicans (72 percent) subscribed to this view. ABC News/*Washington Post* poll, January 12–15, 2010, N = 1,083 adults. In 2002, 80 percent supported allowing adults to "legally use marijuana for medical purposes." *Time*/CNN poll, October 2002, N = 1,007.

3. Similar initiatives have been rejected in the past by voters in other states. In Nevada, a 2002 ballot initiative allowing possession of up to three ounces mustered 39 percent approval, and a 2006 measure allowing one ounce registered 44 percent approval.

4. Roger Parloff, "How Pot Became Legal," *Fortune*, September 28, 2009, pp. 140–162. See also Karl Vick, "In California, Medical Marijuana Laws Are Moving Pot into the Mainstream," *Washington Post*, April 12, 2009.

5. Gallup polls reported in Lydia Saad, "U.S. Support for Legalizing Marijuana Reaches New High," Gallup.com, October 19, 2009, www.gallup.com/poll/123728/U.S.-Support-Legalizing-Marijuana-Reaches-New-High.aspx.

6. In an Angus Reid poll, 53 percent supported the legalization of marijuana (compared to only 8 percent who favored legalizing ecstasy and powder cocaine, 6 percent heroin and meth, and 5 percent crack cocaine), reported in Angus Reid press release, December 9, 2009, poll conducted December 3–4, 2009, N = 1,004. In a Zogby poll, 52 percent agreed that the government should legalize marijuana by "taxing and regulating it," reported in the *Huffington Post*, May 6, 2009 (N = 3,937 registered voters). A 2006 Zogby poll found that 46 percent of Americans supported changing federal law to allow "states to legally regulate and tax marijuana the way they do liquor and gambling" (N = 1,004).

7. Lynn Comella, "Remaking the Sex Industry: The Adult Expo as a Microcosm," in Ronald Weitzer, ed., *Sex for Sale: Prostitution, Pornography, and the Sex Industry*, 2nd ed., New York: Routledge, 2010; Barbara Brents and Teela Sanders, "Mainstreaming the Sex Industry," *Journal of Law and Society* 37 (2010): 40–60.

8. General Social Survey, 2008, N = 824 males, 945 females.

9. Federal Bureau of Investigation, *Crime in the United States*, Washington, DC: Department of Justice, 2009.

10. Bernard Cohen, *Deviant Street Networks: Prostitution in New York City*, Lexington, MA: Lexington Books, 1980, p. 73; John Lowman, "Street Prostitution Control: Some Canadian Reflections on the Finsbury Park Experience," *British Journal of Criminology* 32 (1992): 1–17.

11. See Jeremy Hay, "Spread Your Legs, You Are under Arrest: A Report on the Police Abuse of Prostitutes in San Francisco," *Gauntlet Magazine* 1, no. 7 (1994): 20–32.

12. Merit Audits and Surveys, Merit report, October 15–20, 1983, N = 1,200; Louis Harris poll, January 11–February 11, 1990, N = 2,254.

13. "The Task Force therefore recommends that the City stop enforcing and prosecuting prostitution crimes." San Francisco Task Force on Prostitution, *Final Report*, San Francisco Board of Supervisors, 1996, p. 6.

14. See Ronald Weitzer, "Why Prostitution Initiative Misses: Measure Q in Berkeley Fails on Three Counts," *San Francisco Chronicle*, September 26, 2004, p. E3.

15. Prostitution Task Force, *Workable Solutions to the Problem of Street Prostitution in Buffalo, New York*, 1999.

16. Richard Lake, "Majority Opposes Legalizing Prostitution in Las Vegas," *Las Vegas Review-Journal*, October 30, 2003.

17. Alexandra Lutnick and Deborah Cohan, "Criminalization, Legalization, or Decriminalization of Sex Work," *Reproductive Health Matters* 17 (2009): 38–46.

18. Martin Monto, "Prostitutes' Customers: Motives and Misconceptions," in Weitzer, ed., *Sex for Sale*, 2nd ed., p. 243.

19. Basil Donovan, Christine Harcourt, Sandra Egger, Karen Schneider, Jody O'Connor, Lewis Marshall, Marcus Chen, and Christopher Fairley, *The Sex Industry in Western Australia: A Report to the Western Australian Government*, Sydney: University of New South Wales, 2010, p. x.

20. Wolfenden Committee, *Report of the Committee on Homosexual Offenses and Prostitution*, New York: Lancer, 1964 [1957], para. 227.

21. Ibid., para. 14.

22. Ibid., para. 286.

23. The *strict liability* aspect of the law, applying irrespective of whether the client knew the prostitute had been subjected to coercion, was criticized by the Human Rights Joint Committee in Parliament:

> We are disappointed that the government has failed to provide the evidence which, in its view, demonstrates the necessity for the new strict liability offense. As we have said on a number of previous occasions, legislation should be firmly based on evidence. . . . We conclude that the fact that the offense is one of strict liability will make it difficult for an individual to know how to regulate his conduct given that his knowledge is not an element of the offense. . . . In our view, the proposed offense has the potential to put women into more exploitative or unsafe situations, may not address the problem which the offense aims to target (namely exploitative prostitution), and may discourage reporting of such prostitution.

Human Rights Joint Committee, *Legislative Scrutiny: Policing and Crime Bill 2009, Conclusions and Recommendations*, http://www.publications.parliament.uk/pa/jt200809/jtselect/jtrights/68/6805.htm.

24. The policy is described in more detail in Ronald Weitzer, "Prostitution Control in America: Rethinking Public Policy," *Crime, Law, and Social Change* 32 (1999): 83–102. My discussion of indoor prostitution is restricted to workers who entered the trade voluntarily and does not pertain to those who have been coerced or deceived into selling sex. Law enforcement directed at the protection of such victims is obviously laudable.

25. On Britain, see Catherine Benson and Roger Matthews, "Police and Prostitution: Vice Squads in Britain," in Ronald Weitzer, ed., *Sex for Sale: Prostitution, Pornography, and the Sex Industry*, New York: Routledge, 2000.

26. See, for instance, the six-page investigative report on the policing of massage parlors in Louisville, Kentucky: Jim Adams and Jason Riley, "Louisville Takes Aim at Parlor Prostitution," *Courier-Journal*, July 11, 2004. A study of 16 cities in the mid-1980s by Julie Pearl found that in three of them (Baltimore, Memphis, Milwaukee) indoor prostitution

accounted for between a quarter and a third of their prostitution arrests, and it accounted for half of the arrests in Cleveland. Pearl data cited in Weitzer, "Prostitution Control in America," p. 90.

27. Jessica Logan, "Internet Replacing Streetwalking for Inland Prostitution," *Press-Enterprise* (Riverside, CA), January 1, 2008.

28. *San Francisco Chronicle*, April 6, 1990.

29. Sara Green, "Prostitution Sting Leads to 104 Arrests," *Seattle Times*, November 16, 2006.

30. Quoted in Mike Brunker, "Prostitution Thrives on the Net," *ZD Net News*, June 7, 1999.

31. Jennifer Sullivan and Christopher Schwarzen, "Did Local Vice Cops Cross the Line?" *Seattle Times*, October 7, 2005.

32. Mike Crissey, "State Police Revising Handbook after Sex Sting," Associated Press, September 8, 2001.

33. Jason Riley and Jim Adams, "Officers Have Sexual Contact with Suspects," and Jason Riley, "Undercover Methods Draw Ridicule, Praise," *Courier-Journal*, July 11, 2004, pp. 1, 3.

34. Tom Jackman, "Spotsylvania Deputies Receive Sex Services in Prostitution Cases," *Washington Post*, February 13, 2006, pp. B1, B5.

35. Quoted in Mark Scolforo, "PA Prostitution Case Tossed over Gov't-Funded Sex," Associated Press, November 6, 2009.

36. In some other places, including Phoenix and Houston, vice officers are allowed to undress prior to making an arrest, but these seem to be exceptions to the rule. See Robert Crowe, "Officers Disrobe to Uncover Crime: HPD Changed Its Policy to Crack Down on Spas Fronting for Prostitution," *Houston Chronicle*, January 24, 2005.

37. Ian Demsky, "Police Defend Prostitution Tactic: DA Says Encounters Using Informants Unnecessary," *Tennessean*, February 2, 2005.

38. Cohen, *Deviant Street Networks*, p. 81; Lowman, "Street Prostitution Control."

39. Vice sergeant interviewed by Julie Pearl, May 1985, cited in Weitzer, "Prostitution Control in America."

40. Conversation with three members of the vice squad in Washington, DC, September 14, 1992.

41. San Francisco Committee on Crime, *A Report on Non-Victim Crime in San Francisco, Part 2: Sexual Conduct, Gambling, Pornography*, Mayor's Office, 1971, p. 44.

42. Helen Reynolds, *The Economics of Prostitution*, Springfield, IL: Charles Thomas, 1986, p. 194.

43. Michael Rekart, "Sex-Work Harm Reduction," *Lancet* 366 (December 17, 2005): 2123–2134; Linda Cusick, "Widening the Harm Reduction Agenda: From Drug Use to Sex Work," *International Journal of Drug Policy* 17 (2006): 3–11.

44. San Francisco Committee, *Report on Non-Victim Crime*, p. 38.

45. Special Committee on Pornography and Prostitution, *Pornography and Prostitution in Canada*, Ottawa, ON: Department of Justice, 1985, p. 515.

46. Federal/Provincial Territorial Working Group on Prostitution, *Report and Recommendations in Respect of Legislation, Policy, and Practices Concerning Prostitution-Related Activities*, Ottawa, ON: Department of Justice, 1998, p. 35.

47. Reynolds, *Economics of Prostitution*, p. 192.

48. See the discussion of Boston, Las Vegas, and San Francisco in Barton Child Law and Policy Clinic, *Commercial Sexual Exploitation of Children in Georgia*, Atlanta: Emory Law School, 2008.

49. The Safe Harbor for Exploited Children Act, 2008, New York State.

50. Michael Scott, *Street Prostitution*, Washington, DC: U.S. Department of Justice, 2001; Ronald Weitzer, "The Politics of Prostitution in America," in Ronald Weitzer, ed., *Sex for Sale: Prostitution, Pornography, and the Sex Industry*, New York: Routledge, 2000.

51. Marieke van Doorninck and Rosie Campbell, "Zoning Street Sex Work: The Way Forward?" in Rosie Campbell and Maggie O'Neill, eds., *Sex Work Now*, Portland, OR: Willan, 2006; Hendrik Wagenaar and Sietske Altink, "To Toe the Line: Streetwalking as Contested Space," in David Canter, Maria Ioannou, and Donna Youngs, eds., *Safer Sex in the City: The Experience and Management of Street Prostitution*, Farnham, UK: Ashgate, 2009; Paul van Soomeren and Sander Flight, "Design against Kerb-Crawing: Tippel-zones," paper presented at the International Crime Prevention through Environmental Design conference, Brisbane, Australia, 2004.

52. Lowman, "Street Prostitution Control," p. 2.

53. Adele Weiner, "Understanding the Social Needs of Streetwalking Prostitutes," *Social Work* 41 (1996): 97–105.

54. For a study of one such organization, see Sharon Oselin, "Leaving the Streets," *Deviant Behavior* 30 (2009): 379–406.

55. Marianne Hester and Nicole Westmarland, *Tackling Street Prostitution: Towards an Holistic Approach*, Home Office Research Study 279, London: Home Office, 2004; Jane Pitcher, "Support Services for Women Working in the Sex Industry," in Campbell and O'Neill, eds., *Sex Work Now*; Clarissa Penfold, Gillian Hunter, Rosie Campbell, and Leela Barham, "Tackling Client Violence in Female Street Prostitution: Inter-Agency Working between Outreach Agencies and the Police," *Policing and Society* 14 (2004): 365–379.

56. Atlanta Task Force on Prostitution, *Findings and Recommendations*, Mayor's Office, Atlanta, Georgia, 1986; San Francisco Committee on Crime, *Report on Non-Victim Crime*.

57. Special Committee on Pornography and Prostitution, *Pornography and Prostitution in Canada*.

58. Federal/Provincial Territorial Working Group, *Report and Recommendations*, p. 71; Home Office, *A Coordinated Prostitution Strategy*, London: Home Office, 2006.

59. Angus Reid poll, October 8–9, 2009, N = 1,006. An earlier Canadian survey found much greater public acceptance of indoor than street prostitution: only 11 percent of the public found street prostitution acceptable, compared to 38 percent for brothels, 43 percent for escort services, and 45 percent for prostitution in private premises: Peat Marwick and Partners, *A National Population Study of Prostitution and Pornography*, Ottawa, ON: Department of Justice, 1984.

60. Home Office, *Coordinated Prostitution Strategy*.

61. Amanda Milkovits, "Legislators' Attempts to Quell Prostitution Stall," *Providence Journal*, May 28, 2005; Denise Dowling, "Last Call for Sin," *Rhode Island Monthly*, June 2007.

62. "Rhode Island Law Reform Bills, 2009," press release, sent to all members of the Rhode Island State Legislature, July 31, 2009. The letter was coauthored by me and Elizabeth Wood and signed by scholars from throughout the United States. The press release was quoted in many media outlets, including the state's leading newspaper: "Academics

Urge R.I. to Keep Indoor Prostitution Legal," *Providence Journal*, August 3, 2009. See also my op-ed article, "Some Lurid Prostitution Myths Debunked," *Providence Journal*, June 19, 2009.

63. Donna Hughes, "R.I.'s Carnival of Prostitution," *Providence Journal*, June 24, 2009.

64. Carcieri and Lynch quoted in Lynn Arditi, "New RI Law Banning Indoor Prostitution Leads Some Spas to Close," *Providence Journal*, November 4, 2009.

65. Lynn Arditi, "RI Senate Passes Prostitution Bill, 36–2," *Providence Journal*, October 29, 2009.

66. Quoted in Ray Henry, "RI Lawmakers Adopt Indoor Prostitution Ban," Associated Press, October 30, 2009.

67. Hawaii State Legislature, House of Representatives, HB 982, "Prostitution," 2007, §3 and §6. The companion bill in the Senate was SB 706.

68. Herkes, quoted in Mark Niesse, "Prostitution Bill Gains Support," *Star Bulletin* (Honolulu), February 13, 2007. The bill had 13 cosponsors in the House, one in the Senate.

69. A very similar convergence of interests between the state and prohibitionist forces took place during the Reagan administration in the mid-1980s, when antipornography forces succeeded in shaping the "findings" of the attorney general's commission on pornography, resulting in a major government crackdown on the pornography industry. See Carole Vance, "The Meese Commission on the Road," *Nation*, August 2, 1986, pp. 65, 76–82; and U.S. Department of Justice, *Beyond the Pornography Commission: The U.S. Response*, Washington, DC: Government Printing Office, 1988.

70. Trafficking Victims Protection Act (TVPA), 2000, Public Law 106-386, §103(8).

71. Laura Agustín, *Sex at the Margins: Migration, Labor Markets, and the Rescue Industry*, London: Zed Books, 2007; Sheldon Zhang, "Beyond the 'Natasha' Story: A Review and Critique of Current Research on Sex Trafficking," *Global Crime* 10 (2009): 178–195; Janie Chuang, "Rescuing Trafficking from Ideological Capture: Prostitution Reform and Anti-Trafficking Law and Policy," *University of Pennsylvania Law Review* 158 (2010): 1655–1728. For excellent exposés by investigative journalists, see Jerry Markon, "Human Trafficking Evokes Outrage, Little Evidence," *Washington Post*, September 23, 2007, pp. A1, A8–A9; Nick Davies, "Prostitution and Trafficking: The Anatomy of a Moral Panic," *Guardian* (UK), October 20, 2009; and Jack Shafer, "The Sex-Slavery Epidemic That Wasn't," *Slate*, September 24, 2007. On advocates' use of dramatic visual imagery to alert women about the dangers of migration, such as several poster campaigns launched by the International Organization for Migration in eastern Europe, see Rutvica Andrijasevic, "Beautiful Dead Bodies: Gender, Migration, and Representation in Anti-Trafficking Campaigns," *Feminist Review* 86 (2007): 24–44.

72. Part of the remainder of the chapter draws on two articles: Ronald Weitzer, "The Social Construction of Sex Trafficking: Ideology and Institutionalization of a Moral Crusade," *Politics and Society* 35 (2007): 447–475; and Ronald Weitzer, "The Movement to Criminalize Sex Work in the United States," *Journal of Law and Society* 37 (2010): 61–84.

73. See, for example, Monica O'Connor and Grainne Healy, *The Links between Prostitution and Sex Trafficking: A Briefing Handbook*, CATW and European Women's Lobby, 2006; see also the article by CATW codirector Dorchen Leidholdt, "Prostitution and Trafficking in Women: An Intimate Relationship," *Journal of Trauma Practice* 2 (2004): 167–183.

74. Donna Hughes, "Wolves in Sheep's Clothing: No Way to End Sex Trafficking," *National Review Online*, October 9, 2002, p. 2.

75. Donna Hughes, "Accommodation or Abolition?" *National Review Online*, May 1, 2003, p. 1.

76. U.S. Department of State, "The Link between Prostitution and Sex Trafficking," Bureau of Public Affairs, 2004.

77. E. Benjamin Skinner, *A Crime So Monstrous: Face-to-Face with Modern-Day Slavery*, New York: Free Press, 2008, p. 283.

78. Amy Farrell, Jack McDevitt, and Stephanie Fahy, *Understanding and Improving Law Enforcement Responses to Human Trafficking*, Boston: Institute on Race and Justice, Northeastern University, 2008.

79. Women's Commission for Refugee Women and Children, *The U.S. Response to Human Trafficking: An Unbalanced Approach*, New York: Commission, 2007, p. 14.

80. Trafficking Victims Protection Reauthorization Act (TVPRA), 2003.

81. National Institute of Justice, *Solicitation: Trafficking in Human Beings Research and Comprehensive Literature Review*, Washington, DC: U.S. Department of Justice, 2007, p. 4.

82. See Nicole Masenior and Chris Beyrer, "The U.S. Anti-Prostitution Pledge: First Amendment Challenges and Public Health Priorities," *PLoS Medicine* 4 (2007): 1158.

83. William Fisher, "USAID Sued over Anti-Prostitution Policy," Inter-Press Service News Agency, August 23, 2005.

84. Janice Raymond, "Ten Reasons for *Not* Legalizing Prostitution and a Legal Response to the Demand for Prostitution," *Journal of Trauma Practice* 2 (2003): 315–332, at p. 317.

85. Melissa Farley, *Prostitution and Trafficking in Nevada: Making the Connections*, Prostitution Research and Education, 2007, pp. 118, 119, emphasis added.

86. Ibid., p. 120.

87. Ibid., p. 22.

88. Barbara Brents and Kathryn Hausbeck, "Violence and Legalized Brothel Prostitution in Nevada," *Journal of Interpersonal Violence* 20 (2005): 270–295, at p. 289.

89. Farley, *Prostitution and Trafficking in Nevada*, p. 20.

90. Kathryn Hausbeck, Barbara Brents, and Crystal Jackson, "Vegas and the Sex Industry: Don't Make Assumptions about the Choices Women Make," *Las Vegas Review-Journal*, September 16, 2007.

91. U.S. Department of State, *Trafficking in Persons Report*, Washington, DC: U.S. Department of State, annual.

92. Alison Murray, "Debt Bondage and Trafficking," in Kamala Kempadoo and J. Doezema, eds., *Global Sex Workers*, New York: Routledge, 1998, p. 60.

93. Kamala Kempadoo, "Introduction: Globalizing Sex Workers' Rights," in Kempadoo and Doezema, eds., *Global Sex Workers*, p. 17.

94. Art Hubacher, "Every Picture Tells a Story: Is Kansas City's 'John TV' Constitutional?" *Kansas Law Review* 46 (1998): 551–591.

95. "Curbing Prostitution on Demand Side," *New York Times*, April 20, 1992, p. B8.

96. *Newsweek* poll, January 26–27, 1995, N = 753.

97. Jordan Schrader, "To Reduce Prostitution, Cities Try Shaming Clients," *USA Today*, August 29, 2008.

98. Miyoko Ohtake, "A School for Johns," *Newsweek*, July 24, 2008.

99. Ibid.; Joel Rubin, "Shaming and Scaring Johns into Becoming Average Joes," *Los Angeles Times*, February 26, 2009; Kristin Pisarcik, "Inside a Brooklyn 'John School,'" *20/20*, ABC television, March 20, 2007.

100. Laura Blumenfeld, "In a Shift, Anti-Prostitution Effort Targets Pimps and Johns," *Washington Post*, December 15, 2005, p. A16.

101. End Demand Illinois website, www.enddemandillinois.org.

102. The Predator Accountability Act, 2006, quoted in Shay-Ann Heiser Singh, "The Predator Accountability Act," *DePaul Law Review* 56 (2007): 1035–1064, at p. 1050.

103. A fact sheet produced by the Swedish government describes the rationale for the new law: "Prostitution is not a desirable social phenomenon. The government considers, however, that it is not reasonable to punish the person who sells a sexual service. In the majority of cases at least, this person is a weaker partner who is exploited by those who want only to satisfy their sexual drives." Ministry of Labor, *Fact Sheet*, Stockholm, Sweden, 1998.
Another government publication indicates that the 1999 law was firmly rooted in the oppression paradigm: "In Sweden, prostitution is regarded as an aspect of male violence against women and children, it is officially acknowledged as a form of exploitation of women and children . . . which is harmful not only to the individual prostituted woman or child, but also to society at large." Ministry of Industry, Employment, and Communications, *Prostitution and Trafficking in Human Beings*, Stockholm, Sweden, April 2005.

104. Arthur Gould, "The Criminalization of Buying Sex: The Politics of Prostitution in Sweden," *Journal of Social Politics* 30 (2001): 437–456, at p. 443.

105. TVPA, 2000, §103(3).

106. TVPRA, 2005, §201a.

107. TVPRA, 2005, §204(1b, 1c).

108. Sheila Jeffreys, *The Industrial Vagina*, New York: Routledge, 2009, p. 93.

109. Donna Hughes, *The Demand for Victims of Sex Trafficking*, University of Rhode Island, 2005, pp. 22, 26. Hughes received $108,478 from the State Department to write this report: Attorney General, *Report to Congress on U.S. Government Efforts to Combat Trafficking in Persons in Fiscal Year 2004*, Washington, DC: U.S. Department of Justice, 2005.

110. Hughes, *Demand for Victims*, p. 22.

111. In Mumbai, India, in 2005 the government banned bar dancing, in which women dance seductively but fully clothed at clubs. A survey of 500 dancers found that none had been trafficked, yet the 2005 ban was based in part on the claim that trafficking was rampant. As a result of the ban, 75,000 dancers were thrown out of work. Prabha Kotiswaran, "Labors in Vice or Virtue? Neo-liberalism, Sexual Commerce, and the Case of Indian Bar Dancing," *Journal of Law and Society* 37 (2010): 105–124.

112. Catharine MacKinnon, "Pornography as Trafficking," *Michigan Journal of International Law* 26 (2005): 993–1012, at p. 999.

113. "Appointment of New U.S. Attorney General and Other Matters Regarding Vigorous Enforcement of Federal Obscenity Laws," September 10, 2007, http://www.obscenity-crimes.org/news//Letter-Regarding-Appointment-of-New-U.S.-Atty-General_10Sep2007.pdf. The letter was signed by, inter alia, Donna Hughes, Patrick Trueman, Morality in Media, Family Research Council, Concerned Women for America, Focus on the Family, American Family Association, American Decency Association, and Citizens for Community Values.

114. Patrick Trueman, testimony before the Subcommittee on the Constitution, Civil Rights, and Property Rights, United States Senate, *Hearing on Obscenity Prosecution*, March 16, 2005.

115. Hughes, *Demand for Victims*, p. 26.

116. L. Sullivan, "Justice Department Sets Sights on Mainstream Porn," *Pittsburgh Post-Gazette*, April 11, 2004.

117. U.S. Department of Justice, "Obscenity Prosecution Task Force Established to Investigate, Prosecute Purveyors of Obscene Materials," press release, May 5, 2005; Richard Schmitt, "U.S. Cracking Down on Porn," *Deseret News*, February 15, 2004; Robert Gehrke, "Nation's Porn Prosecutor Fronts War against Obscenity," *Salt Lake Tribune*, February 26, 2007.

118. Schmitt, "U.S. Cracking Down on Porn."

119. Bruce Taylor, transcript of *Frontline* interview, Public Broadcasting Service, June 2001.

120. Ibid.

121. *Miller v. California*, 413 U.S. 15 (1973).

122. Julie Kay, "U.S. Attorney's Porn Fight Gets Bad Reviews," *Daily Business Review*, August 30, 2005.

123. Spencer Hsu, "Judge Drops Porn Case for Insufficient Evidence," *Washington Post*, July 17, 2010, p. A2.

124. Ibid.

125. Stephen Bates, "Outsourcing Justice? That's Obscene," *Washington Post*, July 15, 2007, p. B3.

126. Neil Lewis, "Federal Effort on Web Obscenity Shows Few Results," *New York Times*, August 10, 2007.

127. Josh Gerstein, "Porn Prosecution Fuels Debate," *Politico*, July 31, 2009.

NOTES TO CHAPTER 4

1. Christine Overall, "What's Wrong with Prostitution? Evaluating Sex Work," *Signs* 17 (1992): 705–724, at p. 716.

2. Sheila Jeffreys, *The Industrial Vagina*, New York: Routledge, 2009, p. 177.

3. Janice Raymond, "Ten Reasons for *Not* Legalizing Prostitution and a Legal Response to the Demand for Prostitution," *Journal of Trauma Practice* 2 (2003): 315–332, at p. 322.

4. Mary Sullivan and Sheila Jeffreys, "Legalization: The Australian Experience," *Violence Against Women* 8 (2002): 1140–1148.

5. Mary Sullivan, *What Happens When Prostitution Becomes Work? An Update on Legalization of Prostitution in Australia*, North Fitzroy, Australia: Coalition Against Trafficking in Women, 2005, p. 23.

6. Raymond, "Ten Reasons," p. 322.

7. Melissa Farley, *Prostitution and Trafficking in Nevada: Making the Connections*, San Francisco: Prostitution Research and Education, 2007, p. 118.

8. The two leading prohibitionist groups in the United States are Prostitution Research and Education (founded by Melissa Farley) and the Coalition Against Trafficking in Women (founded by Kathleen Barry). CATW has branches in Europe and Australia, and it is closely allied with the European Women's Lobby.

9. Elizabeth Bernstein, *Temporarily Yours: Intimacy, Authenticity, and the Commerce of Sex*, Chicago: University of Chicago Press, 2007, pp. 146, 164, 166.

10. Laura Agustín, "Sex and the Limits of Enlightenment: The Irrationality of Legal Regimes to Control Prostitution," *Sexuality Research and Social Policy* 5 (2008): 73–86, at p. 76, emphasis added.

11. Ibid., p. 83.

12. Jane Scoular, "What's Law Got to Do with It? How and Why Law Matters in the Regulation of Sex Work," *Journal of Law and Society* 37 (2010): 12–39, at p. 14.

13. Jane Scoular, "Criminalizing Punters: Evaluating the Swedish Position on Prostitution," *Journal of Social Welfare and Family Law* 26 (2004): 195–210; Victor Clausen, "An Assessment of Gunilla Ekberg's Account of Swedish Prostitution Policy," unpublished paper, 2007.

14. Leslie Jeffrey and Barbara Sullivan, "Canadian Sex Work Policy for the 21st Century: Enhancing Rights and Safety, Lessons from Australia," *Canadian Political Science Review* 3 (2009): 57–76, at p. 64.

15. The situation in Daulatoia is illustrated in a documentary: National Geographic Channel, "Prostitution," *Taboo* series, first broadcast on January 17, 2010.

16. Michael Rekart, "Sex-Work Harm Reduction," *Lancet* 366 (December 17, 2005): 2123–2133.

17. Jim Leitzel, *Regulating Vice: Misguided Prohibitions and Realistic Controls*, New York: Cambridge University Press, 2008, p. 198.

18. "Poll: French Want Brothels Legalized," *Boston Globe*, January 22, 1995.

19. Ipsos MORI poll, June 11–12, 2008, N = 1,012, ages 18 and over.

20. Basil Donovan, Christine Harcourt, Sandra Egger, Karen Schneider, Jody O'Connor, Lewis Marshall, Marcus Chen, and Christopher Fairley, *The Sex Industry in Western Australia: A Report to the Western Australian Government*, Sydney: University of New South Wales, 2010, pp. 33, 36.

21. Robert MacCoun and Peter Reuter, *Drug War Heresies*, New York: Cambridge University Press, 2001, pp. 240–248.

22. Jerome Skolnick, "The Social Transformation of Vice," *Law and Contemporary Problems* 51 (1988): 9–29.

23. Simon Lenton, "Pot, Politics, and the Press: Reflections on Cannabis Law Reform in Western Australia," *Drug and Alcohol Review* 23 (2004): 223–233.

24. John Dombrink and Daniel Hillyard, *Sin No More*, New York: NYU Press, 2007, p. 9, citing a 2004 poll.

25. Skolnick, "Social Transformation of Vice."

26. National Commission on Marihuana and Drug Abuse, *Marihuana: A Signal of Misunderstanding*, commissioned by President Richard M. Nixon, 1972.

27. For example, the 2008 voter-approved ballot initiative in Massachusetts decriminalizing possession of marijuana had stiffer penalties for minors than for adults: adults would pay a $100 fine; minors would be subject to parental notification and either participation in a drug-awareness program or paying a $1,000 fine.

28. Ruth Karras, *Common Women: Prostitution and Sexuality in Medieval England*, New York: Oxford University Press, 1996, pp. 32–35.

29. Prostitution Law Review Committee, *Report of the Prostitution Law Review Committee on the Operation of the Prostitution Reform Act 2003*, Wellington, New Zealand: Ministry of Justice, 2008.

30. Bernard Cohen, *Deviant Street Networks: Prostitution in New York City*, Lexington, MA: Lexington Books, 1980, p. 113.

31. Roger Matthews, *Prostitution, Politics, and Policy*, New York: Routledge-Cavendish, 2008, chap. 7.

32. Some of these items have been distilled from Samuel Cameron, "Space, Risk, and Opportunity: The Evolution of Paid Sex Markets," *Urban Studies* 41 (2004): 1643–1657.

33. Donna Guy, *Sex and Danger in Buenos Aires: Prostitution, Family, and Nation in Argentina*, Lincoln: University of Nebraska Press, 1990, chap. 2.

34. Ibid., pp. 57, 64–65.

35. Daniela Danna and Silvia Garcia, "The Situation in Madrid," in Daniela Danna, ed., *Prostitution and Public Life in Four European Capitals*, Rome: Carocci, 2007.

36. In Austria, prostitutes are required to register with local authorities and to undergo periodic medical checks—weekly for STDs and quarterly for HIV. They must carry a card that indicates the results of the tests and must show the card to police officers on request.

37. Barbara Brents, Crystal Jackson, and Kathryn Hausbeck, *The State of Sex: Tourism, Sex, and Sin in the New American Heartland*, New York: Routledge, 2010, p. 234.

38. Ibid.

39. Kathryn Hausbeck and Barbara Brents, "Nevada's Legal Brothels," in Ronald Weitzer, ed., *Sex for Sale: Prostitution, Pornography, and the Sex Industry*, 2nd ed., New York: Routledge, 2010, p. 269.

40. Ibid., p. 272.

41. Brents, Jackson, and Hausbeck, *State of Sex*, pp. 129, 130, 227.

42. Ibid., p. 233.

43. Daria Snadowsky, "The Best Little Whorehouse Is Not in Texas: How Nevada's Prostitution Laws Serve Public Policy and How Those Laws May Be Improved," *Nevada Law Journal* 6 (2005): 217–247, at p. 229.

44. Ibid., p. 226.

45. Alexa Albert, *Brothel: Mustang Ranch and Its Women*, New York: Ballantine, 2001, pp. 30, 100.

46. Hausbeck and Brents, "Nevada's Legal Brothels," p. 271.

47. Albert, *Brothel*; Brents, Jackson, and Hausbeck, *State of Sex*; Snadowsky, "Best Little Whorehouse."

48. Snadowsky, "Best Little Whorehouse," p. 235.

49. Hausbeck and Brents, "Nevada's Legal Brothels," p. 267.

50. Snadowsky, "Best Little Whorehouse," p. 238.

51. Brents, Jackson, and Hausbeck, *State of Sex*, p. 235.

52. Hausbeck and Brents, "Nevada's Legal Brothels."

53. Snadowsky, "Best Little Whorehouse."

54. Ibid.

55. Hausbeck and Brents, "Nevada's Legal Brothels."

56. Brents, Jackson, and Hausbeck, *State of Sex*, p. 174.

57. Patty Kelly, *Lydia's Open Door: Inside Mexico's Most Modern Brothel*, Berkeley: University of California Press, 2008.

58. Ibid., p. 66.

59. Ibid., p. 79.

60. Ibid., p. 212.

61. Yasmina Katsulis, *Sex Work and the City: The Social Geography of Health and Safety in Tijuana, Mexico*, Austin: University of Texas Press, 2008, p. 77.

62. Ibid., p. 65.

63. Ibid., p. 87.

64. World Values Survey, http://www.wvsevsdb.com/wvs/WVSAnalizeQuestion.jsp.

65. Alison Arnot, "Legalization of the Sex Industry in the State of Victoria, Australia," M.A. thesis, University of Melbourne, 2002, pp. 65–69.

66. Ibid., p. 69.

67. Barbara Sullivan, *The Politics of Sex: Prostitution and Pornography in Australia since 1945*, New York: Cambridge University Press, 1997, pp. 214–215.

68. Ibid., pp. 215.

69. Marcus Chen, "Estimating the Number of Unlicensed Brothels in Melbourne," *Australian and New Zealand Journal of Public Health* 34 (2010): 67–71.

70. Crime and Misconduct Commission, *Regulating Prostitution: An Evaluation of the Prostitution Act 1999, Queensland*, Brisbane, Australia: Crime and Misconduct Commission, 2004, pp. 85–86.

71. The illegal market accounts for an estimated 90 percent of prostitution in Queensland. Kate Dennehy, "Queensland Sex Industry Still Largely Illegitimate," *Brisbane Times*, August 16, 2009.

72. Crime and Misconduct Commission, *Regulating Prostitution*, p. 111.

73. Andreas Schloenhardt and Lachlan Cameron, "Happy Birthday, Brothels! Ten Years of Prostitution Regulation in Queensland," *Queensland Lawyer* 29 (2009): 194–220.

74. Prostitution Regulation Act, 2004, Northern Territory (§ 6).

75. Prostitution Laws Amendment Act, 1992, Queensland.

76. Schloenhardt and Cameron, "Happy Birthday, Brothels!"; see also Crime and Misconduct Commission, *Regulating Prostitution*, p. 111.

77. Schloenhardt and Cameron, "Happy Birthday, Brothels!" p. 201.

78. Ibid.

79. Dennehy, "Queensland Sex Industry."

80. Prostitution Act, 1999, Queensland (§ 101[j]).

81. Crime and Misconduct Commission, *Regulating Prostitution*, pp. 75, 89.

82. Ibid., p. 45.

83. Schloenhardt and Cameron, "Happy Birthday, Brothels!" p. 213.

84. Crime and Misconduct Commission, *Regulating Prostitution*, p. 131.

85. Schloenhardt and Cameron, "Happy Birthday, Brothels!" p. 214.

86. Charrlotte Woodward, Jane Fischer, Jake Najman, and Michael Dunne, *Selling Sex in Queensland*, Brisbane, Australia: Prostitution Licensing Authority, 2004, p. 39.

87. Charrlotte Seib, Jane Fischer, and Jackob Najman, "The Health of Female Sex Workers from Three Industry Sectors in Queensland, Australia," *Social Science and Medicine* 68 (2009): 473–478.

88. Crime and Misconduct Commission, *Regulating Prostitution*, p. 71.

89. Schloenhardt and Cameron, "Happy Birthday, Brothels!" p. 215.

90. National Geographic Channel, "Prostitution."

91. I thank Barbara Sullivan for this information.

92. This is the conclusion reached by Barbara Sullivan, "When (Some) Prostitution Is Legal: The Impact of Law Reform on Sex Work in Australia," *Journal of Law and Society* 37 (2010): 85–104.

93. Paul Fitzharris, "Review of the Prostitution Reform Act," in Gillian Abel, Lisa Fitzgerald, and Catherine Healy, eds., *Taking the Crime Out of Sex Work*, Bristol, UK: Policy, 2010, p. 107.

94. "Poll Steels Anti-Prostitution Resolve," *New Zealand Herald*, May 14, 2003.

95. Ronald Weitzer, "Legalizing Prostitution: Morality Politics in Western Australia," *British Journal of Criminology* 49 (2009): 88–105. The legislation was not implemented due to a change in government, but the newly elected regime presented legislation in 2011 that would zone prostitution into designated central-city areas and ban it in suburbs and small towns.

96. Dean Knight, "The Continuing Regulation of Prostitution by Local Authorities," in Abel et al., eds., *Taking the Crime Out of Sex Work*.

97. The three cases are described in ibid.

98. I thank Gillian Abel for this information on the three cities.

99. Knight, "Continuing Regulation."

100. Tim Barnett, Catherine Healy, Anna Reed, and Calum Bennachie, "Lobbying for Decriminalization," in Abel et al., eds., *Taking the Crime Out of Sex Work*, p. 68.

101. Prostitution Law Review Committee, *Report*; Gillian Abel and Lisa Fitzgerald, "Risk and Risk Management in Sex Work Post-Prostitution Reform Act," in Abel et al., eds., *Taking the Crime Out of Sex Work*.

102. Prostitution Law Review Committee, *Report*.

103. Elaine Mossman, "Brothel Operators' and Support Agencies' Experiences of Decriminalization," in Abel et al., eds., *Taking the Crime Out of Sex Work*.

104. Fitzharris, "Review of the Prostitution Reform Act," p. 112.

105. Prostitution Law Review Committee, *The Nature and Extent of the Sex Industry in New Zealand*, Wellington, New Zealand: Ministry of Justice, 2005; Elaine Mossman and Pat Mayhew, *Central Government Aims and Local Government Responses: The Prostitution Reform Act 2003*, Wellington, New Zealand: Ministry of Justice, 2007.

106. Abel and Fitzgerald, "Risk and Risk Management"; Prostitution Law Review Committee, *Report*.

107. Prostitution Law Review Committee, *Report*, p. 152.

108. World Values Survey, http://www.wvsevsdb.com/wvs/WVSAnalizeQuestion.jsp.

109. See Leitzel, *Regulating Vice*, pp. 202–203.

NOTES TO CHAPTER 5

1. Some of these interviews were tape-recorded and others recorded by hand. In Frankfurt, I was introduced to owners of sex businesses by Juanita Henning, director of the local Doña Carmen organization. She accompanied me on my interviews as well.

2. G. J. Ashworth, P. E. White, and H. P. M. Winchester, "The Red-Light District in the West European City: A Neglected Aspect of the Urban Landscape," *Geoforum* 19 (1988): 201–212, at p. 208.

3. Phil Hubbard, "Revisiting the Red Light District: Still Neglected, Immoral, and Marginal?" *Geoforum* 39 (2008): 1743–1755, at p. 1752.

4. See Mara Keire, *For Business and Pleasure: Red-Light Districts and the Regulation of Vice in the United States, 1890–1933*, Baltimore: Johns Hopkins University Press, 2010.

5. Ibid., p. 7.

6. Population figures in 2009 are as follows: Amsterdam, 755,000; Frankfurt, 665,000; Antwerp, 488,000. City Population website, www.citypopulation.de.

7. Figures on city tourist destinations for 2007: Euromonitor International, www.euromonitor.com.

8. Street prostitution is permitted in Hamburg, Germany, and in some Dutch cities that have created special zones, discussed in chapter 6.

9. World Values Survey, 1999, http://www.wvsevsdb.com/wvs/WVSAnalizeQuestion.jsp.

10. World Values Survey, 1990, http://www.wvsevsdb.com/wvs/WVSAnalizeQuestion.jsp.

11. Interview with Antwerp prostitution official, Antwerp, June 24, 2008.

12. Noelle Knox, "In Belgium, Brothels Are Big Business," *USA Today*, November 4, 2003.

13. Email from Antwerp prostitution official, June 21, 2010.

14. Hans Willems, "Schipperskwartier, a Seductive Quarter in Antwerp," Social Welfare Office, Antwerp, Belgium, 2009.

15. Ibid., p. 5.

16. Mayor Patrick Janssens, quoted in Stephen Castle, "Passports and Panic Buttons in the Brothel of the Future," *Independent* (UK), September 23, 2006.

17. The film was commissioned by the Flemish Association for Space and Planning in 2007 and is available on Terenja van Dijk's website, "Skippers' Quarter," http://www.terenjavandijk.net/en/project/schipperskwartier/2/.

18. Interview with Antwerp prostitution official.

19. Willems, "Schipperskwartier," p. 4; the man recalling the former street scene was a poster on Ignatzmice, Will82, January 16, 2011.

20. Interview with Antwerp prostitution official.

21. Dan Bilefsky, "Belgian Experiment: Make Prostitution Legal to Fight Its Ills," *Wall Street Journal*, May 26, 2005.

22. Officer quoted in ibid.

23. Willems, "Schipperskwartier," p. 5.

24. The Antwerp Health House, www.ghapro.be.

25. Willems, "Schipperskwartier," p. 5.

26. Information in this and the following paragraphs provided by Antwerp prostitution official.

27. Interview with Antwerp prostitution official.

28. Ibid.

29. Postings by Davide, September 19, 2009; G.laGaffe, October 15, 2010; and Smurf, April 7, 2010, on www.ignatzmice.com.

30. Clients have complained for years about the curtains and the sofas—for example, a posting on www.worldsexguide.org, April 28, 1998.

31. Client postings in 2009 and 2010 on www.ignatzmice.com.

32. Posting on www.worldsexguide.org, April 15, 1997.

33. Posting by Brad07, www.ignatzmice.com, July 5, 2010.

34. Postings on www.ignatzmice.com.

35. Posting by G.laGaffe, www.ignatzmice.com, September 10, 2008.

36. Interview with Antwerp prostitution official.

37. Dimap poll, 1999, cited in the government's explanation of the prostitution bill that became law in 2002, Parliamentary Paper BT-Drs. 14/5958, May 8, 2001. I thank Gerhard Walentowitz for this source.

38. World Values Survey, http://www.wvsevsdb.com/wvs/WVSAnalizeQuestion.jsp. The 1981 survey was for West Germany; the later polls covered the reunited nation.

39. Barbara Kavemann and Heike Rabe, "The Act Regulating the Legal Situation of Prostitutes: Implementation, Impact, Current Developments," report, Berlin Research Institute for Social Science and Women's Studies, Berlin, 2007, p. 4.

40. Ibid.

41. Annette Jolin, "Germany," in Nanette J. Davis, ed., *Prostitution: An International Handbook on Trends, Problems, and Policies*, Westport, CT: Greenwood, 1993, p. 139.

42. Ibid., p. 131.

43. Susanne Dodillet, "Cultural Clash on Prostitution: Debates on Prostitution in Germany and Sweden in the 1990s," paper presented at Conference on Sex and Sexuality, Salzburg, October 14, 2004.

44. Petra Pau, Party of Democratic Socialism, statement in parliament, quoted in ibid., p. 3.

45. Federal Ministry for Family Affairs, Senior Citizens, Women, and Youth, *Report by the Federal Government on the Impact of the Act Regulating the Legal Situation of Prostitutes* (*Prostitution Act*), Berlin: Ministry, 2007, p. 79.

46. Section 232(1) reads,

> Whosoever exploits another person's predicament or helplessness arising from being in a foreign country in order to induce them to engage in or continue to engage in prostitution, to engage in exploitative sexual activity with or in the presence of the offender or a third person, or to suffer sexual acts on his own person by the offender or a third person shall be liable to imprisonment from six months to ten years. Whosoever induces a person under twenty-one years of age to engage in or continue to engage in prostitution or any of the sexual activity mentioned in the 1st sentence above shall incur the same penalty.

47. Federal Ministry, *Report*, p. 41.

48. Ibid., pp. 79, 61.

49. Ibid., p. 14.

50. Ray Furlong, "German Prostitutes in Rights Plea," *BBC News Online*, June 24, 2005.

51. The amount of unpaid tax within the sex industry was estimated to be €2 billion in 2003, when the annual income from legal prostitution was estimated at €6 billion. There are no recent estimates of the amount of unpaid tax, but the annual income from legal prostitution was estimated at €12.7 billion in 2009. The 2003 figures are from Bundesrechnuupshof, *Bemerkungen zur Haushalts und Wirtschaftführung des Bundes*, Bonn, 2003, p. 185. The 2009 figure is from Erik Kirshbaum, "Global Economic Crisis Hits German Sex Industry," Reuters, April 20, 2009.

52. Kavemann and Rabe, "Act Regulating the Legal Situation of Prostitutes," pp. 15–18.

53. Federal Ministry, *Report*, p. 20.

54. I thank Gerhard Walentowitz for assisting me with these statistics, which were drawn from the Federal Criminal Police Office (Polizeiliche Kriminalstatistik, Kriminalistiches Institut, Wiesbaden, Germany, 2000–2009), http://www.bka.de/pks/.

55. Federal Ministry, *Report*, p. 44.

56. Ibid., p. 79.

57. Ibid., p. 80.

58. Kavemann and Rabe, "Act Regulating the Legal Situation of Prostitutes," p. 8.

59. Interview with Juanita Henning and Gerhard Walentowitz, officials at Doña Carmen, Frankfurt, May 6, 2009.

60. Anne Dölemeyer, Rebecca Pates, and Daniel Schmidt, "Deviant Girls, Small-Scale Entrepreneurs, and the Regulation of German Sex Workers," in Melissa Hope Ditmore, Antonia Levy, and Alys Willman, eds., *Sex Work Matters*, New York: Zed Books, 2010, p. 190.

61. Ibid., p. 191.

62. Ibid.

63. Based on a 2006 survey in Frankfurt reported in Juanita Henning, "Wie Funktioniert die Bordellprostitution in Frankfurt/Main?" in Philipp Thiée, ed., *Menschen Handel: Wie der Sexmarkt Strafrechtlich Reguliert Wird*, Berlin: Vereinigung Berliner Strafverteidiger, 2008, p. 168.

64. "Cologne Leads the Way in Safe Prostitution," *Deutsche Welle*, July 7, 2005, www.DW-World.de.

65. Interview with manager of RTO, Frankfurt, April 29, 2010. See www.rto.de and www.ladies.de.

66. Kamilla la Dee website: www.kamilla-dee.com. Advertised prices are €80 for a half hour, €160 for an hour.

67. Interview with Henning and Walentowitz, May 6, 2009.

68. Crazy Sexy website, www.crazy-sexy-germany.de.

69. Martina Löw and Renate Ruhne, "Domesticating Prostitution: Study of an Interactional Web of Space and Gender," *Space and Culture* 12 (2009): 232–249.

70. Ibid.

71. Henning, "Wie Funktioniert die Bordellprostitution," pp. 168, 170. The average of 920 prostitutes and ten clients per worker is based on Henning's 2006 survey of women working in the area's brothels.

72. Maria Kontos and Kyoko Shinozaki, "Integration of New Female Migrants in the German Labor Market and Society and German State Policies on Integration," Working Paper No. 1, Institut für Sozialforschung an der J. W. Goethe Universität Frankfurt, Frankfurt, 2007.

73. Henning, "Wie Funktioniert die Bordellprostitution," p. 171.

74. Ibid.

75. "Romania Tops EU Sex Worker List," *BBC News Online*, January 26, 2010.

76. Survey conducted by Veronika Munk for TAMPEP (a European nongovernmental organization), cited in Kontos and Shinozaki, "Integration of New Female Migrants."

77. Henning, "Wie Funktioniert die Bordellprostitution," p. 168.

78. Photos of the bar are posted on the website: www.penthouse-no1.com.

79. Postings on www.ignatzmice.com, by ST (August 5, 2007) and Bdltnt (August 1, 2007).

80. Posting by Petertaylor69, www.ignatzmice.com, March 24, 2011.

81. According to outreach workers at Doña Carmen.

82. Email correspondence with Gerhard Walentowitz, November 1, 2009.

83. Rotes Haus website, www.roteshaus.com.

84. Interview with Henning and Walentowitz, May 6, 2009.

85. Posting by Petertaylor69, on www.ignatzmice.com, February 25, 2009.

86. Interview with Eros Center owner, Frankfurt, April 29, 2010, accompanied by Juanita Henning.

87. Juanita Henning, who has close ties to women working in Frankfurt's red-light districts, later confirmed to me that the women are generally good conflict managers and that altercations between workers and clients are relatively infrequent in the hotel-brothels.

88. This is a point made by men who post on www.ignatzmice.com and www.theeroticreview.com, though most of their discourse about the sauna clubs focuses on their sexual experiences and recommendations as well.

89. Posting by Bookguy, www.ignatzmice.com, September 19, 2010. The term "sample" was used by Bookguy.

90. Postings by Monk69, www.theeroticreview.com, July 28 and 29, 2009.

91. Posting by Jman57, www.theeroticreview.com, July 27, 2009.

92. Posting by Makelove and replies, November 28, 2007. Quotations regarding The Palace are by PeachFuzz, December 16, 2010, and LondonBasketCase, March 29, 2011—all on www.ignatzmice.com.

93. Posting by G.laGaffe, www.ignatzmice.com, September 27, 2010.

94. Posting by Guava, www.ignatzmice.com, December 14, 2009.

95. Posting by Derkdiggler, www.theeroticreview.com, May 26 and 27, 2010.

96. Posting by Number 6, www.theeroticreview.com, July 31, 2009.

97. Posting by Number 6, www.theeroticreview.com, August 17, 2009.

98. Posting by Shiatsu and Cordelia, www.ignatzmice.com, May 15, 2006.

99. Posting by Petertaylor69, www.ignatzmice.com, March 22, 2010.

100. Interview with brothel owner and observations of premises, April 29, 2010, accompanied by Juanita Henning.

101. Because we were accompanied by the house manager, our presence seemed to go fairly unnoticed by both the men and the women.

102. Interview with brothel manager and tour of premises, March 19, 2011, accompanied by Juanita Henning.

103. Visit conducted April 30, 2010, accompanied by Juanita Henning.

NOTES TO CHAPTER 6

1. Conversation with author, Amsterdam, 2002.

2. Bylaw quoted in Chrisje Brants, "The Fine Art of Regulated Tolerance: Prostitution in Amsterdam," *Journal of Law and Society* 25 (1998): 621–635, at p. 621.

3. Ibid.

4. Marieke van Doorninck, "History of Prostitution in Amsterdam," unpublished paper, 1999, pp. 4–5.

5. This description is based on ibid.

6. Ibid., p. 7.

7. Brants, "Fine Art of Regulated Tolerance."

8. "Between the Lines," June 1997, newsletter of the de Graaf Foundation for Prostitution Issues.

9. Tineke Oostdam, quoted in Nick Cohen, "Booming Business among Amsterdam's Red Lights," *Independent* (UK), April 24, 2002.

10. Brants, "Fine Art of Regulated Tolerance."

11. Marieke van Doorninck, "A Business like Any Other? Managing the Sex Industry in the Netherlands," in Susanne Thorbek and Bandana Pattanaik, eds., *Transnational Prostitution: Changing Patterns in a Global Context*, London: Zed Books, 2002, p. 196.

12. Interview with Klein Beekman, director of the Association of Operators of Relaxation Businesses (VER), Amsterdam, March 24, 1997.

13. Van Doorninck, "A Business like Any Other?" p. 196.

14. Wim Huisman and Hans Nelen, "Gotham Unbound Dutch Style: The Administrative Approach to Organized Crime in Amsterdam," *Crime, Law, and Social Change* 48 (2007): 87–103; Brants, "Fine Art of Regulated Tolerance."

15. Brants, "Fine Art of Regulated Tolerance."

16. Edgar Danter, "Green Light at Last for Dutch Red Light Districts," Deutsche Presse-Agentur, February 6, 1999, N = 2,600.

17. World Values Survey, conducted in 1990 and 2005, http://www.wvsevsdb.com/wvs/WVSAnalizeQuestion.jsp.

18. Joyce Outshoorn, "Pragmatism in the Polder: Changing Prostitution Policy in the Netherlands," *Journal of Contemporary European Studies* 12 (2004): 165–176.

19. Minister of Justice, quoted in Joyce Outshoorn, "Voluntary and Forced Prostitution: The 'Realistic Approach' of the Netherlands," in Joyce Outshoorn, ed., *The Politics of Prostitution*, New York: Cambridge University Press, 2004, p. 185.

20. Jan Visser, "Prostitution Policy under Construction," unpublished report, Amsterdam, 2008.

21. Sander Flight, Paul Hulshof, Paul van Soomeren, and Peter Soorsma, *Evaluating Lifting the Ban on Brothels: Municipal Policy*, English summary of report by DSP Groep for Ministry of Justice, WODC, 2006, p. 5.

22. Norwegian Ministry of Justice, *Purchasing Sexual Services in Sweden and the Netherlands: Legal Regulation and Experiences*, report by Working Group, October 2004, p. 30.

23. Paul van Soomeren and Sander Flight, "Design against Kerb-Crawing: Tippelzones," paper presented at the International Crime Prevention through Environmental Design conference, Brisbane, Australia, 2004.

24. Ibid.

25. Ibid.

26. Hendrik Wagenaar and Sietske Altink, "To Toe the Line: Streetwalking as Contested Space," in David Canter, Maria Ioannou, and Donna Youngs, eds., *Safer Sex in the City: The Experience and Management of Street Prostitution*, Farnham, UK: Ashgate, 2009.

27. Van Soomeren and Flight, "Design against Kerb-Crawing," p. 12.

28. Anton van Wijk, *Vulnerable Job: An Investigation into the Prostitution Industry in Amsterdam*, Amsterdam: Beke, 2010.

29. Figures are for 2005, cited in Dina Siegel, "Human Trafficking and Legalized Prostitution in the Netherlands," *Temida* (2009): 5–16.

30. Van Wijk, *Vulnerable Job*.

31. In the 1970s, the majority of foreign prostitutes in the country were from Thailand and the Philippines, whereas in the 1980s, the majority of foreigners came from Latin America. Ministry of Foreign Affairs, *FAQ about Dutch Prostitution*, Netherlands, 2005, p. 5.

32. Flight et al., *Evaluating Lifting the Ban*, p. 4.

33. Ibid., p. 6.

34. Hendrik Wagenaar, "Democracy and Prostitution: Deliberating the Legalization of Brothels in the Netherlands," *Administration and Society* 28 (2006): 198–235.

35. Ibid., p. 210.

36. Ibid., p. 211.

37. Interview with Sietske Altink, Amsterdam, March 24, 1997.

38. A. L. Daalder, *Prostitution in the Netherlands since the Lifting of the Brothel Ban*, The Hague: WODC/Ministry of Justice, 2007, p. 74.

39. Ibid., p. 75.

40. Flight et al., *Evaluating Lifting the Ban*, p. 4. The 2009 figure is an extrapolation from the rate of decline in 2000–2006, provided to me by Sander Flight.

41. Based on interview with Andre van Dorst, former director of the Association of Operators of Relaxation Businesses (VER), Amsterdam, May 4, 2009.

42. Bureau of the Dutch National Rapporteur on Trafficking in Human Beings, *Trafficking in Human Beings: Fifth Report of the Dutch National Rapporteur*, The Hague: Bureau, 2007, p. 83.

43. Ministry of Justice, "Full Licensing Required for Prostitution Services," press release, May 20, 2008.

44. Interview with Ministry of Justice official, Amsterdam, May 11, 2009.

45. Regioplan, summary of report, *An Evaluation of the Lifting of the Brothel Ban: The Social Position of Prostitutes*, Amsterdam: Regioplan Beleidsonderzoek, 2006, p. 8.

46. Bureau of the Dutch National Rapporteur, *Trafficking in Human Beings: Fifth Report*, p. 80.

47. Perro de Jong, "Netherlands to Crack Down on Clients of Illegal Prostitutes," *Radio Netherlands Worldwide*, November 9, 2009.

48. Interview with Andre van Dorst, Amsterdam, March 15, 2011.

49. Interview with Hugo Persant Snoep, brothel owner, Amsterdam, June 13, 2008.

50. Interview with van Dorst, March 15, 2011.

51. Interview with Esther Meppelink, director of VER, Amsterdam, March 15, 2011.

52. Interview with window owner, Amsterdam, March 17, 2011.

53. Regioplan, summary of report, pp. 5–6.

54. Interview with Snoep.

55. Regioplan, summary of report; Andre van Dorst, the former director of VER, told me that 97 percent of licensed brothel and escort workers were paying tax as of 2009 (interview, March 15, 2011).

56. Ibid., p. 7.

57. Interview with Snoep.

58. Penny Crofts, "Sex in the Dark: The Brothels Legislation Amendment Act 2007 (NSW)," *Current Issues in Criminal Justice* 19 (2007): 183–196.

59. Elaine Mossman, "Brothel Operators' and Support Agencies' Experiences of Decriminalization," in Gillian Abel, Lisa Fitzgerald, and Catherine Healy, eds., *Taking the Crime Out of Sex Work: New Zealand Sex Workers' Fight for Decriminalization*, Bristol, UK: Policy, 2010, p. 131.

60. Labor Party city councilor Frank de Wolf, quoted in Molly Moore, "Changing Patterns in Social Fabric Test Netherlands' Liberal Identity," *Washington Post*, June 23, 2007.

61. "Majority of Amsterdam Locals Support New Approach to Red Light District," *DutchAmsterdam.nl*, December 24, 2007, originally published in *Het Parool*.

62. The Van Traa Commission, cited in Huisman and Nelen, "Gotham Unbound Dutch Style."

63. Daalder, *Prostitution in the Netherlands*.

64. Ibid., p. 15.

65. "Alkmaar Brothels to Remain Open," *DutchNews.nl*, November 12, 2009.

66. Huisman and Nelen, "Gotham Unbound Dutch Style," p. 101.

67. Frank Bovenkerk, *Loverboys of Modern Pooierschap*, Amsterdam: Augustus, 2006.

68. Asscher, quoted in Catherine Hornby, "Stricter Brothel Rules?" Reuters, January 19, 2010.

69. Ibid.

70. Cohen, quoted in Marlise Simons, "Amsterdam Tries Upscale Fix for Red-Light Area," *New York Times*, February 24, 2008.

71. Cohen, quoted in David Charter, "Half of Amsterdam's Red-Light Windows Close," *Times* (UK), December 27, 2008.

72. De Amsterdamse Prostitutie Monitor, Amsterdam Sociaal, 2010. The survey was administered over six days in February 2010 by female interviewers who went door to door in the large RLD in the Wallen (not the two smaller RLDs in Amsterdam), either interviewing workers on-site or leaving a questionnaire that was later retrieved by the research team. The questionnaire was distributed to all occupants present at the times the survey was fielded, but participation was voluntary, making it impossible to determine how representative it was. Moreover, the questionnaire was in Dutch and English, which may have limited participation among those with rudimentary proficiency in these languages. The results therefore reflect an unknown degree of selection bias, but the sample did include a significant proportion of the window population. I thank Bas Merkx and Laurens Buijs for providing me with the survey instrument and data.

73. "Luxury Amsterdam Sex Club Closed for Good," *Radio Netherlands Worldwide*, July 8, 2009.

74. Interview with Ministry of Justice official, Amsterdam, June 27, 2008.

75. Cyrille Fijnaut, Frank Bovenkerk, Gerben Bruinsma, and Henk van der Bunt, *Organized Crime in the Netherlands*, The Hague: Kluwer, 1998, pp. 102–105. The authors report that eastern Europeans transported women into the Netherlands; some of these individuals ran elaborate operations, while others were involved in networks consisting of a few people.

76. Mariska Majoor, quoted in "Amsterdam Closes a Window on Its Red-Light Tourist Trade," *Guardian* (UK), September 23, 2007.

77. Daalder, *Prostitution in the Netherlands*, p. 84.

78. Transcrime, *Study on National Legislation on Prostitution and the Trafficking in Women and Children*, report to the European Parliament, 2005, p. 121.

79. Bureau of the Dutch National Rapporteur on Trafficking in Human Beings, *Trafficking in Human Beings: Seventh Report of the Dutch National Rapporteur*, The Hague: Bureau, 2010, p. 576.

80. Daalder, *Prostitution in the Netherlands*.

81. Norwegian Ministry of Justice, *Purchasing Sexual Services*, p. 31.

82. Interview with Snoep; interview with van Dorst, May 4, 2009.

83. Interview with Snoep.

84. "Dutch Justice Ministry Unable to Help Sex Industry," *Radio Netherlands* (online), August 4, 2009.

85. Alderman Lodewijk Asscher, as reported in *Het Parool*, February 19, 2009.

86. Regioplan, summary of report, p. 7.

87. Interview with window owner, Amsterdam, May 28, 1998.

88. Interview with window owner, Amsterdam, June 9, 2008.

89. Interview with window owner, Amsterdam, March 17, 2011.

90. Interview with van Dorst, May 4, 2009.

91. Interview with official in window owners' association, Amsterdam, June 11, 2008.

92. Quoted in "Amsterdam's Red Lights: About to Go Out?" *Radio Netherlands Worldwide*, January 21, 2008.

93. Interview with two Amsterdam city officials responsible for prostitution, Amsterdam, May 10, 2010.

94. Interview with Green Party city councilor, Amsterdam, May 9, 2010.

95. Interview with two Amsterdam city officials responsible for prostitution.

96. Interview with Ministry of Justice official, Amsterdam, June 27, 2008.

97. Interview with Ministry of Justice official, Amsterdam, May 11, 2009.

98. Daalder, *Prostitution in the Netherlands*.

99. Bureau of the Dutch National Rapporteur on Trafficking in Human Beings, *Trafficking in Human Beings: Sixth Report of the Dutch National Rapporteur*, Supplementary Figures, The Hague: Bureau, 2008, p. 4.

100. Bureau of the Dutch National Rapporteur on Trafficking in Human Beings, *Trafficking in Human Beings: Third Report of the Dutch National Rapporteur*, The Hague: Bureau, 2005, pp. 94–95.

101. Norwegian Ministry of Justice, *Purchasing Sexual Services*, p. 31.

102. Daalder, *Prostitution in the Netherlands*, p. 80.

103. "Alkmaar Brothels to Remain Open."

104. Daalder, *Prostitution in the Netherlands*.

105. Ibid., pp. 87, 61.

106. De Amsterdamse Prostitutie Monitor.

107. Interview with head police official responsible for prostitution control in Amsterdam, Amsterdam, June 26, 2008.

108. Ibid.

109. Prostitution and Health Center 292 brochure.

110. Interview with director of Prostitution and Health Center 292, Amsterdam, May 10, 2010.

111. Email from director of Prostitution and Health Center 292, May 20, 2010.

112. Interview with two Amsterdam city government officials.

113. Interview with Toos Heemskerk, director of Scharlaken Koord, Amsterdam, March 17, 2011.

114. Posting on www.worldsexguide.org, May 26, 1997.

115. Posting on www.worldsexguide.org, 1994.

116. Posting on www.worldsexguide.org, December 31, 1995.

117. Club Elegance was recently closed by the authorities, because the owner could not demonstrate that all of his income came from legal activities.

118. Mayfair's website: www.themayfair.nl.

119. Ria's website: www.riasmensclub.nl.

120. Jan Bik's website: www.janbik.nl.

121. Posting by Inemetz, www.ignatzmice.com, May 20, 2010.

122. WhyGo Amsterdam, "Amsterdam Sex Clubs: A Complete Guide," www.amsterdamlogue.com/amsterdam-sex-clubs.html.

123. One said that he had been there many times and that "most have been a great time," and he said that most recently, "we had a great time. No rush at all, very passionate, and eager to please." Posting by Iggy1903, www.ignatzmice.com, October 26 and 28, 2009.

124. Ronald de Graaf, *Prostitutes and Their Clients*, The Hague: Gegenens Koninkijke, 1995, p. 15.

125. De Amsterdamse Prostitutie Monitor.

126. Van Wijk, *Vulnerable Job*.

127. Ibid.

128. Interview with Ministry of Justice official, June 27, 2008.

129. Fieldnotes, May 5, 2010, and May 9, 2010.

130. Fieldnotes, May 9, 2010.

131. Posting by Gazza, www.ignatzmice.com, May 18, 2010.

132. Posting by Straton, www.ignatzmice.com, May 21, 2010.

133. Samuel Cameron, "Space, Risk, and Opportunity: The Evolution of Paid Sex Markets," *Urban Studies* 41 (2004): 1643–1657, at p. 1653.

134. The exception is the Candy Club, which is outside the RLD. It bills itself as a dance and swingers club for couples and singles, but freelance prostitutes also work there and take men to curtained rooms for €50. The club's website announces that is has existed for 40 years and is "the cheapest swingers club in the world" and declares, "in our club everything is allowed and nothing is obliged." www.candyclub.nl.

135. G. J. Ashworth, P. E. White, and H. P. M. Winchester, "The Red-Light District in the West European City: A Neglected Aspect of the Urban Landscape," *Geoforum* 19 (1988): 201–212.

136. Fieldnotes, May 11, 2009.

137. Regioplan, summary of report, p. 3. Escorts and street workers were not part of the survey.

138. De Amsterdamse Prostitutie Monitor.

139. Ibid.

140. Manuel Aalbers, "Big Sister Is Watching You: Gender Interaction and the Unwritten Rules of the Amsterdam Red-Light District," *Journal of Sex Research* 42 (2005): 54–62, at p. 58.

141. Quoted in Wendy Chapkis, *Live Sex Acts: Women Performing Erotic Labor*, New York: Routledge, 1997, p. 116.

142. "Red Light District" brochure, Politie, Amsterdam.

143. Aalbers, "Big Sister"; and descriptions on clients' online discussion boards.

144. De Amsterdamse Prostitutie Monitor.

145. Posting by Partylover, www.punternet.com, April 28, 2009.

146. Posting by Straton, www.ignatzmice.com, May 17, 2010.

147. Posting by Bookguy, www.ignatzmice.com, September 8, 2010.

148. Posting by Jerboa, www.punternet.com, October 14, 2009.

149. Postings on www.ignatzmice.com, August 30, 2007, and October 10, 2007.

150. Posting on www.worldsexguide.org, August 27, 1997.

151. Postings on www.ignatzmice.com, April 27, 2010.

152. Posting by BlutoBlutarsky, www.ignatzmice.com, August 18, 2010.

153. Posting by Paebiifm, www.ignatzmice.com, September 8, 2010, and replies.

154. Posting by Drostie, www.ignatzmice.com, August 23, 2008.

155. Posting on www.worldsexguide.org, November 11, 1997.

156. Posting by Brad07, www.ignatzmice.com, May 19, 2010.

157. Posting by Bookguy, www.ignatzmice.com, July 24, 2010.

158. Posting by Bookguy, www.ignatzmice.com, August 8, 2010.

159. Posting by Gladiator99, www.ignatzmice.com, June 12, 2010.

160. Teela Sanders, *Paying for Pleasure: Men Who Buy Sex*, Portland, OR: Willan, 2008.

161. De Amsterdamse Prostitutie Monitor.

162. Conversation with Jasmine, Amsterdam, June 1, 2008. "Jasmine" is a pseudonym.

163. Conversations with Jasmine, Amsterdam, May 8, 2010, and March 15, 2011.

164. Exploitation documented in Sietske Altink and Sylvia Bokelman, *Rechten van Prostituees* [*Rights of Prostitutes*], Amsterdam: Rode Draad, 2006.

165. Email from Sietske Altink to author, January 26, 2010. See also Altink and Bokelman, *Rechten van Prostituees*.

166. Daalder, *Prostitution in the Netherlands*, p. 87.

167. Regioplan, summary of report, p. 7.

168. Daalder, *Prostitution in the Netherlands*, p. 74–75.

169. De Graaf, *Prostitutes and Their Clients*, p. 15.

170. Ministry of Justice, *Report of the Prostitution Law Review Committee on the Operation of the Prostitution Reform Act 2003*, Wellington, New Zealand: Ministry of Justice, 2008.

171. A. L. Daalder, *Lifting the Ban on Brothels*, The Hague: WODC/Ministry of Justice, 2004, p. 30.

172. De Amsterdamse Prostitutie Monitor. The terms "threatening," "harassed," and "abused" were not defined in the survey.

173. Daalder, *Prostitution in the Netherlands*, p. 79.

174. Ibid.

175. Interview with Ministry of Justice official, Amsterdam, June 27, 2008.

176. Bovenkerk, *Loverboys of Modern Pooierschap*.

177. Fieldnotes, June 20, 2008.

178. Daalder, *Prostitution in the Netherlands*, p. 79.

179. Interview with Ministry of Justice official, June 27, 2008.

180. Interview with Toos Heemskerk, director of Scharlaken Koord, Amsterdam, March 17, 2011.

181. The trafficking office reports that 403 possible victims (of all types of trafficking) were identified in 2004 and 579 in 2006 and 826 in 2008, the largest percentage of whom were Dutch citizens, followed by Bulgarians, Nigerians, and Romanians. Bureau of the Dutch National Rapporteur, *Seventh Report*, pp. 611–614.

182. Bureau of the Dutch National Rapporteur, *Trafficking in Human Beings: Seventh Report*, p. 623.

183. Daalder, *Prostitution in the Netherlands*, p. 80; Bureau of the Dutch National Rapporteur, *Trafficking in Human Beings: Seventh Report*.

184. Bureau of the Dutch National Rapporteur, *Trafficking in Human Beings: Third Report*, p. 91.

185. Maaike van Veen, "HIV and Sexual Risk Behavior among Commercial Sex Workers in the Netherlands," *Archives of Sexual Behavior* 39 (2010): 714–723.

186. De Amsterdamse Prostitutie Monitor.

187. Daalder, *Prostitution in the Netherlands*, p. 86.

188. Ibid., p. 87.

189. Ibid., p. 86.

190. Bureau of the Dutch National Rapporteur, *Trafficking in Human Beings: Fifth Report*, p. 49.

191. Damian Zaitch and Richard Staring, "The Flesh Is Weak, the Spirit Even Weaker: Clients and Trafficked Women in the Netherlands," in Andrea Di Nicola, ed., *Prostitution and Human Trafficking: Focus on Clients*, New York: Springer, 2009, p. 98.

192. Interview with Beekman.

193. Ibid.

NOTES TO THE CONCLUSION

1. Discussed in chapter 4.

2. Lars Ericsson, "Charges against Prostitution: An Attempt at a Philosophical Assessment," *Ethics* 90 (1980): 335–366.

3. Christine Overall, "What's Wrong with Prostitution? Evaluating Sex Work," *Signs* 17 (1992): 705–724, at p. 716. Overall is not optimistic that this can be achieved.

4. Carole Pateman, *The Sexual Contract*, Stanford: Stanford University Press, 1988, chap. 7.

5. Feona Attwood, "Sexed Up: Theorizing the Sexualization of Culture," *Sexualities* 9 (2006): 77–94; Barbara Brents and Teela Sanders, "Mainstreaming the Sex Industry," *Journal of Law and Society* 37 (2010): 40–60.

6. On women's role in driving some sex-industry trends, see Lynn Comella, "Remaking the Sex Industry: The Adult Expo as a Microcosm," and Jill Bakehorn, "Women-Made Pornography," both in Ronald Weitzer, ed., *Sex for Sale: Prostitution, Pornography, and the Sex Industry*, 2nd ed., New York: Routledge, 2010.

7. National Organization for Women, *Resolution Calling for the Decriminalization of Prostitution*, Resolution 141 passed at the national NOW conference, 1973.

8. Ericsson, "Charges against Prostitution," pp. 365–366.

9. National Organization for Women, *Resolution*.

10. Prostitution Act, 1999, Queensland, Australia (§ 17).

11. Prostitution Law Review Committee, *Report of the Prostitution Law Review Committee on the Operation of the Prostitution Reform Act 2003*, Wellington, New Zealand: Ministry of Justice, 2008.

12. Federal Ministry for Family Affairs, Senior Citizens, Women, and Youth, *Report by the Federal Government on the Impact of the Act Regulating the Legal Situation of Prostitutes (Prostitution Act)*, Berlin: Ministry, 2007, pp. 79, 80.

13. Pivot Legal Society, *Beyond Decriminalization: Sex Work, Human Rights, and a New Framework for Law Reform*, Vancouver, Canada: Pivot, 2006, p. 2.

14. Special Committee on Pornography and Prostitution, *Pornography and Prostitution in Canada*, Ottawa, ON: Department of Justice, 1985; Federal/Provincial Territorial Working Group on Prostitution, *Report and Recommendations in Respect of Legislation, Policy, and Practices Concerning Prostitution-Related Activities*, Ottawa, ON: Department of Justice, 1998; Pivot Legal Society, *Beyond Decriminalization*.

15. John Lowman, "The 'Left Regulation' of Prostitution: Reconciling Individual Rights and Collective Interests," in John Lowman and Brian D. MacLean, eds., *Realist Criminology: Crime Control and Policing in the 1990s*, Toronto: University of Toronto Press, 1992, p. 172.

16. Hendrik Wagenaar and Sietske Altink, "To Toe the Line: Streetwalking as Contested Space," in David Canter, Maria Ioannou, and Donna Youngs, eds., *Safer Sex in the City: The Experience and Management of Street Prostitution*, Farnham, UK: Ashgate, 2009, p. 167.

17. Ibid.

18. Interview with Jan Visser, official in Red Thread, Amsterdam, May 7, 2010.

19. John Dombrink and Daniel Hillyard, *Sin No More*, New York: NYU Press, 2007.

20. Robert F. Meier and Gilbert Geis, *Victimless Crime? Prostitution, Drugs, Homosexuality, Abortion*, Los Angeles: Roxbury, 1997, p. 28.

21. A survey of (mostly street) prostitutes working in San Francisco found that 71 percent supported decriminalization: Alexandra Lutnick and Deborah Cohan, "Criminalization, Legalization, or Decriminalization of Sex Work," *Reproductive Health Matters* 17 (2009): 38–46. Three-quarters of clients in another survey felt that prostitution should be legalized: Martin Monto, "Prostitutes' Customers: Motives and Misconceptions," in Weitzer, ed., *Sex for Sale*, 2nd ed.

22. Most of these variables are examined in Ronald Weitzer, "Prostitutes' Rights in the United States: The Failure of a Movement," *Sociological Quarterly* 32 (1991): 23–41.

23. Discussed in chapter 3.

24. *Bedford v. Canada*, 2010 ONSC 4264, Superior Court of Justice, Ontario, Justice Himel, September 28, 2010, paras. 3, 536. A court of appeal granted a stay of the judgment until April 29, 2011, to permit appellate review of the case. Since the September ruling, the government has been claiming that the moral fabric of society will unravel if the decision is not overturned.

Bibliography

Aalbers, Manuel, "Big Sister Is Watching You: Gender Interaction and the Unwritten Rules of the Amsterdam Red-Light District," *Journal of Sex Research* 42 (2005): 54–62.

Abel, Gillian, and Lisa Fitzgerald, "Risk and Risk Management in Sex Work Post-Prostitution Reform Act," in Gillian Abel, Lisa Fitzgerald, and Catherine Healy, eds., *Taking the Crime Out of Sex Work: New Zealand Sex Workers' Fight for Decriminalization*, Bristol, UK: Policy, 2010.

"Academics Urge R.I. to Keep Indoor Prostitution Legal," *Providence Journal*, August 3, 2009.

Adams, Jim, and Jason Riley, "Louisville Takes Aim at Parlor Prostitution," *Courier-Journal*, July 11, 2004.

Aggleton, Peter, ed., *Men Who Sell Sex*, Philadelphia: Temple University Press, 1999.

Agustín, Laura, "Sex and the Limits of Enlightenment: The Irrationality of Legal Regimes to Control Prostitution," *Sexuality Research and Social Policy* 5 (2008): 73–86.

———, *Sex at the Margins: Migration, Labor Markets, and the Rescue Industry*, London: Zed Books, 2007.

Albert, Alexa, *Brothel: Mustang Ranch and Its Women*, New York: Ballantine, 2001.

"Alkmaar Brothels to Remain Open," *DutchNews.nl*, November 12, 2009.

Altink, Sietske, and Sylvia Bokelman, *Rechten van Prostituees* [*Rights of Prostitutes*], Amsterdam: Rode Draad, 2006.

"Amsterdam Closes a Window on Its Red-Light Tourist Trade," *Guardian* (UK), September 23, 2007.

"Amsterdam's Red Lights: About to Go Out?" *Radio Netherlands Worldwide*, January 21, 2008.

Anderson, Bridget, and Julia O'Connell Davidson, *Is Trafficking in Human Beings Demand Driven? A Multi-Country Pilot Study*, Geneva: International Organization for Migration, 2003.

Andrijasevic, Rutvica, "Beautiful Dead Bodies: Gender, Migration, and Representation in Anti-Trafficking Campaigns," *Feminist Review* 86 (2007): 24–44.

Anonymous, *Secret Diary of a Call Girl*, New York: Grand Central, 2008.

Arditi, Lynn, "New RI Law Banning Indoor Prostitution Leads Some Spas to Close," *Providence Journal*, November 4, 2009.

———, "RI Senate Passes Prostitution Bill, 36–2," *Providence Journal*, October 29, 2009.

Arnot, Alison, "Legalization of the Sex Industry in the State of Victoria, Australia," M.A. thesis, University of Melbourne, 2002.

Ashworth, G. J., P. E. White, and H. P. M. Winchester, "The Red-Light District in the West European City: A Neglected Aspect of the Urban Landscape," *Geoforum* 19 (1988): 201–212.

Atlanta Task Force on Prostitution, *Findings and Recommendations*, Mayor's Office, Atlanta, Georgia, 1986.

Attorney General, *Report to Congress on U.S. Government Efforts to Combat Trafficking in Persons in Fiscal Year 2004*, Washington, DC: U.S. Department of Justice, 2005.

Attwood, Feona, "Sexed Up: Theorizing the Sexualization of Culture," *Sexualities* 9 (2006): 77–94.

Bakehorn, Jill, "Women-Made Pornography," in Ronald Weitzer, ed., *Sex for Sale: Prostitution, Pornography, and the Sex Industry*, 2nd ed., New York: Routledge, 2010.

Barnett, Tim, Catherine Healy, Anna Reed, and Calum Bennachie, "Lobbying for Decriminalization," in Gillian Abel, Lisa Fitzgerald, and Catherine Healy, eds., *Taking the Crime Out of Sex Work: New Zealand Sex Workers' Fight for Decriminalization*, Bristol, UK: Policy, 2010.

Barry, Kathleen, *The Prostitution of Sexuality*, New York: NYU Press, 1995.

Barton Child Law and Policy Clinic, *Commercial Sexual Exploitation of Children in Georgia*, Atlanta: Emory Law School, 2008.

Bates, Stephen, "Outsourcing Justice? That's Obscene," *Washington Post*, July 15, 2007, p. B3.

Bell, Shannon, *Whore Carnival*, New York: Autonomedia, 1995.

Benson, Catherine, and Roger Matthews, "Police and Prostitution: Vice Squads in Britain," in Ronald Weitzer, ed., *Sex for Sale: Prostitution, Pornography, and the Sex Industry*, New York: Routledge, 2000.

Bernstein, Elizabeth, *Temporarily Yours: Intimacy, Authenticity, and the Commerce of Sex*, Chicago: University of Chicago Press, 2007.

Bilefsky, Dan, "Belgian Experiment: Make Prostitution Legal to Fight Its Ills," *Wall Street Journal*, May 26, 2005.

Blumenfeld, Laura, "In a Shift, Anti-Prostitution Effort Targets Pimps and Johns," *Washington Post*, December 15, 2005, p. A16.

Bovenkerk, Frank, *Loverboys of Modern Pooierschap*, Amsterdam: Augustus, 2006.

Brants, Chrisje, "The Fine Art of Regulated Tolerance: Prostitution in Amsterdam," *Journal of Law and Society* 25 (1998): 621–635.

Brennan, Denise, *What's Love Got to Do with It? Transnational Desires and Sex Tourism in the Dominican Republic*, Durham: Duke University Press, 2004.

Brents, Barbara, and Kathryn Hausbeck, "Violence and Legalized Brothel Prostitution in Nevada," *Journal of Interpersonal Violence* 20 (2005): 270–295.

Brents, Barbara, Crystal Jackson, and Kathryn Hausbeck, *The State of Sex: Tourism, Sex, and Sin in the New American Heartland*, New York: Routledge, 2010.

Brents, Barbara, and Teela Sanders, "Mainstreaming the Sex Industry," *Journal of Law and Society* 37 (2010): 40–60.

Brooks-Gordon, Belinda, *The Price of Sex: Prostitution, Policy, and Society*, Portland, OR: Willan, 2006.

Brown, Annie, "Sex Industry in Scotland: Inside the Deluded Minds of the Punters," *Daily Record* (Scotland), April 28, 2008.

Brown, Louise, "Performance, Status, and Hybridity in a Pakistani Red-Light District: The Cultural Production of the Courtesan," *Sexualities* 10 (2007): 409–423.

Brunker, Mike, "Prostitution Thrives on the Net," *ZD Net News*, June 7, 1999.

Bundesrechnuupshof, *Bemerkungen zur Haushalts und Wirtschaftführung des Bundes*, Bonn, 2003.

Bureau of the Dutch National Rapporteur on Trafficking in Human Beings, *Trafficking in Human Beings: Third Report of the Dutch National Rapporteur*, The Hague: Bureau, 2005,

———, *Trafficking in Human Beings: Fifth Report of the Dutch National Rapporteur*, The Hague: Bureau, 2007.

———, *Trafficking in Human Beings: Sixth Report of the Dutch National Rapporteur*, Supplementary Figures, The Hague: Bureau, 2008.

———, *Trafficking in Human Beings: Seventh Report of the Dutch National Rapporteur*, The Hague: Bureau, 2010.

Cameron, Samuel, "Space, Risk, and Opportunity: The Evolution of Paid Sex Markets," *Urban Studies* 41 (2004): 1643–1657.

Campbell, Russell, *Marked Women: Prostitutes and Prostitution in the Cinema*, Madison: University of Wisconsin Press, 2006.

Carmen, Arlene, and Howard Moody, *Working Women: The Subterranean World of Street Prostitution*, New York: Harper and Row, 1985.

Castle, Stephen, "Passports and Panic Buttons in the Brothel of the Future," *Independent* (UK), September 23, 2006.

Castle, Tammy, and Jenifer Lee, "Ordering Sex in Cyberspace: A Content Analysis of Escort Websites," *International Journal of Cultural Studies* 11 (2008): 108–121.

Celizic, Mike, "Former Call Girl Opens Up about the Industry," MSNBC.msn.com, March 12, 2008.

Chapkis, Wendy, *Live Sex Acts: Women Performing Erotic Labor*, New York: Routledge, 1997.

———, "Power and Control in the Commercial Sex Trade," in Ronald Weitzer, ed., *Sex for Sale: Prostitution, Pornography, and the Sex Industry*, New York: Routledge, 2000.

Charter, David, "Half of Amsterdam's Red-Light Windows Close," *Times* (UK), December 27, 2008.

Chen, Marcus, "Estimating the Number of Unlicensed Brothels in Melbourne," *Australian and New Zealand Journal of Public Health* 34 (2010): 67–71.

Chuang, Janie, "Rescuing Trafficking from Ideological Capture: Prostitution Reform and Anti-Trafficking Law and Policy," *University of Pennsylvania Law Review* 158 (2010): 1655–1728.

Church, Stephanie, Marion Henderson, Marina Barnard, and Graham Hart, "Violence by Clients towards Female Prostitutes in Different Work Settings," *British Medical Journal* 32 (2001): 524–526.

Clausen, Victor, "An Assessment of Gunilla Ekberg's Account of Swedish Prostitution Policy," unpublished paper, 2007.

Cohen, Bernard, *Deviant Street Networks: Prostitution in New York City*, Lexington, MA: Lexington Books, 1980.

Cohen, Erik, "Lovelorn Farangs: The Correspondence between Foreign Men and Thai Girls," *Anthropological Quarterly* 59 (1986): 115–127.

Cohen, Nick, "Booming Business among Amsterdam's Red Lights," *Independent* (UK), April 24, 2002.

"Cologne Leads the Way in Safe Prostitution," *Deutsche Welle*, July 7, 2005, www.DW-World.de.

Comella, Lynn, "Remaking the Sex Industry: The Adult Expo as a Microcosm," in Ronald Weitzer, ed., *Sex for Sale: Prostitution, Pornography, and the Sex Industry*, 2nd ed., New York: Routledge, 2010.

Crime and Misconduct Commission, *Regulating Prostitution: An Evaluation of the Prostitution Act 1999, Queensland*, Brisbane, Australia: Crime and Misconduct Commission, 2004.

Crissey, Mike, "State Police Revising Handbook after Sex Sting," Associated Press, September 8, 2001.

Crofts, Penny, "Sex in the Dark: The Brothels Legislation Amendment Act 2007 (NSW)," *Current Issues in Criminal Justice* 19 (2007): 183–196.

Crowe, Robert, "Officers Disrobe to Uncover Crime: HPD Changed Its Policy to Crack Down on Spas Fronting for Prostitution," *Houston Chronicle*, January 24, 2005.

"Curbing Prostitution on Demand Side," *New York Times*, April 20, 1992, p. B8.

Cusick, Linda, "Widening the Harm Reduction Agenda: From Drug Use to Sex Work," *International Journal of Drug Policy* 17 (2006): 3–11.

Daalder, A. L., *Lifting the Ban on Brothels*, The Hague: WODC/Ministry of Justice, 2004.

———, *Prostitution in the Netherlands since the Lifting of the Brothel Ban*, The Hague: WODC/Ministry of Justice, 2007.

Danna, Daniela, and Silvia Garcia, "The Situation in Madrid," in Daniela Danna, ed., *Prostitution and Public Life in Four European Capitals*, Rome: Carocci, 2007.

Danter, Edgar, "Green Light at Last for Dutch Red Light Districts," Deutsche Presse-Agentur, February 6, 1999.

Davies, Nick, "Prostitution and Trafficking: The Anatomy of a Moral Panic," *Guardian* (UK), October 20, 2009.

Davis, James, and Tom Smith, *General Social Survey: Cumulative Codebook*, Chicago: National Opinion Research Center, 2008.

Decker, John, *Prostitution: Regulation and Control*, Littleton, CO: Rothman, 1979.

de Graaf, Ronald, *Prostitutes and Their Clients*, The Hague: Gegenens Koninkijke, 1995.

de Jong, Perro, "Netherlands to Crack Down on Clients of Illegal Prostitutes," *Radio Netherlands Worldwide*, November 9, 2009.

Delacoste, Frederique, and Priscilla Alexander, eds., *Sex Work: Writings by Women in the Sex Industry*, Pittsburgh: Cleis, 1987.

Demsky, Ian, "Police Defend Prostitution Tactic: DA Says Encounters Using Informants Unnecessary," *Tennessean*, February 2, 2005.

Dennehy, Kate, "Queensland Sex Industry Still Largely Illegitimate," *Brisbane Times*, August 16, 2009.

"Dirty Money: The Business of High-End Prostitution," CNBC, 2008. Documentary.

Dodillet, Susanne, "Cultural Clash on Prostitution: Debates on Prostitution in Germany and Sweden in the 1990s," paper presented at Conference on Sex and Sexuality, Salzburg, October 14, 2004.

Dölemeyer, Anne, Rebecca Pates, and Daniel Schmidt, "Deviant Girls, Small-Scale Entrepreneurs, and the Regulation of German Sex Workers," in Melissa Hope Ditmore, Antonia Levy, and Alys Willman, eds., *Sex Work Matters*, New York: Zed Books, 2010.

Dombrink, John, and Daniel Hillyard, *Sin No More*, New York: NYU Press, 2007.

Donovan, Basil, Christine Harcourt, Sandra Egger, Karen Schneider, Jody O'Connor, Lewis Marshall, Marcus Chen, and Christopher Fairley, *The Sex Industry in Western Australia: A Report to the Western Australian Government*, Sydney: University of New South Wales, 2010.

Dowling, Denise, "Last Call for Sin," *Rhode Island Monthly*, June 2007.

"Downtown Girls: The Hookers of Honolulu," HBO, 2005. Documentary.

"Dutch Justice Ministry Unable to Help Sex Industry," *Radio Netherlands* (online), August 4, 2009.

Dworkin, Andrea, *Life and Death: Unapologetic Writings on the Continuing War against Women*, New York: Free Press, 1997.

———, *Pornography: Men Possessing Women*, New York: Putnam, 1981.

Earle, Sarah, and Keith Sharp, *Sex in Cyberspace: Men Who Pay for Sex*, Aldershot, UK: Ashgate, 2007.

Ericsson, Lars, "Charges against Prostitution: An Attempt at a Philosophical Assessment," *Ethics* 90 (1980): 335–366.

Europap, *Report Questionnaire 2001 in Belgium*, Europap, 2001.

Exner, John, Joyce Wylie, Antonnia Leura, and Tracey Parrill, "Some Psychological Characteristics of Prostitutes," *Journal of Personality Assessment* 41 (1977): 474–485.

Farley, Melissa, "Affidavit of Melissa Farley," in *Bedford v. Attorney General of Canada*, Case No. 07-CV-329807PD1, Ontario, Canada: Superior Court of Justice, 2008.

———, "Bad for the Body, Bad for the Heart: Prostitution Harms Women Even If Legalized or Decriminalized," *Violence Against Women* 10 (2004): 1087–1125.

———, "Prostitution Harms Women Even If Indoors: Reply to Weitzer," *Violence Against Women* 11 (2005): 950–964.

———, "Prostitution, Trafficking, and Cultural Amnesia: What We Must *Not Know* in Order to Keep the Business of Sexual Exploitation Running Smoothly," *Yale Journal of Law and Feminism* 18 (2006): 101–136.

———, *Prostitution and Trafficking in Nevada: Making the Connections*, San Francisco: Prostitution Research and Education, 2007.

———, "Prostitution and Trafficking in Nine Countries," *Journal of Trauma Practice* 2 (2003): 33–74.

Farrell, Amy, Jack McDevitt, and Stephanie Fahy, *Understanding and Improving Law Enforcement Responses to Human Trafficking*, Boston: Institute on Race and Justice, Northeastern University, 2008.

Federal Bureau of Investigation, *Crime in the United States*, Washington, DC: Department of Justice, annual.

Federal Ministry for Family Affairs, Senior Citizens, Women, and Youth, *Report by the Federal Government on the Impact of the Act Regulating the Legal Situation of Prostitutes (Prostitution Act)*, Berlin: Ministry, 2007.

Federal/Provincial Territorial Working Group on Prostitution, *Report and Recommendations in Respect of Legislation, Policy, and Practices Concerning Prostitution-Related Activities*, Ottawa, ON: Department of Justice, 1998.

Fijnaut, Cyrille, Frank Bovenkerk, Gerben Bruinsma, and Henk van der Bunt, *Organized Crime in the Netherlands*, The Hague: Kluwer, 1998.

Fisher, William, "USAID Sued over Anti-Prostitution Policy," Inter-Press Service News Agency, August 23, 2005.

Fitzharris, Paul, "Review of the Prostitution Reform Act," in Gillian Abel, Lisa Fitzgerald, and Catherine Healy, eds., *Taking the Crime Out of Sex Work: New Zealand Sex Workers' Fight for Decriminalization*, Bristol, UK: Policy, 2010.

Flight, Sander, Paul Hulshof, Paul van Soomeren, and Peter Soorsma, *Evaluating Lifting the Ban on Brothels: Municipal Policy*, English summary of report by DSP Groep for Ministry of Justice, WODC, 2006.

Frank, Katherine, *G-Strings and Sympathy: Strip Club Regulars and Male Desire*, Durham: Duke University Press, 2002.

Frank, Katherine, and Michelle Carnes, "Gender and Space in Strip Clubs," in Ronald Weitzer, ed., *Sex for Sale: Prostitution, Pornography, and the Sex Industry*, 2nd ed., New York: Routledge, 2010.

French, Dolores, *Working: My Life as a Prostitute*, New York: Dutton, 1988.

Frohlick, Susan, "'I'm More Sexy Here': Erotic Subjectivities of Female Tourists in the 'Sexual Paradise' of the Costa Rican Caribbean," in Tanu Priya Uteng and Tim Cresswell, eds., *Gendered Mobilities*, Aldershot, UK: Ashgate, 2008.

Furlong, Ray, "German Prostitutes in Rights Plea," *BBC News Online*, June 24, 2005.

Gehrke, Robert, "Nation's Porn Prosecutor Fronts War against Obscenity," *Salt Lake Tribune*, February 26, 2007.

Gerstein, Josh, "Porn Prosecution Fuels Debate," *Politico*, July 31, 2009.

Goldman, Adam, "Scandal Gives Peek inside Call-Girl Ring," Associated Press, March 12, 2008.

Gould, Arthur, "The Criminalization of Buying Sex: The Politics of Prostitution in Sweden," *Journal of Social Politics* 30 (2001): 437–456.

The Great Happiness Space, DVD, Jake Clennell Productions, 2006.

Green, Sara, "Prostitution Sting Leads to 104 Arrests," *Seattle Times*, November 16, 2006.

Guy, Donna, *Sex and Danger in Buenos Aires: Prostitution, Family, and Nation in Argentina*, Lincoln: University of Nebraska Press, 1990.

Gysels, Marjolein, R. Pool, and K. Bwanika, "Truck Drivers, Middlemen, and Commercial Sex Workers," *AIDS Care* 13 (2001): 373–385.

Hallgrimsdottir, Helga, Rachel Phillips, and Cecilia Benoit, "Fallen Women and Rescued Girls: Social Stigma and Media Narratives of the Sex Industry in Victoria, BC from 1980–2005," *Canadian Review of Sociology and Anthropology* 43 (2006): 265–280.

Harcourt, Christine, and Basil Donovan, "The Many Faces of Sex Work," *Sexually Transmitted Infections* 81 (2005): 201–206.

Hausbeck, Kathryn, and Barbara Brents, "Nevada's Legal Brothels," in Ronald Weitzer, ed., *Sex for Sale: Prostitution, Pornography, and the Sex Industry*, 2nd ed., New York: Routledge, 2010.

Hausbeck, Kathryn, Barbara Brents, and Crystal Jackson, "Vegas and the Sex Industry: Don't Make Assumptions about the Choices Women Make," *Las Vegas Review-Journal*, September 16, 2007.

Hay, Jeremy, "Spread Your Legs, You Are under Arrest: A Report on the Police Abuse of Prostitutes in San Francisco," *Gauntlet Magazine* 1, no. 7 (1994): 20–32.

Henning, Juanita, "Wie Funktioniert die Bordellprostitution in Frankfurt/Main?" In Philipp Thiée, ed., *Menschen Handel: Wie der Sexmarkt Strafrechtlich Reguliert Wird*, Berlin: Vereinigung Berliner Strafverteidiger, 2008.

Henry, Ray, "RI Lawmakers Adopt Indoor Prostitution Ban," Associated Press, October 30, 2009.

Herold, Edward, Rafael Garcia, and Tony DeMoya, "Female Tourists and Beach Boys: Romance or Sex Tourism?" *Annals of Tourism Research* 28 (2001): 978–997.

Hershatter, Gail, *Dangerous Pleasures: Prostitution and Modernity in Twentieth-Century Shanghai*, Berkeley: University of California Press, 1999.

———, "The Hierarchy of Shanghai Prostitution: 1870–1949," *Modern China* 15 (1989): 463–498.

Hester, Marianne, and Nicole Westmarland, *Tackling Street Prostitution: Towards an Holistic Approach*, Home Office Research Study 279, London: Home Office, 2004.

Heyl, Barbara, "The Madam as Teacher: The Training of House Prostitutes," *Social Problems* 24 (1977): 545–555.

———, "Prostitution: An Extreme Case of Sex Stratification," in Freda Adler and Rita Simon, eds., *The Criminology of Deviant Women*, Boston: Houghton Mifflin, 1979.

Hoang, Kimberly, "Economies of Emotion, Familiarity, Fantasy, and Desire: Emotional Labor in Ho Chi Minh City's Sex Industry," *Sexualities* 13 (2010): 255–272.

Hoefinger, Heidi, "Professional Girlfriends: Sex Workers and the Bartering of Intimacy in Phnom Penh, Cambodia," M.A. thesis, Hunter College, City University of New York, 2005.

Holt, Thomas, and Kristie Blevins, "Examining Sex Work from the Clients' Perspective," *Deviant Behavior* 28 (2007): 333–354.

Home Office, *A Coordinated Prostitution Strategy*, London: Home Office, 2006.

Hornby, Catherine, "Stricter Brothel Rules?" Reuters, January 19, 2010.

Howe, Cymene, Susanna Zaraysky, and Lois Lorentzen, "Transgender Sex Workers and Sexual Transmigration between Guadalajara and San Francisco," *Latin American Perspectives* 35 (2008): 31–50.

Hsu, Spencer, "Judge Drops Porn Case for Insufficient Evidence," *Washington Post*, July 17, 2010, p. A2.

Hubacher, Art, "Every Picture Tells a Story: Is Kansas City's 'John TV' Constitutional?" *Kansas Law Review* 46 (1998): 551–591.

Hubbard, Phil, "Revisiting the Red Light District: Still Neglected, Immoral, and Marginal?" *Geoforum* 39 (2008): 1743–1755.

Hughes, Donna, "Accommodation or Abolition?" *National Review Online*, May 1, 2003.

———, *The Demand for Victims of Sex Trafficking*, Kingston: University of Rhode Island, 2005.

———, "R.I.'s Carnival of Prostitution," *Providence Journal*, June 24, 2009.

———, "Wolves in Sheep's Clothing: No Way to End Sex Trafficking," *National Review Online*, October 9, 2002.

Huisman, Wim, and Hans Nelen, "Gotham Unbound Dutch Style: The Administrative Approach to Organized Crime in Amsterdam," *Crime, Law, and Social Change* 48 (2007): 87–103.

Human Rights Joint Committee, *Legislative Scrutiny: Policing and Crime Bill 2009, Conclusions and Recommendations*, http://www.publications.parliament.uk/pa/jt200809/jtselect/jtrights/68/6805.htm.

Institute for Population and Social Research, *2007 Survey of Sexual and Reproductive Health of Sex Workers in Thailand*, Salaya, Thailand: Mahidol University, 2007.

Jackman, Tom, "Spotsylvania Deputies Receive Sex Services in Prostitution Cases," *Washington Post*, February 13, 2006.

Jacobs, Andrew, "Call Girls, Updated," *New York Times*, October 12, 2004.

James, Jennifer, "Prostitute-Pimp Relationships," *Medical Aspects of Human Sexuality* 7 (1973): 147–160.

Jeffrey, Leslie, and Barbara Sullivan, "Canadian Sex Work Policy for the 21st Century: Enhancing Rights and Safety, Lessons from Australia," *Canadian Political Science Review* 3 (2009): 57–76.

Jeffreys, Sheila, *The Idea of Prostitution*, North Melbourne, Australia: Spinifex, 1997.

———, *The Industrial Vagina*, New York: Routledge, 2009.

Jolin, Annette, "Germany," in Nanette J. Davis, ed., *Prostitution: An International Handbook on Trends, Problems, and Policies*, Westport, CT: Greenwood, 1993.

Karras, Ruth, *Common Women: Prostitution and Sexuality in Medieval England*, New York: Oxford University Press, 1996.

Katsulis, Yasmina, *Sex Work and the City: The Social Geography of Health and Safety in Tijuana, Mexico*, Austin: University of Texas Press, 2008.

Kavemann, Barbara, and Heike Rabe, "The Act Regulating the Legal Situation of Prostitutes: Implementation, Impact, Current Developments," report, Berlin Research Institute for Social Science and Women's Studies, Berlin, 2007.

Kay, Julie, "U.S. Attorney's Porn Fight Gets Bad Reviews," *Daily Business Review*, August 30, 2005.

Keire, Mara, *For Business and Pleasure: Red-Light Districts and the Regulation of Vice in the United States, 1890–1933*, Baltimore: Johns Hopkins University Press, 2010.

Kelly, Patty, *Lydia's Open Door: Inside Mexico's Most Modern Brothel*, Berkeley: University of California Press, 2008.

Kempadoo, Kamala, "Introduction: Globalizing Sex Workers' Rights," in Kamala Kempadoo and Jo Doezema, eds., *Global Sex Workers*, New York: Routledge, 1998.

———, *Sexing the Caribbean: Gender, Race, and Sexual Labor*, New York: Routledge, 2004.

———, ed., *Sun, Sex, and Gold: Tourism and Sex Work in the Caribbean*, Lanham, MD: Rowman and Littlefield, 1999.

Kimberlin, Joanne, "Women for Hire: Behind Closed Doors in the Escort Industry," *Virginia-Pilot*, May 18, 2008, pp. A1, A10–11.

Kirshbaum, Erik, "Global Economic Crisis Hits German Sex Industry," Reuters, April 20, 2009.

Knight, Dean, "The Continuing Regulation of Prostitution by Local Authorities," in Gillian Abel, Lisa Fitzgerald, and Catherine Healy, eds., *Taking the Crime Out of Sex Work: New Zealand Sex Workers' Fight for Decriminalization*, Bristol, UK: Policy, 2010.

Knox, Noelle, "In Belgium, Brothels Are Big Business," *USA Today*, November 4, 2003.

Koken, Juline, David Bimbi, and Jeffrey Parsons, "Male and Female Escorts: A Comparative Analysis," in Ronald Weitzer, ed., *Sex for Sale: Prostitution, Pornography, and the Sex Industry*, 2nd ed., New York: Routledge, 2010.

Kontos, Maria, and Kyoko Shinozaki, "Integration of New Female Migrants in the German Labor Market and Society and German State Policies on Integration," Working Paper No. 1, Institut für Sozialforschung an der J. W. Goethe Universität Frankfurt, Frankfurt, 2007.

Kotiswaran, Prabha, "Born unto Brothels: Toward a Legal Ethnography of Sex Work in an Indian Red-Light Area," *Law and Social Inquiry* 33 (2008): 579–629.

———, "Labors in Vice or Virtue? Neo-liberalism, Sexual Commerce, and the Case of Indian Bar Dancing," *Journal of Law and Society* 37 (2010): 105–124.

Kulick, Don, *Travesti: Sex, Gender, and Culture among Brazilian Prostitutes*, Chicago: University of Chicago Press, 1998.

Lake, Richard, "Majority Opposes Legalizing Prostitution in Las Vegas," *Las Vegas Review-Journal*, October 30, 2003.

Lambert, Bruce, "As Prostitutes Turn to Craigslist, Law Takes Notice," *New York Times*, September 4, 2007.

Leidholdt, Dorchen, "Prostitution and Trafficking in Women: An Intimate Relationship," *Journal of Trauma Practice* 2 (2004): 167–183.

Leitzel, Jim, *Regulating Vice: Misguided Prohibitions and Realistic Controls*, New York: Cambridge University Press, 2008.

Lenton, Simon, "Pot, Politics, and the Press: Reflections on Cannabis Law Reform in Western Australia," *Drug and Alcohol Review* 23 (2004): 223–233.

Lever, Janet, and Deanne Dolnick, "Call Girls and Street Prostitutes: Selling Sex and Intimacy," in Ronald Weitzer, ed., *Sex for Sale: Prostitution, Pornography, and the Sex Industry*, 2nd ed., New York: Routledge, 2010.

Lewis, Neil, "Federal Effort on Web Obscenity Shows Few Results," *New York Times*, August 10, 2007.

Lim, Lin Lean, *The Sex Sector: The Economic and Social Bases of Prostitution in Southeast Asia*, Geneva: International Labor Office, 1998.

Logan, Jessica, "Internet Replacing Streetwalking for Inland Prostitution," *Press-Enterprise* (Riverside, CA), January 1, 2008.

Löw, Martina, and Renate Ruhne, "Domesticating Prostitution: Study of an Interactional Web of Space and Gender," *Space and Culture* 12 (2009): 232–249.

Lowman, John, "The 'Left Regulation' of Prostitution: Reconciling Individual Rights and Collective Interests," in John Lowman and Brian D. MacLean, eds., *Realist Criminology: Crime Control and Policing in the 1990s*, Toronto: University of Toronto Press, 1992.

———, "Street Prostitution Control: Some Canadian Reflections on the Finsbury Park Experience," *British Journal of Criminology* 32 (1992): 1–17.

Lowman, John, and Chris Atchison, "Men Who Buy Sex: A Survey in the Greater Vancouver Regional District," *Canadian Review of Sociology and Anthropology* 43 (2006): 281–296.

Lowman, John, and Laura Fraser, *Violence against Persons Who Prostitute: The Experience in British Columbia*, Ottawa, Canada: Department of Justice, 1995.

Lucas, Ann, "The Work of Sex Work: Elite Prostitutes' Vocational Orientations and Experiences," *Deviant Behavior* 26 (2005): 513–546.

Lutnick, Alexandra, and Deborah Cohan, "Criminalization, Legalization, or Decriminalization of Sex Work," *Reproductive Health Matters* 17 (2009): 38–46.

"Luxury Amsterdam Sex Club Closed for Good," *Radio Netherlands Worldwide*, July 8, 2009.

MacCoun, Robert, and Peter Reuter, *Drug War Heresies*, New York: Cambridge University Press, 2001.

MacKinnon, Catharine, *Feminism Unmodified*, Cambridge: Harvard University Press, 1987.

———, "Pornography as Trafficking," *Michigan Journal of International Law* 26 (2005): 993–1012.

———, *Toward a Feminist Theory of the State*, Cambridge: Harvard University Press, 1989.

Macleod, Jan, Melissa Farley, Lynn Anderson, and Jacqueline Golding, *Challenging Men's Demand for Prostitution in Scotland*, Glasgow, Scotland: Women's Support Project, 2008.

"Majority of Amsterdam Locals Support New Approach to Red Light District," *DutchAmsterdam.nl*, December 24, 2007, originally published in *Het Parool*.

Markon, Jerry, "Human Trafficking Evokes Outrage, Little Evidence," *Washington Post*, September 23, 2007, pp. A1, A8–A9.

Masenior, Nicole, and Chris Beyrer, "The U.S. Anti-Prostitution Pledge: First Amendment Challenges and Public Health Priorities," *PLoS Medicine* 4 (2007): 1158.

Maticka-Tyndale, Eleanor, "Context and Patterns of Men's Commercial Sexual Partnerships in Northeastern Thailand," *Social Science and Medicine* 44 (1997): 199–213.

Matthews, Roger, *Prostitution, Politics, and Policy*, New York: Routledge-Cavendish, 2008.

May, Tiggey, Alex Harocopos, and Michael Hough, *For Love or Money: Pimps and the Management of Prostitution*, Police Research Series 134, London: Home Office, 2000.

McElroy, Wendy, *XXX: A Woman's Right to Pornography*, New York: St. Martin's, 1995.

McIntosh, Mary, "Who Needs Prostitutes? The Ideology of Male Sexual Needs," in Carol Smart and Barry Smart, eds., *Women, Sexuality, and Social Control*, London: Routledge and Kegan Paul, 1978.

McKeganey, Neil, and Marina Barnard, *Sex Work on the Streets*, Buckingham, UK: Open University Press, 1996.

Meier, Robert F., and Gilbert Geis, *Victimless Crime? Prostitution, Drugs, Homosexuality, Abortion*, Los Angeles: Roxbury, 1997.

Milkovits, Amanda, "Legislators' Attempts to Quell Prostitution Stall," *Providence Journal*, May 28, 2005.

Milrod, Christine, "The Internet Hobbyist: Demographics and Sexual Behaviors of Male Clients of Internet Sexual Service Providers," Ph.D. diss., Institute for Advanced Study of Human Sexuality, San Francisco, 2010.

Ministry of Foreign Affairs, *FAQ about Dutch Prostitution*, Netherlands, 2005.

Ministry of Industry, Employment, and Communications, *Prostitution and Trafficking in Human Beings*, Stockholm, Sweden, April 2005.

Ministry of Justice, *Report of the Prostitution Law Review Committee on the Operation of the Prostitution Reform Act 2003*, Wellington, New Zealand: Ministry of Justice, 2008.

Ministry of Labor, *Fact Sheet*, Stockholm, Sweden, 1998.

Miss S, *Confessions of a Working Girl*, Naperville, IL: Sourcebooks, 2008.

Monto, Martin, "Prostitutes' Customers: Motives and Misconceptions," in Ronald Weitzer, ed., *Sex for Sale: Prostitution, Pornography, and the Sex Industry*, 2nd ed., New York: Routledge, 2010.

Monto, Martin, and Nick McRee, "A Comparison of the Male Customers of Female Street Prostitutes with National Samples of Men," *International Journal of Offender Therapy and Comparative Criminology* 49 (2005): 505–529.

Moon, Katherine, *Sex among Allies: Military Prostitution in U.S.-Korea Relations*, New York: Columbia University Press, 1997.

Moore, Molly, "Changing Patterns in Social Fabric Test Netherlands' Liberal Identity," *Washington Post*, June 23, 2007.

Mossman, Elaine, "Brothel Operators' and Support Agencies' Experiences of Decriminalization," in Gillian Abel, Lisa Fitzgerald, and Catherine Healy, eds., *Taking the Crime Out of Sex Work: New Zealand Sex Workers' Fight for Decriminalization*, Bristol, UK: Policy, 2010.

Mossman, Elaine, and Pat Mayhew, *Central Government Aims and Local Government Responses: The Prostitution Reform Act 2003*, Wellington, New Zealand: Ministry of Justice, 2007.

Murray, Alison, "Debt Bondage and Trafficking," in Kamala Kempadoo and Jo Doezema, eds., *Global Sex Workers*, New York: Routledge, 1998.

National Commission on Marihuana and Drug Abuse, *Marihuana: A Signal of Misunderstanding*, commissioned by President Richard M. Nixon, 1972.

National Geographic Channel, "Prostitution," *Taboo* television series, January 17, 2010.

National Institute of Justice, *Solicitation: Trafficking in Human Beings Research and Comprehensive Literature Review*, Washington, DC: U.S. Department of Justice, 2007.

National Organization for Women, *Resolution Calling for the Decriminalization of Prostitution*, Resolution 141 passed at the national NOW conference, 1973.

Niesse, Mark, "Prostitution Bill Gains Support," *Star Bulletin* (Honolulu), February 13, 2007.

Norwegian Ministry of Justice, *Purchasing Sexual Services in Sweden and the Netherlands: Legal Regulation and Experiences*, report by Working Group, October 2004.

O'Connell Davidson, Julia, "The Anatomy of 'Free Choice' Prostitution," *Gender, Work, and Organization* 2 (1995): 1-10.

———, *Power, Prostitution, and Freedom*, Ann Arbor: University of Michigan Press, 1998.

O'Connor, Monica, and Grainne Healy, *The Links between Prostitution and Sex Trafficking: A Briefing Handbook*, CATW and European Women's Lobby, 2006.

Odzer, Cleo, *Patpong Sisters: An American Woman's View of the Bangkok Sex World*, New York: Arcade, 1994.

Ohtake, Miyoko, "A School for Johns," *Newsweek*, July 24, 2008.

Oppermann, Martin, "Introduction," in Martin Oppermann, ed., *Sex Tourism and Prostitution*, Elmsford, NY: Cognizant Communication, 1998.

Oselin, Sharon, "Leaving the Streets," *Deviant Behavior* 30 (2009): 379–406.

Outshoorn, Joyce, "Pragmatism in the Polder: Changing Prostitution Policy in the Netherlands," *Journal of Contemporary European Studies* 12 (2004): 165–176.

———, "Voluntary and Forced Prostitution: The 'Realistic Approach' of the Netherlands," in Joyce Outshoorn, ed., *The Politics of Prostitution*, New York: Cambridge University Press, 2004.

Overall, Christine, "What's Wrong with Prostitution? Evaluating Sex Work," *Signs* 17 (1992): 705–724.

Padilla, Mark, *Caribbean Pleasure Industry: Tourism, Sexuality, and AIDS in the Dominican Republic*, Chicago: University of Chicago Press, 2007.

Parloff, Roger, "How Pot Became Legal," *Fortune*, September 28, 2009, pp. 140–162.

Pateman, Carole, *The Sexual Contract*, Stanford: Stanford University Press, 1988.

Peat Marwick and Partners, *A National Population Study of Prostitution and Pornography*, Ottawa, ON: Department of Justice, 1984.

Penfold, Clarissa, Gillian Hunter, Rosie Campbell, and Leela Barham, "Tackling Client Violence in Female Street Prostitution: Inter-Agency Working between Outreach Agencies and the Police," *Policing and Society* 14 (2004): 365–379.

Perez-y-Perez, Maria, "Discipline, Autonomy, and Ambiguity: Organizations, Markets, and Work in the Sex Industry, Christchurch, New Zealand," Ph.D. diss., University of Canterbury, Christchurch, New Zealand, 2003.

Perkins, Roberta, and Frances Lovejoy, *Call Girls: Private Sex Workers in Australia*, Crawley: University of Western Australia Press, 2007.

Phillips, Joan, "Tourist-Oriented Prostitution in Barbados: The Case of the Beach Boy and the White Female Tourist," in Kamala Kempadoo, ed., *Sun, Sex, and Gold: Tourism and Sex Work in the Caribbean*, Lanham, MD: Rowman and Littlefield, 1999.

Phua, Voon Chin, "The Love That Binds: Transnational Relationships in Sex Work," *Sexuality and Culture* 13 (2009): 91–110.

Pisarcik, Kristin, "Inside a Brooklyn 'John School,'" *20/20*, ABC television, March 20, 2007.

Pitcher, Jane, "Support Services for Women Working in the Sex Industry," in Rosie Campbell and Maggie O'Neill, eds., *Sex Work Now*, Portland, OR: Willan, 2006.

Pivot Legal Society, *Beyond Decriminalization: Sex Work, Human Rights, and a New Framework for Law Reform*, Vancouver, Canada: Pivot, 2006.

Plumridge, Libby, and Gillian Abel, "A Segmented Sex Industry in New Zealand: Sexual and Personal Safety of Female Sex Workers," *Australian and New Zealand Journal of Public Health* 25 (2001): 78–83.

"Poll: French Want Brothels Legalized," *Boston Globe*, January 22, 1995.

"Poll Steels Anti-Prostitution Resolve," *New Zealand Herald*, May 14, 2003.

Popper, Karl, *The Logic of Scientific Discovery*, New York, Basic Books, 1959.

Porter, Judith, and Louis Bonilla, "The Ecology of Street Prostitution," in Ronald Weitzer, ed., *Sex for Sale: Prostitution, Pornography, and the Sex Industry*, 2nd ed., New York: Routledge, 2010.

Prince, Diana, "A Psychological Study of Prostitutes in California and Nevada," Ph.D. diss., U.S. International University, San Diego, California, 1986.

Prostitution Law Review Committee, *The Nature and Extent of the Sex Industry in New Zealand*, Wellington, New Zealand: Ministry of Justice, 2005.

———, *Report of the Prostitution Law Review Committee on the Operation of the Prostitution Reform Act 2003*, Wellington, New Zealand: Ministry of Justice, 2008.

Prostitution Task Force, *Workable Solutions to the Problem of Street Prostitution in Buffalo, New York*, 1999.

Pruitt, Deborah, and Suzanne LaFont, "For Love and Money: Romance Tourism in Jamaica," *Annals of Tourism Research* 22 (1995): 422–440.

Quan, Tracy, *Diary of a Manhattan Call Girl*, New York: Three Rivers, 2003.

Raphael, Jody, and Deborah Shapiro, *Sisters Speak Out: The Lives and Needs of Prostituted Women in Chicago*, Chicago: Center for Impact Research, 2002.

Ratliff, Eric, "Women as 'Sex Workers,' Men as 'Boyfriends': Shifting Identities in Philippine Go-Go Bars and Their Significance in STD/AIDS Control," *Anthropology and Medicine* 6 (1999): 79–101.

Raymond, Janice, "Prostitution Is Rape That's Paid For," *Los Angeles Times*, December 11, 1995, p. B6.

———, "Prostitution on Demand: Legalizing the Buyers as Sexual Consumers," *Violence Against Women* 10 (2004): 1156–1186.

———, "Ten Reasons for *Not* Legalizing Prostitution and a Legal Response to the Demand for Prostitution," *Journal of Trauma Practice* 2 (2003): 315–332.

Regioplan, summary of report, *An Evaluation of the Lifting of the Brothel Ban: The Social Position of Prostitutes*, Amsterdam: Regioplan Beleidsonderzoek, 2006.

Rekart, Michael, "Sex-Work Harm Reduction," *Lancet* 366 (December 17, 2005): 2123–2134.

Reynolds, Helen, *The Economics of Prostitution*, Springfield, IL: Charles Thomas, 1986.

Rhodes, Hillary, "Prostitution Advances in a Wired World," Associated Press, March 11, 2008.

Riley, Jason, "Undercover Methods Draw Ridicule, Praise," *Courier-Journal*, July 11, 2004.

Riley, Jason, and Jim Adams, "Officers Have Sexual Contact with Suspects," *Courier-Journal*, July 11, 2004.

Rissel, Chris, "Experiences of Commercial Sex in a Representative Sample of Adults," *Australian and New Zealand Journal of Public Health* 27 (2003): 191–197.

"Romania Tops EU Sex Worker List," *BBC News Online*, January 26, 2010.

Romans, Sarah, Kathleen Potter, Judy Martin, and Peter Herbison, "The Mental and Physical Health of Female Sex Workers," *Australian and New Zealand Journal of Psychiatry* 35 (2001): 75–80.

Rubin, Gayle, "Thinking Sex: Notes for a Radical Theory of the Politics of Sexuality," in Carole S. Vance, ed., *Pleasure and Danger: Exploring Female Sexuality*, Boston: Routledge and Kegan Paul, 1984.

Rubin, Joel, "Shaming and Scaring Johns into Becoming Average Joes," *Los Angeles Times*, February 26, 2009.

Saad, Lydia, "U.S. Support for Legalizing Marijuana Reaches New High," Gallup.com, October 19, 2009, www.gallup.com/poll/123728/U.S.-Support-Legalizing-Marijuana-Reaches-New-High.aspx.

Sanders, Teela, *Paying for Pleasure: Men Who Buy Sex*, Portland, OR: Willan, 2008.

———, *Sex Work*, Portland, OR: Willan, 2005.

Sanders, Teela, and Rosie Campbell, "Designing Out Vulnerability, Building In Respect," *British Journal of Sociology* 58 (2007): 1–19.

San Francisco Committee on Crime, *A Report on Non-Victim Crime in San Francisco, Part 2: Sexual Conduct, Gambling, Pornography*, Mayor's Office, 1971.

San Francisco Task Force on Prostitution, *Final Report*, San Francisco Board of Supervisors, 1996.

Sausa, Lydia, JoAnne Keatley, and Don Operario, "Perceived Risks and Benefits of Sex Work among Transgender Women of Color in San Francisco," *Archives of Sexual Behavior* 36 (2007): 768–777.

Schloenhardt, Andreas, and Lachlan Cameron, "Happy Birthday, Brothels! Ten Years of Prostitution Regulation in Queensland," *Queensland Lawyer* 29 (2009): 194–220.

Schlosser, Eric, "The Business of Pornography," *U.S. News and World Report*, February 10, 1997.

Schmitt, Richard, "U.S. Cracking Down on Porn," *Deseret News*, February 15, 2004.

Schrader, Jordan, "To Reduce Prostitution, Cities Try Shaming Clients," *USA Today*, August 29, 2008.

Scolforo, Mark, "PA Prostitution Case Tossed over Gov't-Funded Sex," Associated Press, November 6, 2009.

Scott, Michael, *Street Prostitution*, Washington, DC: U.S. Department of Justice, 2001.

Scoular, Jane, "Criminalizing Punters: Evaluating the Swedish Position on Prostitution," *Journal of Social Welfare and Family Law* 26 (2004): 195–210.

———, "What's Law Got to Do with It? How and Why Law Matters in the Regulation of Sex Work," *Journal of Law and Society* 37 (2010): 12–39.

Seib, Charrlotte, Michael Dunne, Jane Fischer, and Jackob Najman, "Commercial Sexual Practices before and after Legalization in Australia," *Archives of Sexual Behavior* 39 (2010): 979–989.

Seib, Charrlotte, Jane Fischer, and Jackob Najman, "The Health of Female Sex Workers from Three Industry Sectors in Queensland, Australia," *Social Science and Medicine* 68 (2009): 473–478.

Shafer, Jack, "The Sex-Slavery Epidemic That Wasn't," *Slate*, September 24, 2007.

Shaver, Frances, "Sex Work Research: Methodological and Ethical Challenges," *Journal of Interpersonal Violence* 20 (2005): 296–319.

Sherman, William, "The Naked Truth about Strip Clubs," *New York Daily News*, July 8, 2007.

Siegel, Dina, "Human Trafficking and Legalized Prostitution in the Netherlands," *Temida* (2009): 5–16.

Simons, Marlise, "Amsterdam Tries Upscale Fix for Red-Light Area," *New York Times*, February 24, 2008.

Singh, Shay-Ann Heiser, "The Predator Accountability Act," *DePaul Law Review* 56 (2007): 1035–1064.

Skinner, E. Benjamin, *A Crime So Monstrous: Face-to-Face with Modern-Day Slavery*, New York: Free Press, 2008.

Skolnick, Jerome, "The Social Transformation of Vice," *Law and Contemporary Problems* 51 (1988): 9–29.

Smith, Michael, Christian Grov, and David Seal, "Agency Based Male Sex Work," *Journal of Men's Studies* 16 (2008): 193–210.

Snadowsky, Daria, "The Best Little Whorehouse Is Not in Texas: How Nevada's Prostitution Laws Serve Public Policy and How Those Laws May Be Improved," *Nevada Law Journal* 6 (2005): 217–247.

Special Committee on Pornography and Prostitution, *Pornography and Prostitution in Canada*, Ottawa, ON: Department of Justice, 1985.

Sprinkle, Annie, "The Forty Reasons Why Whores Are My Heroes," *Social Alternatives* 18 (1999): 8.

Stein, Martha, *Lovers, Friends, Slaves*, New York: Berkeley, 1974.

Steinfatt, Thomas, *Working at the Bar: Sex Work and Health Communication in Thailand*, Westport, CT: Ablex, 2002.

Strossen, Nadine, *Defending Pornography*, New York: Anchor, 1995.

Sturdevant, Saundra, and Brenda Stoltzfus, *Let the Good Times Roll: Prostitution and the U.S. Military in Asia*, New York: New Press, 1993.

Stychin, Carl, "Exploring the Limits: Feminism and the Legal Regulation of Gay Male Pornography," *Vermont Law Review* 16 (1992): 857–900.

Suchetka, Diane, and Jim Nichols, "Sex for Sale: The Men Who Buy It," *Cleveland Plain Dealer*, March 21, 2008.

Sullivan, Barbara, *The Politics of Sex: Prostitution and Pornography in Australia since 1945*, New York: Cambridge University Press, 1997.

———, "When (Some) Prostitution Is Legal: The Impact of Law Reform on Sex Work in Australia," *Journal of Law and Society* 37 (2010): 85–104.

Sullivan, Jennifer, and Christopher Schwarzen, "Did Local Vice Cops Cross the Line?" *Seattle Times*, October 7, 2005.

Sullivan, L., "Justice Department Sets Sights on Mainstream Porn," *Pittsburgh Post-Gazette*, April 11, 2004.

Sullivan, Mary, *What Happens When Prostitution Becomes Work? An Update on Legalization of Prostitution in Australia*, North Fitzroy, Australia: Coalition Against Trafficking in Women, 2005.

Sullivan, Mary, and Sheila Jeffreys, "Legalization: The Australian Experience," *Violence Against Women* 8 (2002): 1140–1148.

Takeyama, Akiko, "Commodified Romance in a Tokyo Host Club," in Mark McLelland and Romit Dasgupta, eds., *Genders, Transgenders, and Sexualities in Japan*, New York: Routledge, 2005.

Taylor, Jacqueline Sanchez, "Dollars Are a Girl's Best Friend: Female Tourists' Sexual Behavior in the Caribbean," *Sociology* 34 (2001): 749–764.

———, "Female Sex Tourism: A Contradiction in Terms?" *Feminist Review* 83 (2006): 43–59.

Thomas, Joe, "Gay Male Pornography since Stonewall," in Ronald Weitzer, ed., *Sex for Sale: Prostitution, Pornography, and the Sex Industry*, 2nd ed., New York: Routledge, 2010.

Transcrime, *Study on National Legislation on Prostitution and the Trafficking in Women and Children*, report to the European Parliament, 2005.

Trotter, Henry, *Sugar Girls and Seamen: A Journey into the World of Dockside Prostitution in South Africa*, Auckland Park, South Africa: Jacana, 2008.

Trueman, Patrick, testimony before the Subcommittee on the Constitution, Civil Rights, and Property Rights, United States Senate, *Hearing on Obscenity Prosecution*, March 16, 2005.

Urbina, Ian, "For Runaways, Sex Buys Survival," *New York Times*, October 26, 2009.

U.S. Department of Justice, *Beyond the Pornography Commission: The U.S. Response*, Washington, DC: Government Printing Office, 1988.

———, "Obscenity Prosecution Task Force Established to Investigate, Prosecute Purveyors of Obscene Materials," press release, May 5, 2005.

U.S. Department of State, "The Link between Prostitution and Sex Trafficking," Bureau of Public Affairs, 2004.

———, *Trafficking in Persons Report*, Washington, DC: U.S. Department of State, annual.

Uy, Jude, Jeffrey Parsons, David Bimbi, Juline Koken, and Perry Halkitis, "Gay and Bisexual Male Escorts Who Advertise on the Internet: Understanding the Reasons for and Effects of Involvement in Commercial Sex," *International Journal of Men's Health* 3 (2007): 11–26.

Vance, Carole, "The Meese Commission on the Road," *Nation*, August 2, 1986, pp. 65, 76–82.

van Doorninck, Marieke, "A Business like Any Other? Managing the Sex Industry in the Netherlands," in Susanne Thorbek and Bandana Pattanaik, eds., *Transnational Prostitution: Changing Patterns in a Global Context*, London: Zed Books, 2002.

———, "History of Prostitution in Amsterdam," unpublished paper, 1999.

van Doorninck, Marieke, and Rosie Campbell, "Zoning Street Sex Work: The Way Forward?" in Rosie Campbell and Maggie O'Neill, eds., *Sex Work Now*, Portland, OR: Willan, 2006.

van Soomeren, Paul, and Sander Flight, "Design against Kerb-Crawing: Tippelzones," paper presented at the International Crime Prevention through Environmental Design conference, Brisbane, Australia, 2004.

van Veen, Maaike, "HIV and Sexual Risk Behavior among Commercial Sex Workers in the Netherlands," *Archives of Sexual Behavior* 39 (2010): 714–723.

Vanwesenbeeck, Ine, "Another Decade of Social Scientific Work on Prostitution," *Annual Review of Sex Research* 12 (2001): 242–289.

———, *Prostitutes' Well-Being and Risk*, Amsterdam: VU University Press, 1994.

Vanwesenbeeck, Ine, Ron de Graaf, Gertjan van Zessen, Cees Straver, and Jan Visser, "Professional HIV Risk Taking, Levels of Victimization, and Well-Being in Female Prostitutes in the Netherlands," *Archives of Sexual Behavior* 24 (1995): 503–515.

van Wijk, Anton, *Vulnerable Job: An Investigation into the Prostitution Industry in Amsterdam*, Amsterdam: Beke, 2010.

Vick, Karl, "In California, Medical Marijuana Laws Are Moving Pot into the Mainstream," *Washington Post*, April 12, 2009.

Visser, Jan, "Prostitution Policy under Construction," unpublished report, Amsterdam, 2008.

Wagenaar, Hendrik, "Democracy and Prostitution: Deliberating the Legalization of Brothels in the Netherlands," *Administration and Society* 28 (2006): 198–235.

Wagenaar, Hendrik, and Sietske Altink, "To Toe the Line: Streetwalking as Contested Space," in David Canter, Maria Ioannou, and Donna Youngs, eds., *Safer Sex in the City: The Experience and Management of Street Prostitution*, Farnham, UK: Ashgate, 2009.

Waite, Mark, "Prostitutes Dispute Trummell Charges," *Pahrump Valley Times* (Nevada), October 5, 2007.

Weinberg, Martin, Frances Shaver, and Colin Williams, "Gendered Prostitution in the San Francisco Tenderloin," *Archives of Sexual Behavior* 28 (1999): 503–521.

Weiner, Adele, "Understanding the Social Needs of Streetwalking Prostitutes," *Social Work* 41 (1996): 97–105.

Weitzer, Ronald, "Legalizing Prostitution: Morality Politics in Western Australia," *British Journal of Criminology* 49 (2009): 88–105.

———, "The Movement to Criminalize Sex Work in the United States," *Journal of Law and Society* 37 (2010): 61–84.

———, "The Mythology of Prostitution: Advocacy Research and Public Policy," *Sexuality Research and Social Policy* 7 (2010): 15–29.

———, "The Politics of Prostitution in America," in Ronald Weitzer, ed., *Sex for Sale: Prostitution, Pornography, and the Sex Industry*, New York: Routledge, 2000.

———, "Prostitutes' Rights in the United States: The Failure of a Movement," *Sociological Quarterly* 32 (1991): 23–41.

———, "Prostitution Control in America: Rethinking Public Policy," *Crime, Law, and Social Change* 32 (1999): 83–102.

———, "Sex Work: Paradigms and Policies," in Ronald Weitzer, ed., *Sex for Sale: Prostitution, Pornography, and the Sex Industry*, 2nd ed., New York: Routledge, 2010.

———, "The Social Construction of Sex Trafficking: Ideology and Institutionalization of a Moral Crusade," *Politics and Society* 35 (2007): 447–475.

———, "Sociology of Sex Work," *Annual Review of Sociology* 35 (2009): 213–234.

———, "Some Lurid Prostitution Myths Debunked," *Providence Journal*, June 19, 2009.

———, "Why Prostitution Initiative Misses: Measure Q in Berkeley Fails on Three Counts," *San Francisco Chronicle*, September 26, 2004, p. E3.

Whittaker, Dawn, and Graham Hart, "Managing Risks: The Social Organization of Indoor Sex Work," *Sociology of Health and Illness* 18 (1996): 399–414.

Willems, Hans, "Schipperskwartier, a Seductive Quarter in Antwerp," Social Welfare Office, Antwerp, Belgium, 2009.

Wilson, Ara, *The Intimate Economies of Bangkok*, Berkeley: University of California Press, 2004.

Wolfenden Committee, *Report of the Committee on Homosexual Offenses and Prostitution*, New York: Lancer, 1964 [1957].

Women's Commission for Refugee Women and Children, *The U.S. Response to Human Trafficking: An Unbalanced Approach*, New York: Commission, 2007.

Woodward, Charlotte, Jane Fischer, Jake Najman, and Michael Dunne, *Selling Sex in Queensland*, Brisbane, Australia: Prostitution Licensing Authority, 2004.

Zaitch, Damian, and Richard Staring, "The Flesh Is Weak, the Spirit Even Weaker: Clients and Trafficked Women in the Netherlands," in Andrea Di Nicola, ed., *Prostitution and Human Trafficking: Focus on Clients*, New York: Springer, 2009.

Zatz, Noah, "Sex Work/Sex Act: Law, Labor, and Desire in Constructions of Prostitution," *Signs* 22 (1997): 277–308.

Zhang, Sheldon, "Beyond the 'Natasha' Story: A Review and Critique of Current Research on Sex Trafficking," *Global Crime* 10 (2009): 178–195.

Zheng, Tiantian, *Red Lights: The Lives of Sex Workers in Postsocialist China*, Minneapolis: University of Minnesota Press, 2009.

Index

Adult Entertainment Expo, 5
adult industry trade shows, 5
Agustín, Laura, 74–75
Albert, Alexa, 89
Alkmaar, the Netherlands, 152, 166
Allentown, Pennsylvania, 55
Altink, Sietske, 154
Amsterdam, 159–196; Belle, statue of, 184, *185*; brothel owners in, 163–165; brothel workers in, 187; brothels in, 146–147, 151, 160, 170–176, 187; call girls/escorts in, 151; Candy Club, 247n134; Casa Rosso live sex show, 164; clients of sex workers in, 176–177; Club Elegance brothel, 171, *173*; Club Mayfair brothel, 172; De Fonteyn brothel, 146–147; Dominicus Kerk, 177; Golden Key brothel, 172, *174*; health centers for sex workers, 167–168; home-based sex work, 147, 151; Jan Bik brothel, 174–176; La Vie En Proost strip club, 183; Labor Party, 160; Love Club 21 massage parlor, 186; municipal prostitution control teams, 164, 167; organized crime, 159, 161–162; Oude Kerk (Old Church), 184, 188; pimping in, 161–162, 198–199; police in, 163–164, 167–168; prostitutes, rates charged by, 172, 176, 187, 195; prostitutes in, 166–170, 177; Prostitution Information Center, 184; red-light districts (RLDs), 105–107, 113–114, 147–148, 151–152, 159–160, 176–196; Ria's Men's Club brothel, 172, *175*; Ruysdaelkade red-light district, 177, 179–181, 184; Singel red-light district, 165, 177–179, 184; Societe Anonyme brothel, 171, *172*; "stag parties" from Britain, 190–191; street prostitution in, 147, 151; Thai Massage parlor, 186; tourists per annum, 108; trafficking in, 161, 199–201; transgender sex workers, 186; the Wallen red-light district, 177, 181–186, 190, 199; window workers in, 18, 147–148, 160–166, *165*, 177, 186–196, 201; working conditions for sex workers, 148; Yab Yum Club, 162, 170–171

Antwerp, 109–115; brothel owners in, 111; organized crime, 109; red-light district, 105–107, 109–115, 145, 162, 181, 184; "Skippers' Quarter" (documentary film), 110; street prostitution in, 109; tourists per annum, 108; Villa Tinto brothel, 111, *112*; window workers in, 18, 109, 111, 114

Argentina, 86–87
Arnhem, the Netherlands, 151
Arnot, Alison, 92–93
Asscher, Lodewijk, 160–161
Association of Operators of Relaxation Businesses, 153
Atlanta, Georgia, 59
Auckland, New Zealand, 98
Australia, 92–96; brothel workers in, 28; call girls/escorts in, 28, 38; Labor Party, 16; legal prostitution in, 92–96; legalization of prostitution, 76, 78; New South Wales, 96, 159, 205, 208; Northern Territory, 93; percentage of men who have paid for sex, 4; prostitution, attitudes toward, 79, 80; Prostitution Control Act (1995), 93; Prostitution Licensing Authority, 94; Queensland, 32, 93–96, 210; Sydney, 96; Victoria, 92–93, 94; Western Australia (*see* Western Australia)

Austria, 122, 236n36

Index | 275

streetwalkers, 23–28; age of entry into prostitution, 58; assistance in leaving the streets, 57; in California, 28; childhood abuse, 25; clients of, 30–32; desperation, 58; drug abuse, 18; duration of encounters, 31; exploitation by third parties, 17; generalizations/myths about, 13–14; homelessness, 58; "honeymooning" to, 38; impact on community, 17, 23, 57–58; indoor prostitutes compared to, 25–26, 27–28, 32; job satisfaction, 28; location of services, 17; mental health, 27; in New Zealand, 220n91; pimping, relationship with, 25; potential clients' attitudes toward, 21; prices charged, 17; protection against violence toward, 57; public visibility, 17; runaways among, 18, 58; self-image/esteem, 28; socioeconomic backgrounds, 23; victimization while working, 24, 25–26, 95; well-being, 27

strip clubs: African American women, 9; Frankfurt, 121; La Vie En Proost (Amsterdam), 183; targeting of, 69; trafficking, 69; in United States, 4, 6

Sudfass Sauna Club (Frankfurt), 140, *141*

"survival sex," 58

Sweden: antiprostitution activities, 68; clients of sex workers, criminalization of, 68, 75, 76, 233n103; indoor prostitution in, 74; oppression paradigm in, 68; prostitution, attitudes toward, 79, 80; prostitution policy, 74, 75; street prostitution in, 75

Switzerland, 80, 122, 149

Sydney, Australia, 96

Taiwan, 78

Takeyama, Akiko, 43

Taylor, Bruce, 70–71

Taylor, Jacqueline Sanchez, 43

telephone sex, 6

Thai Massage parlor (Amsterdam), 186

Thailand: Bangkok, 8–9, 24; bar or casino workers in, 26, 39, 41–42; indoor prostitution in, 22; Patpong, 8–9; Pattaya, 24; prostitutes in, 14, 24, 28–29; prostitution, attitudes toward, 79, 80; sex tourists in, 40; sex work in, 8–9

third parties: in Amsterdam, 147; in Belgium, 108, 145; exploitation by, 17; in Germany, 115; in legal prostitution regimes, 198–199; legalization of prostitution, 25; in the Netherlands, 149; Policing and Crime Act (UK, 2009), 53, 228n23; in red-light districts (RLDs), 108; roles in indoor prostitution, 25; in Spain, 80; in Uganda, 222n10. *See also* pimping

Thomas, Joe, 9

Tijuana, Mexico, 91–92

Tippelzones (strolling zones), 150–151, 186, 208

Tokyo, 43

tourism and indoor prostitution, 39–44

trafficking: in Amsterdam, 161, 199–201; conflation with all sexual commerce, 63; convictions for, 200; criminalization of prostitution, 66; in Germany, 116, 118, 120; legal prostitution, 199–201; in Mumbai, India, 233n111; pornography, 13, 69; prostitution, 63–66, 204; strip clubs, 69

Trafficking in Persons Report (U.S. State Department), 66

Trafficking Victims Protection Act (USA, 2000), 48

Trafficking Victims Protection Reauthorization Act (TVPRA) (USA, 2005), 69

transgender sex workers: age of entry into prostitution, 201; in Amsterdam, 186; in Antwerp, 111; in Brazil, 9; in the Netherlands, 201; oppression paradigm, 11; in San Francisco, 9–10; window workers, 111, 186

Trotter, Henry, 40–41

Trueman, Patrick, 70

two-track prostitution policy, 52–62; in Atlanta, 59; in Canada, 59; harm reduction principle, 57; indoor prostitution, 53–57; in Nevada, 59, 61; precedents for, 59–62; in Rhode Island, 59–60, 61; in San Francisco, 59; Street Offenses Act (UK, 1959), 53; street prostitution, 53, 56–59; Wolfenden Committee, 53

About the Author

RONALD WEITZER is Professor of Sociology at George Washington University and author or editor of several books, including *Sex for Sale: Prostitution, Pornography, and the Sex Industry* and *Race and Policing in America: Conflict and Reform.*